Echoes of Survival
Unravelling My Iranian Zoroastrian Ancestors' Enduring Legacy

Tale of Perseverance: A Family and Community's Triumph Across Four Centuries, Defying All Odds

Mehrborzin Jamshid Soroushian

Echoes of Survival

Copyright © 2024 Mehrborzin Soroushian

Dedication

To the memory of my parents and all the ancestors who came before them for their steadfastness and sacrifice to keep ablaze the flame of their faith and identity.

Dedicated to all Zoroastrians of Iran who persevered through the centuries of genocidal acts directed against them but still managed to keep the flame of faith alive and prevail against all odds.

Table of Contents

Dedication iii
Chapter 1 Introduction 1
   Historical Background 1
   Focus of this Book 4
Chapter 2 My Paternal Ancestry 6
   2.1   Kaykhosrow Hormuzd & Daulat Jamshid 6
        2.1.1   Kaykhosrow Hormuzd 6
        2.1.2   Daulat Jamshid Marzban 8
   2.2   Bahram Kaykhosrow Hormuzd & Rudabeh Shahriar Mehrab 10
        2.2.1   Bahram Kaykhosrow Hormuzd 10
        2.2.2   Rudabeh Shahriar Mehrab 12
   2.3   Jamshid Bahram Kaykhosrow & Firozehe Bahman Khodabux 15
        2.3.1   Jamshid Bahram Kaykhosrow 15
        2.3.2   Firozehe Bahman Khodabux 18
   2.4   Shahriar Jamshid Bahram & Gohar Hormuzdyar Esfandiyar 23
        2.4.1   Shahriar Jamshid Bahram 23
        2.4.2   Gohar Hormuzdyar Esfandiyar 25
   2.5   Khodabux Shahriar Jamshid & Katayun Faridun Kaykhosrow 29
        2.5.1   Khodabux Shahriar Jamshid 29
        2.5.2   Katayun Faridun Kaykhosrow 31
   2.6   Shahriar Khodabux-Shahriar & Banu Gushtasp-Dinyar-Bahram-Klantar 36
        2.6.1   Shahriar Khodabux Shahriar 36
        2.6.2   Banu Gushtasp Dinyar Bahram Klantar 44
   2.7   Soroush Shahriar Khodabux and IranBanu Esfandiyar Khodabux 53
        2.7.1   Soroush Shahriar Khodabux Shahriar Jamshid 53
        2.7.2   IranBanu Esfandiyar Khodabux 71
   2.8   Jamshid Soroush Shahriar and Homayun Sohrab Rustom 82
        2.8.1   Jamshid Soroush Shahriar Khodabux Shahriar Jamshid Soroushian 82
        2.8.2   Homayun Sohrab Rustom Kaikhosrow Viraf Kianian 108

2.9	Mehrborzin Jamshid Soroushian and Mehrbanou Mehraban Zartoshty	119
	2.9.1 Mehrborzin Jamshid Soroush Soroushian	119
	2.9.2 Mehrbanou Mehraban Jamshid Zartoshty	128

Chapter 3 Other Descendancies of Khodabux Shahriar Jamshid 136

3.1	Esfandiyar Khodabux Shahriar and Sultan Khosrow Hormuzdyar	136
	3.1.1 Esfandiyar Khodabux Shahriar Jamshid	136
	3.1.2 Sultan Khosrow Hormuzdyar	137
3.2	Mahindokht Soroush Soroushian and Manutchehr Dinyar Shahriari	140
	3.2.1 Mahindokht Soroush-Shahriar Soroushian	140
	3.2.2 Manutchehr Dinyar-Bahram Shahriari	141
3.3	Tooran Shahriar Shahriari and Bahram Bahman Bahrami	147
	3.3.1 Tooran Shahriar Bahman Shahriari	147
	3.3.2 ShahBahram Bahman Bahrami	148
3.4	Banu Faridun-Shahriar Soroushian and Mehraban Kaykhosrow	153
	3.4.1 Banu Faridun-Shahriar Soroushian	153
	3.4.2 Mehraban Kaykhosrow-Rustom Hormozdi	154
3.5	Rustom Kaikhosrow Soroushian Kermani and Winifred Audrey Sutherland	160
	3.5.1 Rustom Kaikhosrow Soroushian Kermani	160
	3.5.2 Winifred Audrey Sutherland	162
3.6	Khodamorad Kaikhosrow Khodabux and Ruth Phinney	168
	3.6.1 Khodamorad (Rod) Kaikhosrow-Khodabux Soroushian Kermani	168
	3.6.2 Ruth Phinney	169

Chapter 4 My Maternal Ancestry 174

4.1	Bahram Sohrab Viraf and Firozeh Marzban Rustom	174
	4.1.1 Bahram Sohrab Viraf	174
	4.1.2 Firozeh Marzban Rustom	175
4.2	Feridon Bahram Sohrab and Morwarid Dinyar Khosrow	175
	4.2.1 Feridon Bahram Sohrab	175
	4.2.2 Morwarid Dinyar Khosrow	176
4.3	Karshasp Feridon Bahram and Homayun Dinyar Parviz	177
	4.3.1 Karshasp Feridon Bahram	177

		4.3.2 Homayun Dinyar Parviz	177
4.4	Viraf Karshasp Feridon and Khorshid Mehran Shahpur		178
	4.4.1	Viraf Karshasp Feridon	178
	4.4.2	Khorshid Mehran Shahpur	178
4.5	Kaikhosrow Viraf Karshasp and Kian Feridon Rustom		179
	4.5.1	Kaikhosrow Viraf Karshasp	179
	4.5.2	Kian Feridon Rustom	179
4.6	Rustom Kaikhosrow Viraf and Mahasti Khodadad Firoze		180
	4.6.1	Rustom Kaikhosrow Viraf	180
	4.6.2	Mahasti Khodadad Firoze	180
4.7	Sohrab Rustom Kaikhosrow and Simin Khosrow ShahJahan		181
	4.7.1	Sohrab Rustom Kaikhosrow	181
	4.7.2	Simin Khosrow ShahJahan	182

Chapter 5 Conclusion 185

Acknowledgments 187

List of Figures

Figure 1: Ruins of the Zoroastrian Fire Temple of Gonabad in use through the mid-18th century. 6

Figure 2: Natural Springs inside a mountainous cave close to Historic Tabas, Khorasan 12

Figure 3: Descendants of Bahram Kaykhosrow and Rudabeh Shahriar 15

Figure 4: Photos of direct descendants of Jamshid Bahram and Firozeh Bahman in the course of 20th century who served in the military or security services 23

Figure 5: Descendants of Shahriar Jamshid Bahram and Gohar Hormuzdyar Esfandiyar 28

Figure 6: A drawing produced by a traveler depicting a Zoroastrian family in Kerman in 1838 28

Figure 7: Descendants of Khodabux Shahriar & Katayun Faridun 34

Figure 8: Descendants of Khodamorad Khodabux, and Firozehe Bahram 34

Figure 9: Descendants of Kaikhosrow Khodabux Shahriar & his spouses 35

Figure 10: Extract from a Telegram sent from Percy Sykey, the British Consul in Kerman, to his superiors regarding the Zoroastrians of Kerman 43

Figure 11: Descendants of Shahriar Khodabux and Banu Gushtasp 48

Figure 12: Deed of Purchase for a real property in 1868 issued to Shahriar by a local Islamic Clergy, where Shahriar is identified as "Obedient to Islam, Shahriar a Gaber, son of Obedient to Islam, Khodabux a Gaber" 48

Figure 13: 1894, Kerman: Leaders of the Naseri Zoroastrian Anjuman of Kerman, is 2nd sited from right Shahriar Khodabux, 3rd one is Kaikhosorow Shahrokh, 4th one is Dastur Rustom Jahangir, 6th one is Arbab Gushtasp Dinyar 49

Figure 14: 1894, Kerman: Governor of Kerman, FarmanFarmayan, and the British Counsel, Percy Sykes, sited in the middle of the First row. Shahriar Khodabux (4th from right)) and Kaikhosorow Shahrokh (5th from right) in the second row 49

Figure 15: 1896, Kerman: Front row (right to left) Percy Sykes (British Counsel in Kerman), Shahriar Khodabux (5th president of the Zoroastrian Association), Dastur Rustom Jahangir (3rd president), Gushtasp Dinyar (4th president) 50

Figure 16: 1904, Kerman: (from Left to Right) Gohar Shahriar, IranBanu Esfandiyar, GoharBanu Bahram Dinyar, Banu Gushtasp Dinyar, Morwarid Gushtasp Dinyar 51

Figure 17: 1905 Kerman, Shahriar Khodabux (sited 5th from the left) at his Commercial office with the rest of his staff. His youngest brother, Kaikhsorow, is sited 4th from the right. 52

Figure 18: 1944 Kerman, Banu Gushtasp, sat in the front a month before her passage. Her family and members of the household have assembled for the memorial photo 53

Figure 19: Descendants of Soroush Shahriar and IranBanu Esfandiyar 74

Figure 20: 1895 Kerman: Soroush (*), his younger brother Faridun (**) at school with their teacher, Kaikhosrow Shahrokh (+) and other Zoroastrian pupil. 75

Figure 21: 1905, Bombay: Soroush (seated to the right), his brother Faridun (standing behind him), and two other Zoroastrians posing for this photo in Bombay. 76

Figure 22: 1920, Kerman: Family photo taken a year after the passage of Shahriar Khodabux. His two sons, Faridun (seated, first from left) and Soroush, seated to the left of their mother, Banu Gushtasp. The three children to the left are Faridun's oldest son, Shahriar, his oldest daughter, Banu, and his second son, Kaikhosrow, cuddled in the back row. The four children are shown to the left. 77

Figure 23:1922, Kerman: Special election of the Anjuman witnessed by an inspector from Tehran holding the ballot box – center stage. Soroush Soroushian is standing to his left. 78

Figure 24:1929, Kerman: Katayun Soroush Soroushian with her fiancé, Jamshid Jahangir Fravahar, featured with the Oakland car imported from America; she learned to drive the car from a young age and was amongst the first females in Iran to operate an automobile. 80

Figure 25:1930, Kerman: Commemorative photo taken on the occasion of the visit of Mr. Petit (a Parsi Philanthropist) from Bombay (sited 6th from right). Soroush Soroushian, the president of Kerman Anjuman, is seated between Mr. and Mrs. Petit. Other dignitaries and community members are in attendance. 80

Figure 26:1936, Kerman: Zoroastrian Community Celebration of the National unveiling of Iranian Women (Hijab-baradari) 81

Figure 27: 1959, Kerman: Wedding of Esfandiyar, the third son of IranBanu to Ms. Katayun Shahriari 81

Figure 28: 1936, Yazd: Homayun Sohrab Kianian's Sixth Grade Graduation Certificate 112

Figure 29: 1934, Kerman: Jamshid Soroushian during his Mandatory Military Service 113

Figure 30: 1945, Kerman: Wedding photo taken in Kerman upon arrival of Homayun and Jamshid from Yazd. Jamshid's uncle, Faridu, and his wife, GoharBanu, are sitting on his left side. His mother and his sister, Katayun, are sitting on the right side of Homayun. 113

Figure 31: 1949, Kerman: Visit of Professor Pour-Davoud (3rd from right in the front row) to Kerman as a guest of Jamshid Soroushian. 114

Figure 32: 1957, Kerman Airport: Jamshid Soroushian (first from right) welcoming Mohamed Reza Shah Pahlavi to Kerman for a Royal Visit. Standing next to Jamshid is Mr. Shahpur Kaikhosrow Kianian 115

Figure 33: 1963, Kerman: A family photo of Jamshid and Homayun Soroushian with their five offspring and Homayun's older sister, KhorshidBanu. 116

Figure 34: 1964, Kerman: Novruz community-wide celebration hosted by the Zoroastrian Association. Jamshid (second from right in the second row) was the president of the Anjuman. 116

Figure 35: 1965, Kerman: Jamshid Soroushian in the audience with Mohamed Reza Shah Pahlavi during a royal visit to Kerman...117

Figure 36: Decorative Wall Carpet commissioned by Jamshid Soroushian depicting the artist's impression of the burning of Persepolis by Alexander of Macedonia in 330 BCE 118

Figure 37: 1956, Kerman: Mehrborzin (1st from right) standing next to his father at a reception for a group of Parsis visiting from India. 131

Figure 38: 1956, Tehran: Mehrbanou standing in front of her mother with the rest of her family posing for a family portrait.. 132

Figure 39: 1963, Kerman: Iranshahr School Boy Scout Troops at the Main Kerman Stadium 133

Figure 40: February 1964, Kerman: Birth Day celebration for Mehrborzin and his sisters, Armity and Anahita, at home with Cousins, Aunts, Uncles, and friends......................... 133

Figure 41: 1980, London, UK: Wedding Ceremony of Mehrbanou and Mehrborzin at the Zoroastrian House in London.. 134

Figure 42: September 1992, Vancouver, Canada: NovJote Ceremony of Vishtasp (left) and Viraf (right) sited with their parents Mehrborzin and Mehrbanou 135

Figure 43: 1935, Kerman: Arastu (standing behind his parents). Hamayun & Khosrow Soroushian (holding their second daughter, PouranDokht Sitting in the Front row: Parvin and her brother Aflatoon. 139

Figure 44: 1941, Tehran: From left: Khosrow Esfandiyar and Rustom Esfandiyar................ 139

Figure 45: 1938, Kerman: Standing from Left, Hormuzd, Mahindokht, Katayun Seated in the front is their grandmother, Banu Gushtasp Dinyar, and Katayun's firstborn daughter, IranBanu 145

Figure 46: 1945, Kerman: Manuchehr Dinyar Shahriari 145

Figure 47: 1951, London: Front row (L to R) Mrs. Mehrabi, Kiandokht Kianian, Mahindokht Soroushian. Back row (L-R) Mr. Khodadad Mehrabi, IranBanu Jamshid Fravahar............... 146

Figure 48: 1957, Germany: Mahindokht and Manutcher...................................... 146

Figure 49: 1934, Kerman: Tooran seated in the front (right side) for a family photo............ 151

Figure 50: 1957, Tehran: Tooran (seated first from left) with her first daughter, Homa, husband, Bahram mother, Gohar, and her two brothers, Siross and Shahrokh. 151

Figure 51: 1961 Tehran, Family photo taken in their home garden in Tehran, Bahram (holding Vida),Tooran (holding Mitra) and Homa are standing. 152

Figure 52: 1944, Kerman: Banu standing between her brother Shahriar and father Faridun behind her grandmother (seated)... 157

Figure 53: 1945, Kerman: Wedding of Banu Soroushian and Mehraban Hormuzdi surrounded by family members 157

Figure 54: 1953 Tehran's Shah Reza Boulevard. Photograph captured by Dr. Hormuzdi depicting the return of Shah Mohamed Reza Pahlavi and Queen Sorraya from Italy amidst the constitutional crisis involving Prime Minister Mosadeq. 158

Figure 55: 1958, Kermanshah: Banu and Mehraban Hormuzdi with their four daughters 158

Figure 56: 1992 Payke Mehr Publication Report on Dedication of a Residential unit in Tehran in Memory of Dr. Mehraban Hormuzdi and his siblings for Zoroastrian Philanthropical use in Tehran 159

Figure 57: 1940, Albany: Building housing Rustom's Retail Carpet and Luxury Goods Store 164

Figure 58: 1940, Albany: Rustom (seated on the right) and Winifred, seated across from him and his friends 165

Figure 59: 1952, Albany: Rustom and his son Peter, daughter Karen, along with his cousin, Khosrow Esfandiyar Soroushian, visiting from Iran 165

Figure 60: 1956, Albany Times Union Newspaper Interview with Rustom Kermani 166

Figure 61: 1970, Middle East-Iran report on Rustom Kermani School Dedication 166

Figure 62: 1971, Cover Page of Hukht Publication in Iran carrying an interview with Mr. Rustom Kermani 167

Figure 63: 1939, Kerman: Khodamorad (second row, second from right) posing for a family photo before his departure for the US. Standing in the middle (dark suit) is Soroush Shahriar Soroushian 171

Figure 64: 1939, NY Harbor: Khodamorad's US Landing Permit 171

Figure 65 October 2, 1933: Albany Evening News Report Announcing Arrival of Khodamorad 172

Figure 66: 1945, Albany, NY: Khodamorad and Ruth's Wedding Photo (center of the photo)) 173

Figure 67: 2023, Upstate New York: Ruth and Khodamorad's offspring, (L to R) Ronald, David and Karyl 173

Figure 68: A page from Yazd's Naseri Anjuman Annual of 1893 indicating Rustom Kaikhosrow Viraf and Khosrow Shahjahan as signatories. 181

Figure 69: Descendents of Rustom and Mahasti family gathering in Kerman in 1934 181

Figure 70: 1957 Yazd Airport: Sohrab Kianian (3rd from Right) leading the Zoroastrian delegation in welcoming the Shah of Iran on his inspection of flood relief operations in Yazd. 183

Figure 71: 1956 Yazd, Second row: Sohrab Kianian (1st Left), Simin Khosrow ShahJahan (1st Right) on the occasion of the wedding of their second son Feridon (2nd from Right) with Simin Mazdeh (second from the left), In the back row, left to right, Jamshid Soroushian, Homayun

Mehrborzin Jamshid Soroushian

Sohrab Kianian, KhorshidBanu Sohrab Kianian, and Rustom Sohrab Kianian, Sitted in the front from left to right, Soroush Jamshid Soroushian, Mahvash Jamshid Soroushian, Mehrborzin Jamshid Soroushian... 184

Chapter 1
Introduction

The aim of this book is to narrate the history of the Zoroastrians of Iran in the past three centuries on a micro level of singular families. We follow the struggles of the successive generations of two Zoroastrian families. Each of these families managed to endure the hostile environment that permeated the dominantly Islamic State as it related to the treatment of the non-Moslems in general and in particular to the treatment of the remaining packets of Zoroastrians who had managed to persevere in their ancestral land. The span of time for this family history is from the early 18th century to the early 21st century.

The information captured in this book is mostly from documented as well as from orally transmitted family history passed from one generation to the next. Additional sources included community and family business records covering the period from the late 19th century to the 21st century. Another source of information was personal recollections of family members and community[1] elders who were still alive in the late 20th century and early 21st century and who, in their youth years, had contact with the prior generations of these families. As for the life story of the generations of the family who lived in the 18th century and early 19th century, given the scarcity of recorded family history for that period, the scant evidence on the resettlements of remaining Zoroastrians from various localities in Khorasan and their likely landing points in Yazd and Kerman was drawn upon. Furthermore, information about the growth of Yazd City and the Zoroastrian quarters of Yazd City was factored in to determine the likely arrival period for these families in the city of Yazd, which became a regional commercial hub in the course of the 19th century. The growing Zoroastrian presence in the city was a contributing factor to the thriving business environment in Yazd,[2] and that outcome itself resulted in attracting more Zoroastrian arrivals from Khorasan to relocate to the city of Yazd.

Relative to the names of the earlier generations of the family living in the 18th century, in a few cases, the traditional naming convention was drawn upon to come up with their likely forenames.

Historical Background

The past three centuries were a make-or-break period for the survival of a viable Zoroastrian community in their ancestral land. The 18th century witnessed the end of the Safavid dynasty, which had consolidated power over Iran under the banner of Shiite Islam. Non-

---

[1] Reference is to the Zoroastrian community of Kerman, and to the Moslems who were in close contact with members of this family whose lineage is .reviewed in the following chapters.

[2] The rise of British Raj and the port city of Bombay as a major business center in the course of the 19th century was a factor. The Parsis had a dominant position in business and commerce in India and were mostly centered in Bombay. The British Raj extended its influence to the Persian Gulf and Southern Persia. The Zoroastrians of Yazd in particular benefited from conducting business with their coreligionists in India. That connection gave them an advantage.

Moslems were discriminated against and, on many occasions, massacred, with the net result that the population of Zoroastrians dropped from about four million at the beginning of the Safavid rule in 1500 to just over 90,000[3] in 1722 when the Safavids were defeated by the Sunni militia from the Eastern flank of the Iranian territory.[4] The continuous genocidal acts of massacres, kidnapping of their youngsters, burdensome taxation, and unjust rules and restrictions imposed on the Zoroastrians by the local rulers and carried out by mobs and ruffians had taken its toll.

The bloodshed and insecurity that marked much of the 18th century in Iran, including in the Eastern province of Khorasan, resulted in the displacement of the remaining Zoroastrians from that province. They sought refuge in the environmentally harsh central regions on the southern rim of the Iranian desert in Yazd and later in Kerman due to the relative remoteness of those localities.

In 1856 an accurate census of the Zoroastrians of Iran was taken by Maneckji Limji Hataria.[5] Only 7,300 were found to have managed to survive in Yazd, Kerman, and Kermanshah.[6]

Since the family stories covered in this book all had their origin in 18th-century Khorasan[7], more specifics about the condition of the remaining Zoroastrians in that Northeastern province are described below.

Over the years leading to the 18th century, Zoroastrians had been driven out of major cities in Khorasan. They could live in the proximity of the cities. Going back to the 7th century A.C., when the Arab invaders waging the banner of Islam arrived in Khorasan, Zoroastrians were dominant in all aspects of the life of that prosperous province. Notwithstanding all the war crimes that were perpetuated against the populace of Khorasan by the invaders, the process of Islamization of that province only went into full gear some two centuries after the initial assault. As successive local rulers vying for dominance came to power, they imposed discriminatory rules on the Zoroastrians, who were amongst the most vulnerable segments of the population.

---

3 A 98% reduction in the number of adherents of the Zoroastrians of Iran during the reign of the Safavids (span of 220 years)

4 Present day Southern Afghanistan

5 Maneckji Limji Hataria was dispatched to Iran by the Bombay based Society for the Amelioration of the Zoroastrians of Iran in 1854. At the time of arrival, he was 41 years old and spent much of the rest of his life in Iran and did much towards improving the conditions of the Zoroastrians in Iran.

6 The reduction in the number of adherents of the Zoroastrian religion in Iran from 4 million at the beginning of the 16th century to just under 7300 in the year 1856 meant a 99% decrease that had brought the community to the verge extinction.

7 Historically Khorasan ranks amongst the most agriculturally rich and populace provinces. The Silk Road trade benefited Khorasan and was a source of livelihood for the merchant class in Khorasan that included Zoroastrian families who lived close to major cities and or close to trading hubs in Khorasan. Over the course of years, some of the Zoroastrian families had established business relationship with merchants in other countries as well as in the interior of Iran. These trading contacts had typically been further fostered by successive generations, as in most cases the sons would follow in the footsteps of their fathers in continuation of the family business. Besides agricultural products Khorsan also had a rich artisanry and carpet weaving production base that were suited for trade.

Echoes of Survival

The local rulers who were Moslem converts, found it advantageous to be aligned with the Arab caliphs ruling from Baghdad and were considered as vassals of the Caliphs. The harsh treatment of Zoroastrians and non-Moslems was their way of proving their adherence and loyalty to the Caliph's rule.

The ongoing discrimination perpetuated against the Zoroastrians and the frequent political upheavals over the years took its toll on the Zoroastrians of Iran, including those in the Khorasan province. As a result, their number kept shrinking. By the 16th century, the Zoroastrians were barred from holding bureaucratic positions and driven out of major cities in Khorasan. With the increased pressure and limitations imposed on the Zoroastrians, an ever-decreasing number could sustain themselves as adherents of their ancestral faith. The others who felt powerless had to abandon their ancestral faith and convert to Islam in order to get relief from excessive taxation and discrimination. Clusters of Zoroastrians could be found living in the proximity of major cities in Khorasan. They typically had a Zoroastrian priest family living amongst them or within reasonable proximity of them. They also understood the importance of making sure their children gained some level of education and were well-versed in the tenets of their religion.

Increasingly, only merchants, especially the ones who were engaged in trading with other locations and outside of Khorasan, as well as farm owners and agriculturists, had the means to sustain themselves. The excessive taxes and discriminatory measures imposed on Zoroastrians had made their lives very difficult. Some of the Zoroastrian merchants had trustworthy Moslem partners who provided them a useful shield and allowed them to pursue their business activities with less encumberment. In the case of one of my maternal ancestral lines, part of their family in Khorasan had converted to Islam but continued to work closely with their Zoroastrian family members. Subsequent to the Zoroastrian portion of the family abandoning their livelihoods in Khorasan and fleeing to Yazd, the Moslem relatives also followed them due to increased insecurity and turmoil.

Despite their religious zeal, the local Moslem rulers seemed to have understood the contribution the Zoroastrians were making to the economies in their domains. As such most local rulers would exercise some degree of tolerance towards this enterprising community. It was usually during periods of political upheavals and uncertainty involving outside forces that the Zoroastrians were very vulnerable. During such periods, their physical safety and livelihood would be in serious jeopardy.

The upheavals of the 18th century caused the remaining packets of Zoroastrians who had survived in various regions of Khorasan[8] to once and for all upend their livelihoods and move to safer sanctuaries around Yazd. After that period, we find no trace of any remaining Zoroastrians in Khorasan. Likely those who remained were eventually forced to convert to Islam.

---

[8] By 18th century packets of Zoroastrians had survived in the suburbs of few of major cities and trade hubs in Western Khorasan, such as Bardaskan, Neyshabur, Herat and Gonabad.

The factors that had made Yazd villages more of a sanctuary were the harshness of its landscape and their undesirability to invading armies. The new Zoroastrian arrivals ended up developing villages in remote areas where underground water could be brought to the surface at lower elevations compared to the source of the underground water reservoirs, usually at the base of mountains. The qanat systems that they had to construct delivered continuous water and enabled them to cultivate the land and turn the desert into fertile agricultural oases. Some of the new arrivals would use these landing points, as a staging area to plan their next move into the city.

Focus of this Book

The life stories of eight generations of my paternal and maternal ancestry are related in this book. It turns out that both my paternal and maternal ancestries trace back to various localities in the Western part of the greater Khorasan province of the early 18th century (vicinity of three cities - Gonabad in South-Central, and Bardaskan and Neyshabur further North). There is no evidence these families knew each other and or were in contact with one another during their years in Khorasan. Suffice it to say each family found it necessary to uproot themselves from their ancestral abodes in Khorasan in the course of the 18th century and to flee to safer localities in the Yazd province. That meant abandoning the livelihoods they had built over the years in Khorasan and to re-establish themselves in their new abodes.

As much detail about the life conditions of each generation that could be sourced has been reflected in the chapters of this book.

The coverage narrates the life events of both the husband and the wife heads for each generation of the family. Information about the successive generations of each family was mostly available on the paternal side, and that is reflected here. In the case of my paternal ancestry my paternal grandfather and my paternal grandmother were first cousins, and so they had the same paternal grandparents; as such, the coverage for their prior generations is identical.

I also captured the information relevant to my mother's ancestry from the paternal branch.

I hope this information gives the reader insights into the great sacrifice that each generation made to safeguard their heritage and pass it on to those who came after them. The tale of their heroic struggle to overcome adversity and prevail should be an inspiration to us all.

The life stories of the generations of these families from the 18th century to the 21st century can be categorized as follows.

1. 18th century - Flight of Survival (fleeing Khorasan)

2. 19th century - Resilience Born of Acute hardship (Resettlements in new abodes – Yazd and Kerman)

3. 20th century (first half) – Regeneration - (seizing opportunities and prevailing)

4. 20th century (1945 Onwards) - Continued Upward Mobility

5. 20th century (1979 – 1999) - Flight Westwards (Departing their ancestral land for North America and the West)

Echoes of Survival

6. 21st Century (1980s – 2120s) - Establishing themselves in the West

Chapter 2
My Paternal Ancestry

The genesis of my paternal ancestry study begins with a generation compelled to uproot their lives in Khorasan and seek refuge in safer environs near Yazd on the periphery of the central desert. They represent the final generation of our family born in Khorasan driven by the imperative to safeguard their Zoroastrian heritage by leaving the region.

2.1 Kaykhosrow Hormuzd & Daulat Jamshid
2.1.1 Kaykhosrow Hormuzd
1724 – 1772 (Gonabad, Khorasan – Mehdi Abad, Yazd)

Figure 1: Ruins of the Zoroastrian Fire Temple of Gonabad in use through the mid-18th century.

Kaykhosrow was the eldest son of Hormuzd Gushtasp and his wife Firozeh, born in the vicinity of Gonabad in the southwestern part of Greater Khorasan during the early 18th century. Growing up amidst a community of Zoroastrian families, Kaykhosrow and his siblings received their education at home, guided by two neighbors. They also witnessed Zoroastrian ceremonies performed by a local priest on special occasions at the still-active Zoroastrian Fire Temple nearby.

During his formative years, Kaykhosrow developed a keen interest in his father's farming business and often accompanied him on horseback during inspection tours. Hormuzd Gushtasp was also involved in trading farm products with merchants in other locations.

The relative remoteness of their home shielded them from the periodic warfare that afflicted major cities in Khorasan. As a precautionary measure against the vulnerability felt by Zoroastrians, they had arranged safe hideaways stocked with water and food to sustain the family for several weeks at a time.

Echoes of Survival

The turmoil that unfolded in Eastern Iran following the fall of the Safavids disrupted trade, presenting challenges that Kaykhosrow's father had to address. This experience imparted valuable lessons to Kaykhosrow, which proved beneficial throughout his life. Additionally, there were years of minimal farm yields due to severe cold, during which Kaykhosrow learned resilience and the importance of contingency planning from his family.

At the age of twenty-four, Kaykhosrow tied the knot with Daulat Jamshid, whom he had encountered at community gatherings during their upbringing. Daulat subsequently moved in with Kaykhosrow, and within a year, they welcomed their first child, a son named Bahram. The couple had two daughters as well, Morwarid and Sarvar.

The absence of a robust central government during the first half of the 18th century rendered security conditions in provinces like Khorasan exceedingly precarious. The downfall of Safavid rule, centered in Isfahan, at the hands of rebellious Sunnis from the eastern regions exacerbated these conditions. Ragtag bands began to form, often targeting the vulnerable inhabitants of prosperous settlements left defenseless due to the absence of local rulers' who were able to provide protection to the inhabitants.

Among the most vulnerable were the Zoroastrians, who faced increasing harassment and perilous circumstances. With the escalating Sunni-Shiite conflict and the questioning of Shiites' Islamic faith by Sunnis, many Shiites directed hostility towards their long-standing Zoroastrian neighbors as a means of asserting their own Islamic credentials. Faced with these mounting dangers, an increasing number of Zoroastrians began to make plans to abandon their homes in Khorasan in favor of safer locales.

There was a prevailing belief that greater safety could be found in remote areas of the Yazd province. Consequently, many Zoroastrians began to consider liquidating whatever wealth they could from their holdings and to resettle in more secure areas surrounding Yazd city. These areas promised not only safety but also the potential to rebuild their livelihoods.

As their children matured, Kaykhosrow and Daulat came to the realization that they needed to relocate in order to secure a better future for their offspring. Their intention was to relocate to Yazd, aligning their move with other family members.

In anticipation of his impending departure from Khorasan, Kaykhosrow had already secured a deal with a prosperous Muslim merchant interested in acquiring farmland around Gonabad. For the buyer, who had thoroughly assessed the agricultural holdings and the accompanying residence, it represented an opportunity to acquire prime property at a discounted rate. For Kaykhosrow, cognizant of the potential for his property to be confiscated without compensation due to his minority status, it offered a chance to receive partial compensation and to escape the tumult of Khorasan. The buyer's ability to make payments in valuable coins and his past track record of being honorable in his business dealings were a factor.

Kaykhosrow's brother had similarly arranged a deal with the same buyer. Both brothers found it a bitter pill to swallow, considering the arduous efforts their father and grandfather had invested in developing those farming lands. They had to balance their sentimental attachment with the prospects for future generations.

Shortly after the passing of Kaykhosrow's father, Hormuzd, in 1765, Kaykhosrow and his brother relocated to MehdiAbad, situated to the north of Yazd, where some of their relatives and Zoroastrian acquaintances had already settled. Kaykhosrow's mother would accompany his family to MehdiAbad, though she would sadly pass away five years later.

The move itself required careful coordination. Typically, the family embarked on their journey quietly at night so as not to arouse suspicion among their non-Zoroastrian neighbors. They also had to pay a group to accompany them and provide protection from potential harm during their flight.

Daulat's family also relocated to Yazd, settling in a village further west of MehdiAbad. Family reunions occurred only a few times a year, as each family focused on their own livelihoods and sustenance. The initial village accommodation they settled into resembled miniature versions of the houses they had left behind in Khorasan.

Twelve years after arriving in MehdiAbad, Kaykhosrow succumbed to the harshness of a severe winter and passed away. His wife, Daulat, and their children had to carry on. Bahram, the eldest offspring, 19 years old at the time, continued the family's farming and trading business. Fortunately, his paternal uncle had also relocated to MehdiAbad with his own family and was there to offer guidance and support whenever needed.

2.1.2 Daulat Jamshid Marzban
1731 - 1780 (Gonabad, Khorasan – MehdiAbad, Yazd)

Daulat was Jamshid's and Mahasti's third child. She and her four siblings were raised in a modest house situated near the farmland owned by their father to the north of Gonabad. At least four other Zoroastrian families resided nearby, among them one whose head would conduct Zoroastrian religious ceremonies for all Zoroastrian families in and around Gonabad. The majority of other Zoroastrian families lived to the south and west of them.

As they grew up, Daulat, her siblings, and the other Zoroastrian children living nearby would frequently gather to receive schooling from one of the neighbor's wives. They were taught basic reading, writing, mathematics, and basic tenets of the Zoroastrian faith. From childhood, they were emphatically instructed not to wander away from the supervision of adults and to exercise caution when approached by unfamiliar adults.

At a young age, their parents also acquainted them with hiding spots near the house, instructing them that in the event of an attack on the house, they should seek refuge there. These hideaways were stocked with preserved food and water to sustain them for several weeks if necessary. Years later, their parents recounted the tragic attack on two of their Zoroastrian neighbors, whose brutal killings went unpunished.

As Daulat and her siblings entered their teenage years, their parents occasionally voiced their concerns about the increasing threat faced by the remaining Zoroastrian families. They discussed the three alternatives each family would have to consider: either selling their holdings at a discount and fleeing to safer locations to preserve their religious identity, taking the risk to stay and protect their property, or trying to retain their holdings at the expense of sacrificing their religious identity which was the least desirable option. The parents expressed dismay at the possibility that some families might opt for the third alternative, which could ultimately result in them losing their property despite their efforts.

Daulat often fondly reminisced about her childhood, recalling how she helped with the practice of drying fruits by slicing some of the produce from their orchards and spreading them on the roof to dry in the sun. These dried fruits became a staple snack during the winter, with most of them being sold to retailers. Daulat also treasured memories of annual feasts such as NovRuz, Ordibehshtgan, Tirgan, Mehrgan, Yalda, and Sadeh.[9] She, along with other Zoroastrian families, continued to hold these celebrations for their new generations to enjoy and become familiar with.

There were occasions when Zoroastrians from around Gonabad would come together for festivities, providing opportunities for the youth to socialize. It was during these community events that Daulat met Kaykhosrow on several occasions.

Shortly after turning 18, Daulat received a proposal to marry Kaykhosrow Hormuzd. They were soon wed, and Daulat relocated to Kaykhosrow's farmhouse. With the birth of their children, the couple grew increasingly concerned about their offspring's safety and future prospects. They received news that more and more Zoroastrians from various parts of Khorasan were migrating to Yazd and Kerman. With escalating Shia-Sunni conflicts, the Zoroastrians sensed an existential threat to them in Khorasan. Consequently, Daulat and Kaykhosrow began to plan their departure from the region. The circumstances surrounding their relocation to the Yazd province were detailed in the preceding section.

In MehdiAbad, they constructed a modest house on a farm they had purchased while simultaneously establishing their livelihood as their children grew up. They instilled in their offspring lofty ideals, emphasizing the importance of overcoming discrimination and life's challenges. Despite limited trading opportunities compared to Gonabad, Kaykhosrow imparted to his children the lessons he had gleaned from his trading experiences, encouraging them to seek out business opportunities. Meanwhile, Daulat instilled in her children a sense of pride in their Zoroastrian heritage, making them aware of the sacrifices made by previous generations.

Twelve years after their arrival, Kaykhosrow passed away, leaving their son Bahram to step in and continue his father's work. Three years later, Bahram married Rudabeh Shahriar, whose family had relocated to MehdiAbad from Tabas, another locality in Khorasan.

Daulat lived long enough to witness all her children marry and establish their own lives. While her two sons and one daughter remained in MehdiAbad, her youngest daughter married a Zoroastrian man from a different village and moved to his farmhouse. Although she was only a half day's journey away from MehdiAbad, she would only visit from time to time.

---

[9] These were the annual celebrations observed by Zoroastrians and many Iranians. Nowruz marks the first day of spring and the beginning of the new year. Tirgan is the summer festival, Mehrgan is the fall festival, Yalda is the winter festival, and Sadeh is a fire festival held 50 days before the start of spring.

Outliving her husband by eight years, Daulat had the opportunity to meet some of her grandchildren, including Jamshid Bahram, before her passing.

2.2 Bahram Kaykhosrow Hormuzd & Rudabeh Shahriar Mehrab
2.2.1 Bahram Kaykhosrow Hormuzd
1750 – 1797 (Gonabad, Khorasan – MehdiAbad, Yazd)

Bahram was Kaykhosrow's and Daulat's eldest child. He was ten years old when his family left Khorasan and took the risky journey to MehdiAbad. Years later, Bahram would still have nightmares about their flight from Gonabad to MehdiAbad. On that dangerous trip, he had to constantly comfort his younger siblings so they could cope with the demands of the long land trip without crying and drawing attention to themselves until they reached their destination. Later he came to appreciate the sacrifice his elders had made for his and his siblings' future sakes in making the move. As he was settling in MehdiAbad, the news they were getting from new arrivals from Khorasan was that Khorason was becoming increasingly unsafe for the remaining Zoroastrian families there.

Bahram realized some of these small hamlets around Yazd did not exist before the 18th century due to the harshness of the environment and the lack of surface water needed to cultivate the land for agriculture. It was the remoteness and the undesirable nature of the landscape that had appealed to the Zoroastrian families fleeing prejudice and genocidal acts directed at them in other parts of Islamized Iran. The Zoroastrians constructed underground aqueducts, called Qanats, to channel water typically from the base of mountains many miles away to irrigate the vacant lands and transform them into farms. Most of the settlements had no Moslem population at the beginning, but as the farms and fruit orchards around the hamlets became fertile and self-sustaining, Moslems were also attracted. Once a Moslem priest arrived, trouble for the Zoroastrians would usually follow. This included the kidnapping and abduction of young Zoroastrians and their forcible conversion into Islam at the hands of the fanatical Moslems.

While the provincial rulers in Yazd city took a hands-off approach towards these new villages at first while the hard-working Zoroastrian refugees were developing the land, once a conflict broke out between a Zoroastrian and a Moslem, they would take the side of the Moslem. As the Moslem population of these villages increased, the names of the villages were changed to Arab-sounding names, and, in some cases, the Zoroastrians would be coerced into converting to Islam or be driven off their properties.

As the oldest son, Bahram knew that he needed to help his father with the farm, including extending the waterway so more of the raw land could be used for agriculture. Bahram was also a good mentor to his younger brother.

The experience Bahram gained working closely with his father gave him the confidence to carry on once his father passed away. Bahram was twenty years old at the time. Bahram and his younger brother had to carry the work forward and expand their farmland.

Two years later, in a nearby village, Bahram came across a young Zoroastrian girl by the name of Rudabeh, whose family had moved from Tabas, Khorasan. The chance encounter blossomed into a lasting bond. Soon, Bahram's mother and siblings were introduced to Rudabeh and her family. At twenty-two, Bahram married Rudabeh. Subsequently Rudabeh moved in with Bahram in MehdiAbad. The following year, their daughter was born, followed two years later by the birth of their first son who was given the forename of Jamshid. The couple had another daughter and son years later.

In the meantime, Bahram's operation was expanding. Bahram started transporting produce grown on the farm by donkey to nearby settlements to sell or barter. He then extended his operation in coordination with farmers from nearby villages, including his father-in-law; they would transport the produce to Yazd city and sell it to bazaari merchants. He managed to identify the Moslem Bazari merchants[10] who would buy farm products from Zoroastrians. Bahram also had to figure out when and how to travel to avoid becoming a victim of highway robbers. The travel to the city took more than a day and usually required resting on the way. He would coordinate and travel with a number of other farmers and had guard dogs accompanying them.[11] Bahram also expanded his operation by transporting other local farmers' produce to Yazd city and selling it there in exchange for a service fee. Bahram's sons helped him operate the farm and accompanied him on some of his trips.

In 1794, a calamity befell the family when the governor's militia came to the village looking for able young men to be taken away. Several Zoroastrian youth, including Jamshid Bahram, were spotted and snatched by the militia and taken away swiftly before the villagers could mount any form of resistance. Other militias conducted similar raids on other villages and seized many young Zoroastrian boys. The families were never told the reason for the seizure and the fate of their youth. The loss of his son caused too much grief for Bahram, who passed away the following year. The rest of the family was left to carry on.

Bahram left behind a profound legacy. Within one generation of his family's relocation to a new environment, he was able to expand his father's farming business, add more dimensions to it, and make it profitable. He also established reliable business contacts outside his immediate surroundings and effectively mentored his children. They all became committed to their community and to the cause of safeguarding their heritage.

---

10 Some of the more prejudicial Moslem would not buy farm products or food items from Zoroastrians.

11 Once they reached the safe vicinity of the city, one of the farmers would stay behind with the dogs due to the Moslem's negative view of dogs on religious grounds.

2.2.2 Rudabeh Shahriar Mehrab
1754 – 1805 (Tabas, Khorasan – MehdiAbad, Yazd)

Figure 2: Natural Springs inside a mountainous cave close to Historic Tabas, Khorasan

Rudabeh and her three siblings were born in an agrarian area close to Tabas, Khorasan, where their parents, uncles, and grandparents also lived. The family settled around Tabas several generations before and engaged in trade and farming. Their family was amongst the remaining Zoroastrians in the area that managed to sustain themselves despite all the challenges to which non-Moslems were subjected. Rudabeh's father, Shahriar, was a productive and successful merchant who established business contacts with a number of merchants in other parts of Khorasan and adjoining provinces, as well as in other major settlements further to the east of Khorasan. Shahriar would, on occasion, travel to other locations in pursuit of his business interests. His travel experience became very handy when, in 1770, he felt the need to move his family to Yazd province due to the worsening conditions for the remaining Zoroastrians in Tabas. The exodus of Zoroastrians from Khorasan had accelerated several decades earlier, and Shahriar and his family were among the last to flee to Yazd from Tabas. Assaults on Zoroastrians in

Echoes of Survival

Khorasan and raids on their businesses by fanatical Moslems had increased in recent months. Rudabeh was 16 years old when this life-changing relocation took place in the spring. Although this was her first long-distance trip, she felt reassured by her father who was a seasoned traveler leading the departing party. Their destination was a settlement close to MehdiAbad in the Yazd province that another group of Zoroastrians from Tabas, including one of her uncles, had founded years earlier. It took a few years of planning, several months of preparation, and over two weeks of travel for the family to move to Yazd.[12]

A significant amount of effort from each member of the family contributed to the construction of their new home. Situated on a farm they had recently acquired, the house was modest in size compared to their previous residence near Tabas. Rudabeh and her siblings were actively involved in assisting their parents as they settled into their new home. Despite the demands of relocating, her mother remained dedicated to homeschooling her children. Like the few remaining Zoroastrian families in 18th-century Khorasan, Rudabeh's parents were literate and adept at staying informed about events beyond their region. They made a concerted effort to impart knowledge and cultivate resilience in their children, particularly in the face of prejudice and hostility directed towards them.

The serendipitous encounter between Rudabeh and Bahram Kaykhosrow, who hailed from MehdiAbad, sparked regular gatherings between their families. Rudabeh, along with her parents, embraced Bahram's marriage proposal,[13] leading to their union when Rudabeh turned twenty. The fact that her father, Shahriar, held Bahram in high regard further facilitated their union. Following their marriage, Rudabeh relocated to MehdiAbad, where the couple welcomed their first child, a daughter named Narguess, the subsequent year. Two years later, their first son, Jamshid, was born, expanding the family. Several years down the line, they were blessed with the arrival of a second daughter and a second son, further enriching their household.

Rudabeh dedicated herself to the upbringing and education of her children, following the example set by her own parents. Additionally, she assisted Bahram with farm duties and managed household chores. From a young age, Rudabeh involved her children in household and farm tasks. She remained mindful of the precautionary advice imparted by her parents, passing it on to her own children. These lessons included guidance on how to respond if they were ever abducted, encouraging resilience and seeking opportunities to escape to safety. They were taught to be discerning of strangers, assessing whether they posed a threat. As a conclusion to these survival teachings, the children were advised to uphold their family values and traditions, striving for excellence even in the face of adversity. Rudabeh and Bahram emphasized the

---

12 Despite the relocation to the remote area in Yazd province, Shahriar managed to stay in contact with some of the merchants in Tabas with whom he had established long-standing business dealings, and he made a few trips back to Khorasan in pursuit of his business interests.

13 The customary tradition would have involved Bahram's parents formally extending the marriage proposal to Rudabeh's parents.

importance of retaining these lifelong lessons and passing them on to future generations when they themselves became parents.

When Rudabeh's first son, Jamshid, was abducted by the governor's militia, she was forty years old. The following year, her husband Bahram passed away, leaving her grief-stricken. Despite facing both tragedies, Rudabeh remained resilient, caring for her three remaining children and managing the farm. At just eleven years old, her youngest son, along with her two sisters, stepped up to fill the void left by the loss of their father and brother, Jamshid.

Rudabeh's father, Shahriar, was still alive when these hardships befell the family. Determined to support Rudabeh and her grandchildren, he devoted himself to helping them move forward despite his advanced age. The family endured, with Shahriar providing as much assistance as he could in the time he had left.

Despite the challenges, Rudabeh lived for another ten years, witnessing her daughters' marriages and her younger son taking on the responsibility of managing the family farm and business.

Reflection on Rudabeh's life: With Rudabeh's passing, the 18th-century chapter of our family's narrative draws to a close. Yet, her unwavering dedication, determination, and steadfastness, mirroring those who preceded her, ensured the continuity of our Zoroastrian lineage, community, and the enduring traditions that have sustained us throughout history. Rudabeh epitomized the pivotal role played by Zoroastrian women in nurturing their children to confront the prejudices and adversities they would inevitably encounter as they matured. Equipping them with life survival skills, imparting education, and preparing them for the responsibilities of adulthood were integral facets of her maternal duties.

Reflecting on her life, we, her descendants three centuries later, stand as fortunate heirs to her legacy. Our lineage traces back to her eldest son, Jamshid, who endured abduction and forced labor in Kerman. Despite the hardships, Jamshid persevered, paving the way for his descendants to ascend and fulfill their potential.

Furthermore, certain descendants of Rudabeh's eldest daughter, Narguess, who ventured further west to Ardakan, flourished during the course of the 20th century within the context of Pahlavi Iran. Many have since resettled in the United States and Canada, contributing to the rich tapestry of our family's diaspora.

Bahram Kaykhosrow
1750 – 1795
(Gonabad, Khorasan – MehdiAbad, Yazd)

Rudabeh Shahriar
1754 – 1805
(Tabas, Khorasan – MehdiAbad, Yazd)

Nargues Bahram
1775- 1826 (MehdiAbad)

Jamshid Bahram
1777 -1823 (MehdiAbad – Kerman)

Firozeh Bahram
1780 - ? (MehdiAbad - ?)

Borzu Bahram
1784 - ? (MehdiAbad - ?)

Figure 3: Descendants of Bahram Kaykhosrow and Rudabeh Shahriar

2.3 Jamshid Bahram Kaykhosrow & Firozehe Bahman Khodabux
2.3.1 Jamshid Bahram Kaykhosrow
1777 - 1823 (MehdiAbad, Yazd – Kerman)

Jamshid spent his formative years in the quaint village of Mehdi-Abad, nestled in the heart of Yazd, alongside other Zoroastrian families who, like his own, had migrated from Khorasan in preceding decades. The meager agricultural yields in Yazd posed a constant challenge to livelihoods, compelling families to meticulously ration grain and dried fruits for sustenance during the harsh autumn and winter months. Life in the village was undeniably arduous.

Raised by their parents, Bahram and Rudabeh, Jamshid and his siblings were instilled with lofty ambitions and encouraged to seek opportunities beyond the confines of their rural existence. Bahram and Rudabeh imparted invaluable lessons to their children, preparing them for the inevitability of encountering discrimination and urging them to cultivate resilience in the face of adversity. They emphasized the importance of perseverance in pursuit of their aspirations.

With no formal educational infrastructure in the village, knowledge was imparted by parents and elders, who shared the wisdom they had acquired firsthand. Ensuring the youth were well-versed in the tenets of the Zoroastrian faith and acquainted with the struggles of previous generations to uphold their religious heritage was a priority for the elders. Through oral tradition, they preserved the rich history of resilience and determination that defined their community.

As the eldest son, Jamshid often joined his father on various excursions, actively assisting in the management of their family farm. His bond with his grandfather, Shahriar, was particularly strong, as Shahriar occasionally accompanied them on trips to Yazd city. Shahriar served as another influential figure in Jamshid's life, leaving an indelible mark on his character.

However, the trajectory of Jamshid's life was soon to be influenced by the unfolding geopolitical events of the region. A concise overview of these events follows.

Mehrborzin Jamshid Soroushian

1. In 1748, Mohammad Taghi Khan, the son of Mirza Mohammad Baghar, seized control of the governorship of Yazd. Despite the tumultuous power struggles and shifting allegiances across Iran, he maintained his grip on power in Yazd until his death in 1798. Taghi Khan wielded authority with a formidable militia at his command. To erect the governor's opulent mansion in Yazd, known as Daulat Abad, Taghi Khan resorted to egregious tactics, exploiting Zoroastrians from nearby villages as forced laborers. Shockingly, even pregnant women were compelled to bear heavy construction materials on their backs.[14] This cruel exploitation extended to the governor's sinister intention of inducing miscarriages, thereby diminishing the future population of Zoroastrians.

2. In 1794, Agha Mohammed Qajar conquered the city of Kerman. A brutal death was dealt to LotfAli Khan Zand[15], who had sought refuge in Kerman. The Qajars assumed control on a national level. Agha Mohammed resorted to vengeful and inhumane measures to punish the inhabitants of Kerman city for harboring the final Zand ruler. He implemented several measures aimed at the city's obliteration before departing for the Caucasus. Among his directives was the deliberate filling of all water wells with soil, effectively depriving the city of its access to drinking water.

3. In late 1793, Mohammad Taghi Khan, the governor of Yazd, who enjoyed the favor of Agha Mohammed Qajar, appealed to the Qajar ruler to spare Kerman from further harm. Eventually, the Qajar ruler acquiesced, and Mohammad Taghi Khan's son, Ali-Naghi Khan,[16] was appointed as the governor of Kerman. Upon arriving in Kerman City and witnessing the extensive devastation, Ali-Naghi Khan requested his father to provide him with a reliable workforce to aid in the city's restoration, focusing on reconstructing the city walls and infrastructure.

Once again, Mohammad Taghi Khan resorted to enslaving Zoroastrians, dispatching them for this laborious task. The governor's militia scoured Yazd villages, forcibly seizing young and capable Zoroastrian males to be sent to Kerman for forced labor. Among those forcibly separated from their families was the 17-year-old Jamshid Bahram. Shortly thereafter, Jamshid and a group of Zoroastrians embarked on their journey to Kerman. Sadly, Jamshid never had the opportunity to bid a final farewell to his family. The family likely learned of their son's fate as

---

14 Social History of the Zoroastrians of Yazd, Volume I, (in Farsi), by Dr. Ali Akbar Tashakori, UCI (University of California, Irvine) Jordan Center for Persian Studies sponsored, Year 2020, Page 189

15 LotfAli Khan Zand was the grandson of Karim Khan Zand.

Karim Khan's reign, spanning from 1751 to 1779, was characterized by a relatively peaceful period in the tumultuous 18th century Iran. Upon the demise of his father, Jafar Khan Zand, in 1789, the young prince LotfAli Khan asserted his claim to the throne, sparking a challenge from Mohammed Khan Qajar. However, LotfAli's reign proved short-lived. In March 1794, he was captured and brutally executed by order of Mohammed Qajar, who subsequently established the Qajar dynasty. The Qajar dynasty, which endured until 1924, marked a period of decline for Iran, coinciding with the ascent of colonial powers.

16 His father had installed him in charge of the Taft district in Yazd prior to this assignment.

other youths from their village and neighboring villages were similarly captured and taken away. It is believed that Jamshid's ties to his family were severed once he departed his village in Yazd and was sent to Kerman.

Upon arrival in Kerman, Jamshid and his fellow Zoroastrians, who had been forcibly relocated, found themselves housed in temporary shelters and immediately immersed in the arduous task of rebuilding Kerman's infrastructure. Despite the challenges, Kerman became Jamshid's lifelong home until his passing in 1920, tragically without ever reuniting with his parents and siblings.

Conditions for the Zoroastrian community saw a modest improvement under the governance of Ibrahim Khan Zahir Ul-Doleh, a Qajar Khan appointed by the second ruler of the Qajar dynasty in 1803. Endowed with funds specifically designated for the revitalization of Kerman, Ibrahim Khan focused his efforts on the restoration of the vital Qanat systems that served as lifelines for the city and its surrounding villages. Notably, some of these villages situated northeast of the city still retained a residual Zoroastrian population.

In one of these villages, 27-year-old Jamshid Bahram, engrossed in a construction project, crossed paths with a 22-year-old Zoroastrian woman named Firozeh Bahman. Within a year, the two were united in marriage.

Under the auspices of the new governor, Zoroastrians found themselves able to secure a decent livelihood. Before long, Jamshid Bahram had amassed sufficient savings to acquire a residence in the Zoroastrian enclave of Kerman city. This enclave, slowly recovering from the devastation wrought by Agha Mohammad Qajar, was witnessing a gradual return to normalcy. Other Zoroastrian migrants, primarily hailing from Yazd, Khorasan, and Zabol, were also settling in.

In 1807, the couple welcomed their first child, whom they named Shahriar (Jamshid Bahram), paying homage to Jamshid's maternal grandfather. Three more children followed in due course.

Despite enduring forced labor from a tender age, along with the wrenching separation from his family and the grueling toil in unfamiliar surroundings, Jamshid remained steadfast in his commitment to higher principles. He understood the imperative of imparting the same value system and ideals that had sustained his forebears to his descendants and the generations yet to come.

For Jamshid, it was akin to running a relay race towards a brighter future for his family, community, and country, even if it would take a century to fully materialize. Despite facing pervasive prejudice against Zoroastrians, they persevered, buoyed by the vision of a better, prejudice-free life not only for themselves but also for their kin and fellow beings. This optimistic outlook fueled their efforts to strive for a better tomorrow.

The reinstatement of the burdensome Jazya tax by the governor, with its stringent enforcement of annual collections, added to their challenges. The devastating loss of his young daughter Nahid, a victim of kidnapping, weighed heavily on Jamshid's heart. Nevertheless, he felt compelled to remain resilient, determined to safeguard his remaining family for as long as possible.

2.3.2 Firozehe Bahman Khodabux
1785 -1831 (Kerman)

Firozehe and her siblings were raised in a village northeast of Kerman city. Their father, Bahman, tirelessly tended to their modest-sized farm, an inheritance from his father. To supplement their income, he also served as a foreman on farmland belonging to a Muslim landlord residing in the city. Meanwhile, Firozehe's mother juggled household chores, child-rearing, tending to the livestock, and assisting her husband on the farm.

Bahman's lineage is traced back several generations in the city, where they once owned property until they were forcibly expelled due to their Zoroastrian faith. Forced to retreat to nearby villages, they were among the fortunate Zoroastrians who survived various political upheavals in Kerman and its environs while steadfastly resisting conversion to Islam. Throughout these trials, the burdensome Jazya tax remained a constant, though their farm remained intact, a stroke of luck amid adversity. Over time, however, the original farm holding dwindled as it was divided among successive inheritors.

Living in close proximity to other Zoroastrians in their village and nearby hamlets fostered a sense of community. It provided an opportunity for communal celebrations of Zoroastrian festivities away from prying eyes. These shared occasions were especially cherished by the younger villagers, affording them the chance to socialize with peers while learning about the religious significance of the celebrations.

Firozehe possessed a curious intellect, drawing knowledge and wisdom from her elders. Her keen instincts, honed through practical experience, guided her away from perilous situations that endangered vulnerable Zoroastrians. Thanks to her astuteness, she avoided the tragic fate that befell some of her peers who were kidnapped from the village.

A serendipitous encounter introduced her to Jamshid Bahram. His Dari accent and demeanor immediately signaled to Firozehe that she was meeting a fellow Zoroastrian. Their acquaintance flourished, eventually leading to marriage.

Impressed by Jamshid's sincerity and noble character, Firozehe's parents welcomed him into their family. They admired his resilience in overcoming the hardships of forced labor and his unwavering commitment to building a better future.

Determined to forge a fulfilling life together, Firozehe and Jamshid faced the pervasive prejudice against Zoroastrians and the onerous Jazya tax with fortitude. Each child they welcomed into the world meant an additional financial burden due to the tax, yet they remained undeterred in their desire to raise a family. The financial assistance provided by Firozehe's family in the first year of each child's birth proved invaluable, helping them fulfill their Jazya obligations and shield their family from the harsh consequences of non-compliance with the tax collectors.

Echoes of Survival

Three children born to the couple reached adulthood. Unfortunately, little information has been passed down regarding the life and faith of their second child, a daughter, and their third surviving child, a son.

Tragically, their youngest child, Nahid, was abducted at the tender age of six and never reunited with her family. The loss devastated Firozehe, her husband, and their remaining children, leaving them reeling from the trauma. Despite the immense grief, they found strength in the necessity of persevering.

Their firstborn, Shahriar, was named in homage to Jamshid's beloved maternal grandfather, whose influence left an indelible mark on him during his formative years. The tale of Shahriar and his lineage, rooted in Kerman, unfolds through the remainder of the century and into the mid-20th century.

Jamshid (Jam) Bahram	mt	*Firozehe Bahman Khodabux*
1777 -1823		1785-1831
(MehdiAbad, Kerman)		(Kerman)

Shahriar Jamshid	*Kaykhosrow Jamshid*	*Rudabeh Jamshid*	*Nahid Jamshid*
1807-1850	1809-?	1812-1862	1814-?
Kerman	Kerman – India	Kerman-Yazd	Kerman - ?
	(Fled to India, fate unknown)		(kidnapped at young age)

Jamshid adeptly transformed himself within a new environment, a realm from which he found himself permanently distanced from his parents and the wider family circle. Embodying the invaluable lessons imparted by his parents, he ensured the perpetuation of his Zoroastrian heritage, steadfastly passing it down through subsequent generations. Though visual records of him and Firozehe are regrettably absent, we present images of their descendants, spanning three to four generations. These illustrious progeny, serving with valor, contributed to military and security endeavors in defense of their respective homelands throughout the 20th century.[17]

---

[17] Notable absences from the collection below include the image of a great-grandson descending from Sultan Khodabux-shahriar-Jamshid, who served with distinction in the US Air Force during the latter half of the 20th century. Additionally, the photos of two descendants of ShirinBaii Daulat Esfandiyar-Khodabux-Shahriar Jamshid are absent; both individuals served in the US Marines during the early 21st century.

Mehrborzin Jamshid Soroushian

Jamshid and Firozeh's great grand son Rustom Kaykhosrow-Khodabux-Shahriar-Jamshid Lietunant in the Southern Persian Rifles, 1910

Faridun and Firozeh's great grandson Bahram Faidun-Khodabux-Shahriar-Jamshid Officer in the Imperial Iranian Army, 1933

Echoes of Survival

Jamshid and Firozeh's great grandson, Parviz - Soroush-Shahriar-Khodabux-Shahriar-Jamshid, an officer In the Imperial Iranian Army, 1941

Jamshid and Firozeh's great grandson, Khodamorad Kaykhosrow-Khodabux-Shahriar-Jamshid, commissioned in the US Army during WWII, 1943

Jamshid and Firozeh's great grandson, Kaykhosrow Faridun-Shahriar-Khodabux-Shahriar-Jamshid Enlisted in the US Armay, 1944

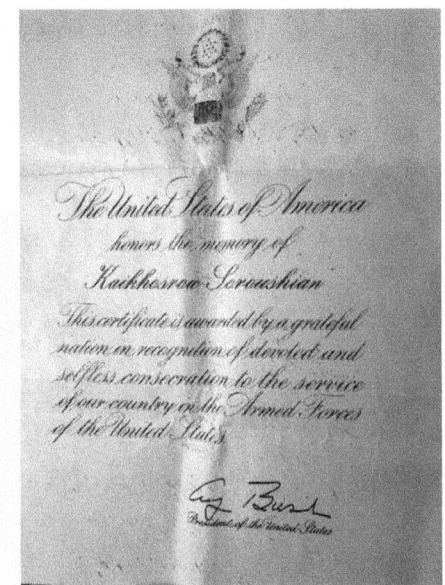

Commendation received upon passage of Kaykhosrow from the US President, 1991

Jamshid and Firozeh's great grandon, Arastu -- Khosrow-Esfandiyar-Khodabux-Shahriar-Jamshid, Officer of the Iranian Imperial Army, 1951

Jamshid and Firozeh's great grandon Siross (son of Gohar Khodamorad-Khodabux-Shahriar-Jamshid), Commissioned officer in the Iranian Security Forces, 1952

Figure 4: Photos of direct descendants of Jamshid Bahram and Firozeh Bahman in the course of 20th century who served in the military or security services

2.4 Shahriar Jamshid Bahram & Gohar Hormuzdyar Esfandiyar
2.4.1 Shahriar Jamshid Bahram
1807 -1850 (Kerman)

Shahriar, the eldest of four siblings born to Jamshid and Firozehe, was raised with a firm emphasis on self-assurance and street smarts by his parents. Growing up, they imparted cautionary tales about the perils that targeted Zoroastrian youth, drawing from their own harrowing experiences. Shahriar later realized that his father spoke from the heart, having endured forced labor and separation from his loved ones, while his mother shared her firsthand observations of Zoroastrian youngsters vanishing, never to return.

Despite their diligent precautions, tragedy struck when Shahriar was twelve: his six-year-old sister Nahid went missing, presumed kidnapped. This devastating loss weighed heavily on Shahriar's parents, particularly his father, who passed away four years later, burdened with remorse for not shielding his daughter from harm. The absence of Nahid also left Shahriar and his remaining siblings with a profound sense of vulnerability.

At the tender age of sixteen, Shahriar found himself thrust into a newfound responsibility as the eldest male in the family following his father's demise. He assumed a pivotal role in providing for his younger siblings and caring for his grieving mother.

Mehrborzin Jamshid Soroushian

A few years after Shahriar's birth, his father, Jamshid, began working on his father-in-law's farm, assisting on other farms managed by his father-in-law as well. Jamshid swiftly became an independent worker,[18] and Shahriar, from a tender age, joined his father in laboring on the farm. Jamshid, in addition to his farm duties, undertook the responsibility of transporting harvested produce to the bustling Kerman bazaar for sale or storage. Over time, Jamshid forged strong relationships with the bazaar's merchants, who relied on him for both the quality of farm goods and punctual deliveries.

Accompanying his father on these delivery trips, Shahriar familiarized himself with the bazaar's merchants and their establishments. Possessing an inquisitive nature and quick learning abilities, Shahriar keenly observed and absorbed his father's adept negotiation skills.

However, one recurring source of frustration for both father and son was the necessity of wearing distinct dark-yellow attire that marked them as Zoroastrians, making them vulnerable to harassment and harm from hostile Muslim groups targeting minorities. This perpetual threat compelled Jamshid and Shahriar to meticulously plan their routes and timing to avoid areas with a high concentration of Muslims, minimizing the risk of confrontation. Moreover, as minorities, they were prohibited from riding on the backs of donkeys and were required to walk alongside them, except when out of sight from Muslim observers.

His parents imparted the rudiments of reading and writing to Shahriar and his siblings to the best of their ability. One task Shahriar and his siblings undertook was painstakingly transcribing the text from the family Vendidad into new blank books. Unintentionally, this activity facilitated their education in basic literacy. The primary purpose was to present these books to tax collectors as partial payment for the annual Jazya tax, alleviating the financial burden.

Aside from copying religious texts, opportunities for formal education were scarce. However, exposure to poetry recitals from the Shahnameh and other literary works, including those of Hafez, at Zoroastrian communal gatherings enriched their learning during their formative years.

At the age of sixteen, following his father's passing, Shahriar, as the eldest son, assumed the role of breadwinner for the family. His maternal uncle provided crucial support, offering financial assistance to meet the daunting Jazya tax obligation, a major concern for Zoroastrian families. Shahriar successfully navigated this responsibility, spending much of his time shuttling between nearby villages and the Kerman bazaar and engaging in the trade of farm produce. He also managed the small farm left behind by his father, with his younger brother actively assisting him in agricultural endeavors.

Developing adept negotiation skills, Shahriar secured favorable prices for his sourced produce at the bazaar. He also became proficient in evading highway robbers and hostile Muslim groups, experiencing only occasional encounters with such threats. Shahriar invested in several donkeys for transporting both farm produce to the bazaar and fertilizers from the city to the farm, ensuring smooth logistical operations.

Shahriar had forged business connections with a merchant specializing in wool for export. Some of the villagers he had befriended also owned flocks of sheep. Each year, as the sheep were sheared, Shahriar would purchase the wool from these villages and resell it to the bazaar merchant, turning a profit.

---

[18] The mentorship that Jamshid received from his father, Bahram, and his maternal grandfather, Shahriar, starting at a young age, provided invaluable guidance and support throughout his life.

His workdays commenced before dawn and stretched into the late hours, a routine he had inherited from his father and internalized over time. Shahriar had honed a keen sense of where to direct his efforts to maximize productivity and achieve optimal outcomes.

Within a few years, Shahriar had amassed enough savings to purchase his own modest house in the Zoroastrian quarter. Following tradition, his younger brother would inherit their parents' home and raise his family there. It had become customary for Zoroastrians residing in the Zoroastrian quarters, also known as Gaber Mahella, to stash away silver coins and other easily exchangeable non-perishable items, burying them deep within their house yards in locations easily accessible when needed. This precautionary measure served as a means of survival in the event of fanatical Muslim mobs assaulting the Zoroastrian quarters, ransacking homes, and disrupting the livelihoods of the inhabitants. Once the threat had passed and the residents felt safe to return from hiding, they would have the financial resources to procure essential goods for their sustenance.

The most harrowing periods for them occurred during the annual observances by Muslims commemorating the murders of their imams twelve centuries prior. At times, impassioned speeches by leading Mullahs would incite hatred against Zoroastrians and other minorities, falsely linking them to events that transpired centuries ago in distant lands. Such vitriolic sermons often culminated in Muslim mobs descending upon Zoroastrian quarters, wreaking havoc on the lives of the residents in a misguided quest for vengeance.

With Shahriar moving into his own house, the silver coins previously buried in their father's residence were left for his younger brother, who now occupied the home. Shahriar embarked on the task of saving his own coins and burying them in his yard. It was anticipated that Shahriar's sister would relocate to her husband's home, where the newlywed couple would begin their own tradition of saving and burying coins in their own yard.

At the age of 24, Shahriar married Gohar, a neighbor he had known for years. Their families shared a close bond, having been acquainted for some time. Sadly, by the time Shahriar and his siblings were marrying, their mother, Firozeh, had passed away. Shahriar's maternal uncle, aunt, cousins, and siblings were the sole attendees from his side at the wedding celebration.

A year into their marriage, Gohar and Shahriar welcomed their first child, a son. During infancy, the child fell gravely ill, nearly succumbing to the illness. Miraculously, he recovered, prompting his name to be changed to Khodabux, signifying God's intervention in sparing his life. Tragically, Khodabux's younger brother passed away in infancy due to illness. Several years later, a daughter was born to Gohar and Shahriar, who grew to adulthood and married a Zoroastrian man from Kerman in her early twenties. Subsequently, Shahriar and Gohar had another daughter, who was unfortunately kidnapped as a young girl, separating her from the rest of the family. Limited information is available about her subsequent life.

2.4.2 Gohar Hormuzdyar Esfandiyar
1811 -1860 (Kerman)

Gohar's lineage traces back generations in Kerman, where her ancestors established roots. Her maternal great-grandfather, Rustom, endured Mahmud Hatok's brutal assault on the Zoroastrian villages northeast of Kerman in 1719. As a young boy, Rustom displayed remarkable agility, narrowly escaping Mahmud's invading army from the eastern province of Qandahar. Amidst the chaos of the attack, Rustom found refuge by leaping into a vertical well, an integral part of the Qanat water system supplying the fortified city of Kerman. Safely reaching the well's depths, Rustom traversed the underground aqueduct, following its current until emerging at the foot of the city's protective walls. Moved by compassion, the guards atop the walls opened the gates, allowing Rustom and other fleeing Zoroastrians to seek sanctuary within the fortified city.

On his paternal side, Gohar's grandparents made a significant relocation to Kerman during their teenage years, leaving behind their ancestral homes in the Sistan province. Their families, among the dwindling Zoroastrian communities in Zabol, persevered as adherents of their faith until circumstances in Sistan became untenable. Faced with worsening conditions, they opted to seek refuge in Kerman, as the land routes to India posed too great a peril during that era.

Gohar's parents, Hormuzdyar Esfandiar and Turan Mehrab were raised in the Zoroastrian quarters of Kerman, where they endured persecution and violence from fanatical Muslim aggressors. Despite facing numerous beatings and attacks, Hormuzdyar remained resilient, enduring severe injuries inflicted by these ruffians. Turan, too, had her share of harrowing experiences, narrowly escaping multiple kidnapping attempts. The heartbreaking abduction of a neighbor's daughter, who happened to be Turan's close childhood friend, deeply affected her, prompting her to take proactive measures to safeguard her own family.

Determined to protect their children, Gohar's parents, who also had an older son, Esfandiar, two years her senior, and younger siblings, Mahin and Gushtasp, made education a priority. They arranged for their children to receive schooling from an elderly Zoroastrian couple in the neighborhood who were willing to impart knowledge to the local children. In exchange, Gohar and her siblings assisted their teachers with household chores. Additionally, Hormuzdyar and Turan would provide farm produce and dairy products from their small farms outside the city to support the elderly couple.

Gohar, influenced by her mother and grandmother, learned valuable skills such as knitting and cooking. She took on the responsibility of preparing family meals and crafting clothing for her siblings.

Hormuzdyar cultivated fruit trees on his farm, a tradition that led to a family ritual each late summer. They would gather excess apricots and grapes, laying them out in the sun to dry. Come late autumn and winter, these dried fruits, often mixed with nuts, became a staple in their household. Beyond their own consumption, Hormuzdyar would also trade or sell surplus dried fruits.

Gohar and her siblings were all too familiar with the annual burden of the Jazya tax, imposed on every Zoroastrian regardless of age. The tax was not only excessive but also collected in a dehumanizing manner. Tax collectors would descend upon the Zoroastrian quarter, resorting to violence and even hostage-taking of children if payments were not met. They accepted Zoroastrian religious texts as payment, destroying them to discourage literacy in the community. Despite this oppression, the family faithfully copied passages from their Vendidad, inadvertently fostering literacy among the youth.

Despite the hardships, Gohar and her peers found solace in the seasonal communal celebrations held safely away from Muslim persecution. These events provided opportunities for socializing and forming enduring friendships. It was during one such gathering that Gohar met Shahriar Jamshid, with whom she forged a deep friendship that blossomed into marriage at the age of 21. Aware of the challenges ahead, including the escalating Jazya tax and the pressure to convert, the couple remained resolute in preserving their Zoroastrian heritage and raising their children accordingly.

Their determination stemmed from a profound appreciation for their ancestors' sacrifices to maintain their religious identity and uphold ethical principles. They instilled these values in their children, ensuring the legacy of resilience and pride in their Zoroastrian heritage endured.

Echoes of Survival

Hormuzdyar cultivated fruit trees on his farm, a tradition that led to a family ritual each late summer. They would gather excess apricots and grapes, laying them out in the sun to dry. Come late autumn and winter, these dried fruits, often mixed with nuts, became a staple in their household. Beyond their own consumption, Hormuzdyar would also trade or sell surplus dried fruits.

Gohar and her siblings were all too familiar with the annual burden of the Jazya tax, imposed on every Zoroastrian regardless of age. The tax was not only excessive but also collected in a dehumanizing manner. Tax collectors would descend upon the Zoroastrian quarter, resorting to violence and even hostage-taking of children if payments were not met. They accepted Zoroastrian religious texts as payment, destroying them to discourage literacy in the community. Despite this oppression, the family faithfully copied passages from their Vendidad, inadvertently fostering literacy among the youth.

Despite the hardships, Gohar and her peers found solace in the seasonal communal celebrations held safely away from Muslim persecution. These events provided opportunities for socializing and forming enduring friendships. It was during one such gathering that Gohar met Shahriar Jamshid, with whom she forged a deep friendship that blossomed into marriage at the age of 21. Aware of the challenges ahead, including the escalating Jazya tax and the pressure to convert, the couple remained resolute in preserving their Zoroastrian heritage and raising their children accordingly.

Their determination stemmed from a profound appreciation for their ancestors' sacrifices to maintain their religious identity and uphold ethical principles. They instilled these values in their children, ensuring the legacy of resilience and pride in their Zoroastrian heritage endured.

Shahriar Jamshid Bahram	mt	Gohar Hormuzdyar Esfandiyar
1807-1850		1811-1860
Kerman		Kerman

Khodabux Shahriar	Bahram Shahriar	Firozehe Shahriar
1832-1868 (Kerman)	1837 -?	1839-?

Figure 5: Descendants of Shahriar Jamshid Bahram and Gohar Hormuzdyar Esfandiyar

Figure 6: A drawing produced by a traveler depicting a Zoroastrian family in Kerman in 1838

2.5 Khodabux Shahriar Jamshid & Katayun Faridun Kaykhosrow
2.5.1 Khodabux Shahriar Jamshid
1832 – 1868 (Kerman)

As Khodabux matured in Kerman, assisting his father Shahriar from an early age, the conditions across Iran were deteriorating. To the north, Russian encroachment on Iranian territory became increasingly pronounced. Meanwhile, the British endeavored to extend their influence eastward, particularly in regions such as Herat, which lay closer to Kerman, aiming to establish a buffer against Russian advances toward India.

The presence of foreign travelers passing through Kerman on official business for their countries was more visible. A number of foreign visitors would visit Kerman's Zoroastrian quarter and interview the inhabitants about their conditions.[19] Khodabux remembered that when he was about ten years old, a European scholar passed through Kerman and stayed at the house of a Zoroastrian priest for about a week looking for old religious books. His harmless presence in the community had created a buzz, and the inhabitants noticed that the fanatical Moslems had mostly stayed away from the Zoroastrian neighborhood during his stay.[20]

During this era, a number of Zoroastrian men from Kerman and Yazd resorted to an "underground railroad" to escape to India, seeking refuge from the prevailing conditions. Widespread poverty and the persistence of contagious diseases continued to afflict the populace, taking a heavy toll on the community. For Zoroastrians, the relentless burden of the oppressive Jazya tax, lack of state protection, inheritance laws favoring conversion to Islam, and discriminatory dress codes made them vulnerable targets for persecution by Muslim authorities, with no respite in sight.

Periodically, distressing reports circulated within Zoroastrian communities of youth being abducted, families succumbing to pressure and converting to Islam, or individuals fleeing to India. For those determined to persevere despite escalating hardships, resilience and steadfastness became indispensable virtues. Their reputation for diligence, integrity, and reliability provided them with a competitive advantage. Despite being barred from operating storefronts in the bazaar, Zoroastrians exerted a notable influence in its commercial activities. Some even secured leases for shops, such as Namdar, Khodabux's brother-in-law.

At the time of his father Shahriar's passing, 16-year-old Khodabux had already mastered the fundamentals of his father's trade. With unwavering resolve, Khodabux chose to follow in his father's footsteps. Over time, he expanded his father's enterprise to encompass villages

---

[19] Zoroastrians, drawing from past encounters, often hesitated to divulge the injustices they faced to foreign visitors, fearing reprisal. They feared that any inquiries made by these visitors to Muslim authorities regarding their complaints would result in severe consequences for those suspected of collaborating with outsiders.

[20] The individual referred to is likely the Danish scholar Niel Ludvig Westergaard, who journeyed to Kerman and Yazd in search of ancient Zoroastrian manuscripts for acquisition and transport to Denmark. It is probable that he had arranged his accommodation with the governor of the time, which could account for the level of security provided to him during his stay.

situated south and southwest of Kerman city, areas that were more distant and posed greater travel risks.

At the age of 21, Khodabux's mother, Gohar, encouraged him to consider marriage. Gohar suggested Katayun as a potential match, as she was acquainted with Katayun's mother, Morwarid, from their childhood. Katayun, four years younger than Khodabux, had left a strong impression on him with her resilience and determination, qualities reminiscent of Khodabux's own mother, whom he greatly admired. The union between Khodabux and Katayun proved enduring. Despite being aware of the considerable challenges facing them as a Zoroastrian couple raising children, they remained steadfastly devoted to each other and to building a family.

As the sole surviving son, Khodabux stood to inherit his parents' home. Consequently, Katayun relocated to Khodabux's residence, where his mother and sister also resided. Within a year, Khodabux's sister married and moved out of the house.

A year into their marriage, Khodabux and Katayun welcomed their first child, a son. In homage to his father, Khodabux named the boy Shahriar. The following year, their second child, another son, was born while Khodabux's mother, Gohar, was still alive. In honor of Katayun's maternal grandfather, this son was named Esfandiyar. Ultimately, the couple had eight children—five sons and three daughters. To sustain his growing family, Khodabux labored diligently, not only to provide for their needs but also to fulfill the annual Jazya tax obligation for all family members.

Drawing from the foundational knowledge acquired from his father, Khodabux expanded the family business. Utilizing additional transport donkeys, he facilitated the transportation of agricultural produce from more distant villages to the Kerman bazaar. On return trips, he transported essential goods back to the villages for sale. Khodabux's business primarily involved transporting harvested produce to the Kerman city bazaar, where he would either sell it outright or on consignment to trusted merchants with whom he had forged strong relationships based on mutual trust. Simultaneously, Khodabux would procure essential items such as clothing, cooking utensils, and foodstuffs needed by the villagers for resale. Due to the trust and reliability he had established, villagers preferred to conduct transactions with Khodabux, entrusting him with the transportation of their produce to the bazaar for sale, with compensation arranged upon completion of sales. Similarly, bazaari merchants trusted Khodabux to transport their products on credit to the villages, with compensation provided after the sale. However, Khodabux bore sole responsibility for any losses incurred during transportation.

Through accumulated experience, Khodabux developed strategies to mitigate transport risks, such as selecting optimal departure times and safer routes. During the offseason, when trips to the villages were less frequent, Khodabux worked on farms near the city. Additionally, he acquired a small parcel of agricultural land with water rights in a nearby village, enabling him to cultivate wheat and fruit primarily for his family's consumption. Despite the demanding and high-risk nature of his business, Khodabux's efforts ensured the provision of his family's needs.

Just a few months after the birth of his youngest son, Kaikhosrow, Khodabux fell ill during the winter and passed away at the age of 36. His eldest son, Shahriar, who was fourteen years old at the time, assumed the role of provider for the family. Shahriar had accompanied his father on several excursions to the villages and around the city, allowing him to become acquainted with some of the villagers and bazaari merchants his father dealt with. However, no one anticipated that Shahriar would be conducting business at such a young age. Fortunately, the goodwill fostered by Khodabux with both the villagers and the merchants proved invaluable. Despite his youth, Shahriar found that villagers and merchants were willing to engage in business with him, thanks to the reputation and trust established by his father.

2.5.2 Katayun Faridun Kaykhosrow
1836 -1882 (Kerman)

Katayun's upbringing in the Kerman Zoroastrian quarter, known as Gaber Mahella, left an enduring mark on her young psyche. Witnessing a Zoroastrian neighbor publicly lashed by tax collectors for failing to meet the exact Jazya tax payment had a profound impact, with the haunting cries of her humiliated neighbor echoing in her memory.

At the tender age of nine, the abduction of a neighbor's child casts a shadow of despair over the community. The anguish of the grieving parents, etched in Katayun's mind, reflected the harsh realities faced by those around her.

As a teenager, Katayun narrowly escaped kidnapping attempts, a harrowing experience that fueled her determination to defy the prejudices aimed at her and her peers. Alongside her older brother Namdar and younger siblings Sohrab and Morwarid, she supported her parents in navigating life's challenges. They learned essential literacy skills, spending afternoons transcribing passages from the family's Vendidad book to submit as partial payment to tax collectors. As they matured, they assisted with farm chores culinary duties, and learned knitting from their mother.

Katayun's marriage to Khodabux Shahriar brought joy and stability, strengthened by their families' close bonds. Impressed by Khodabux's entrepreneurial acumen, Katayun found reassurance in his ability to inherit and expand his father's business.

Their growing family reflected their optimism, with each child named after esteemed ancestors. Despite the financial burden of the Jazya tax, Khodabux's thriving business provided for their needs.

The couple welcomed their first child, Shahriar, within a year of their marriage. Subsequently, they were blessed with four sons—Esfandiar, Hormuzdyar, Khodamorad, and Kaykhosrow—and three daughters—Daulat, Firozeh, and Sultan. Each child bore the name of an esteemed ancestor from either Katayun's or Khodabux's lineage, with Firozeh being a poignant tribute to Khodabux's late mother, who had passed away just a few years prior.

Their decision to expand their family reflected both their optimism and their favorable circumstances. Khodabux's thriving business provided financial stability, enabling them to comfortably support their growing household, including meeting the demanding Jazya tax obligations imposed on each family member.

The couple welcomed their eighth child, a boy they named Kaykhosrow, continuing the tradition of naming each child after an ancestor of Katayun or Khodabux.

Tragically, Khodabux fell seriously ill in the middle of winter and never recovered, leaving his wife and eight children devastated by his sudden passing.

With the support of Katayun's family, neighbors, and friends, Khodabux's remains were laid to rest in Kerman's Tower of Silence. Dastoor Jahangir Rustom Manochehr,[21] a family friend, led prayers for him.

At just fourteen years old, Shahriar, the eldest son, took on the responsibility of providing for the family. Katayun became a pillar of strength for her sons, offering encouragement and wisdom drawn from her own experiences. Her family assisted as much as possible, with Katayun's mother, Sultan Soroush Manochehr, moving in to help care for the younger children.

As the family's primary breadwinner, Katayun took on odd jobs, including baking bread for neighbors. Each baking session yielded 25 to 30 loaves, providing sustenance for her family in exchange for a few loaves as compensation.

A skilled knitter, Katayun also secured knitting jobs to support her growing family. As her children, especially the youngest, Kaykhosrow, reached school age, Katayun's workload intensified. Despite the challenges, she devoted herself tirelessly to her family until her passing at the age of 46.

Her eldest child, Shahriar, was 26 at the time, while her youngest, Kaykhosrow, was just 14. Daulat, her eldest daughter, was twenty and expecting her first child. Firozeh, seventeen, was engaged, and Sultan, fourteen, would later marry Rustom, the son of Dastoor Jahangir.

Katayun's hard work, dedication, and leadership within the community earned her widespread respect and admiration. Others frequently sought her help and moral support in overcoming life's challenges.

In reflecting on Katayun's life, we find inspiration in her unwavering courage and commitment to her family and community. Despite facing immense adversity, she remained resolute in upholding her Zoroastrian heritage and ensuring the continuity of her family's legacy. Katayun's enduring legacy serves as a beacon of strength and determination for future generations to emulate.

From that juncture onward, Shahriar, the eldest son at fourteen years old, assumed the role of provider for the family. Katayun remained a steadfast source of encouragement and guidance to her sons, sharing the wisdom gleaned from her own observations and experiences. The family rallied together to support one another as best they could. Katayun's mother, Sultan Soroush Manochehr, moved in with them, offering invaluable assistance in caring for the younger children during her time with them.

In due course, it fell upon Shahriar and his younger brothers, particularly Esfandiyar, to carry forward their father's business to sustain the family. Meanwhile, Katayun took on various

---

[21] In later years, Dastoor Rustom, son of Dastoor Jahangir, would enter matrimony with Sultan, the third daughter of Khodabux and Katayun.

odd jobs to help put food on the table. Among these, she would visit neighbors' homes to bake bread, skillfully molding the dough into large loaves and expertly tending to them in the oven, typically producing 25 to 30 loaves per session. In exchange for her labor, she would receive two to three loaves to nourish her own family. Additionally, Katayun's proficiency in knitting occasionally provided her with employment opportunities.

As her children grew, particularly when the youngest, Kaykhosrow, reached the age of five, the demands of Katayun's work intensified. From that point until the final year of her life, she toiled tirelessly, effectively becoming the primary breadwinner for her family. Tragically, Katayun passed away at the age of 46, leaving behind a legacy of hard work, devotion to her family, and leadership within the community, earning the respect and admiration of all who knew her. She was often sought out for her assistance and moral support in navigating life's challenges.

At the time of her passing, Shahriar, her eldest child, was 26 years old, while her youngest, Kaikhosrow, was 14. Daulat, her eldest daughter, was 21 and had been married for less than a year, expecting her first child. Firozeh, her second daughter, was 17 and engaged. Sultan, her third daughter, was 14 at the time of Katayun's passing and would later marry Rustom, the son of Dastoor Jahangir, in the years that followed.

Reflection on Katayun's life: The 19th-century era of the family concluded with the passing of Katayun. Her indomitable spirit, characterized by her ability to overcome adversity and her unwavering commitment to her family and community, ensured the continuity of the Zoroastrian lineage and the traditions that had sustained them throughout history. Katayun epitomized courage and steadfastness, exemplifying a resolute dedication to righteousness. Following her husband's untimely demise, she assumed the responsibility of caring for her family without hesitation or faltering, leaving behind a legacy of resilience and determination that continues to inspire us today.

Below are timelines tracing the descendants of Khodamorad Khodabux and Firozeh Bahram, as well as those of Kaikhosrow Khodabux Shahriar and his spouses

Khodabux Shahriar *Katayun Faridun Kaykhosrow*

(1832– 1868) Kerman (1836 – 1882) Kerman

    Shahriar
    1854-1919 (Kerman)

    Esfandiyar
    1856-1910 (Kerman)

        Daulat Shahriari
        1859-1918 {Kerman)

            Hormuzdyar
            1862-1897 (Kerman)

                Firozeh Farahi
                1864-1933 (Kerman)

                Khodamorad
                1866-1933 (Kerman)

                    Sultan Hormuzdi
                    1867-1929 (Kerman)

                        Kaikhosrow
                        1868-1942 (Kerman)

Figure 7: Descendants of Khodabux Shahriar & Katayun Faridun

Khodamorad Khodabux Shahriar[22] mt *Firozehe Bahram Jamshid*
  1866 – 1920 (Kerman) 1872 – 1928 (Kerman)

  Faridun Khodamorad
  1894 – 1943 (Kerman)

              Gohar Khodamorad
              1898 – 1967 (Kerman – Tehran)

Figure 8: Descendants of Khodamorad Khodabux, and Firozehe Bahram

---

[22] The descendancy charts for two of Khodabux's sons, Khodamorad, and Kaykhosrow are also shown below. The charts for two other sons of his, Shahriar and Esfandiyar are shown in subsequent chapters.

Kaikhosrow Khodabux Shahriar[23]	*mt (in1899)*	*Morwarid Darvish Dinyar*
1868 – 1942 (Kerman)		1871 – 1903 (Kerman)

Banu Hormuzdyar Khodabux
1893 – 1954 (Kerman)

Rustom Kaikhosrow Khodabux
1901 – 1976 (Kerman – NYC)

Kaikhosorw Khodabux Shahriar[24]	*mt (in 1905)*	*Khorshid Iraj Falahzadeh*
1868-1954 (Kerman)		1882-1957 (Yazd – Kerman)

Khodayar Kaikhosrow Khodabux
1909-1977 (Kerman – Tehran)

    Jamshid Kaikhosrow Khodabux
    1912-1974 (Kerman-Tehran)

        Zarbanu Kaikhosrow Khodabux
        1916-1978 (Kerman)

            Khodamorad Kaikhosrow Khodabux
            1920-2009 (Kerman, Albany-NY)

                Zomorood Kaikhosrow Khodabux
                1922 – 1932 (Kerman)

                    Khodarahm Kaikhosrow Khodabux
                    1925 – 2002 (Kerman, San Francisco)

Figure 9: Descendants of Kaikhosrow Khodabux Shahriar & his spouses

---

[23] First marriage

[24] Second marriage

2.6 Shahriar Khodabux-Shahriar & Banu Gushtasp-Dinyar-Bahram-Klantar

2.6.1 Shahriar Khodabux Shahriar

1856 – 1919 (Kerman)

Shahriar, the first child of Khodabux (also written as Khodabakhsh) and Katayun, spent more time helping his father with his business than his younger siblings did. He had accompanied his father on many of his trips to the villages, including to Jupar which was to the southwest of Kerman city. Shahriar came to know the merchants in the bazaar his father did business with, as well as the merchants who bought wholesale sheep wool and other farm products. On these trips to the villages, Shahriar also got to know the villagers with whom his father was doing business.

Shahriar, in his youth, apprenticed with his maternal uncle, Namdar, who merchandized fabrics from his store in the bazar. Namdar's reputation for honesty as a Zoroastrian resulted in the wealthier buyers patronizing his business. The exposure Shahriar got from this apprenticeship was valuable in terms of learning how to source material from wholesalers. He also learned how to competitively price the products. Shahriar was compensated by his uncle for his hard work.

Upon the unexpected death of his father, young Shahriar had to fill in for him. He believed that there should be no lapse in meeting the trade needs of the bazaari merchants and the villagers who had come to depend on his father. The timing of his father's passing during winter gave him some breathing room, as winter was typically a slow season.

Shahriar learned the basics of conducting business from his father. The mentorship of his maternal uncle, Namdar, also helped him develop more business acumen. Namdar continued to mentor Shahriar after Khodabux's death, and by the first spring following his father's passage, Shahriar felt prepared to continue the business on his own. Shahriar was intent on continuing the business relationships his father had fostered with villagers and the Bazaari merchants. Given his young age, this desire was reassuring to the villagers and the bazaari merchants who had come to value their business dealings with Khodabux. Shahriar also managed to identify and connect with the contacts his father had made in other villages.

Shahriar realized he had to overcome one significant obstacle to safely travel in the countryside and in the city. Given his youthful appearance, he could become a target for robbers on the open roads looking to seize his donkeys and cargo. His minority status (made apparent by the color of the attire he was forced to wear) contributed to this vulnerability, as no one would likely come to his rescue if he were attacked. To mitigate the risk, Shahriar planned to wear bulky clothing and to carry himself with confidence to give the appearance of an older person. In addition, he prepared to defend himself and take evasive action in the event of an attack.

However, his first experience with a sandstorm is something he had not planned for, and it became a defining moment for him. As he recounted the event, he embarked alone on one of his first excursions to Jupar with two donkeys: one for carrying goods and one to ride.[25] He left early in the morning for Jupar, carrying an assortment of cooking utensils and fabrics the villagers needed. As he approached his destination, he encountered an expansive sandstorm. Shahriar had no prior exposure to blinding sand storms and did not know how best to protect himself and his transport donkeys, and he was moving forward. Before long, he fell to the ground, partially covered by sand, and he almost lost consciousness. In about half an hour, the storm subsided, and calm returned. Shahiar recounted that three old men clad in white picked him up from the ground and shook him back to consciousness. Then, they poured water into his mouth and reassured him that he was safe. Then, one of them gave him a coin and encouraged him to move forward in life and to be persistent. By the time Shahriar's orientation returned to him, the men had found Shahriar's donkeys. They also poured water from their containers into the donkeys' mouths. Then they reloaded the canvases containing the material Shahriar was transporting onto the back of one of the donkeys, and pointed Shahriar in the direction of Jupar and walked away. Shahriar, having regained his composure, mounted the donkey and resumed his journey. When he looked back, the three men had disappeared from view. Shortly thereafter, he reached Jupar and was able to sell all his merchandise for a profit. He then purchased a load of farm products and headed back to the city, where he arrived late at night. His mother and siblings had stayed up waiting for him. They were relieved to see him back safe. He delivered the farm products to a bazaari merchant the next day. Shahriar learned tremendously from that experience, and his business really took off. He always carried the coins the three mysterious men had given him from that point onwards.

By the time Shahriar was coming of age, the conditions in Kerman and Iran, more generally were changing. Before continuing Shahriar's story, I briefly review the external changes occurring at the time that serve as important context to history.

1. In the course of the 19th century, the prosperous Zoroastrian community in India (Parsis) concentrated mostly in the port city of Bombay, were becoming increasingly concerned about the deteriorating condition of their brethren in Iran. They dispatched a representative by the name of Maneckji Limji Hataria to Iran to investigate the condition of the remaining Zoroastrians and to recommend ways of improving their lives. Maneckji's arrival in the mid-1850s happened a few years before Shahriar was born. Maneckji Hataria's tireless efforts, continuing through the end of his life, resulted in improvements in the lives of the Zoroastrians of Iran, including Nasser-ul-Dinshah's rescission of the Jazya tax (excessive head tax imposed on Zoroastrians and other minorities) in 1882.

2. The advent of telegram lines in the first half of the 1830s and the establishment of a telegraph line from India through Iran (known as Persia at the time) enroute to London

---

[25] Sand storms happened infrequently to the south of Kerman city. Although Shahriar had traveled to Jupar in the company of his father several times before, he never encountered a sand storm in that time.

in the second half of the 19th century meant cities like Kerman and Yazd gained electronic connectivity to other major cities.

3. The increased British presence in southern Persia resulted in the establishment of a major British consulate in Kerman towards the latter part of the 19th century, years after Maneckji's arrival. British Subjects, including Parsis, could avail themselves of the support of the local British representatives. Czarist Russia also established a consulate in Kerman in the beginning years of the 20th century.

The young Shahriar Khodabux was immersed in the conduct of his own business. He was focused on expanding his business and managed to involve his younger brothers as well. Shahriar developed a keen sense of selecting profitable ventures and cultivating new business contacts. His reliability and innate inclination to treat his business contacts with fairness and respect helped his business flourish. Whenever encountering insults and physical threats due to the religious prejudice of the fanatical Moslems, Shahriar would manage to remain unfazed and look past those experiences and continue with his mission unimpeded.

Shahriar's boldness in expanding his business and his shrewdness enabled him to establish business connections in the Kerman Bazaar. Many of the merchants did business with him, and some of them even partnered with him in joint ventures. Soon, he realized he needed to expand into farm ownership and property ownership. He expanded the business operation with a number of employees and, eventually, with his two sons, and this enabled him to source sheep wool and hand-woven carpets produced around Kerman that were fit for export domestically and internationally. In time, "Shahriar Khodabux & Sons'" trading business expanded to other major cities and countries, including India, England, and the United States.

Furthermore, by joining forces with his father-in-law's business, Shahriar established a network of business contacts in major Iranian cities and international locations to trade with and let him expand into banking services. Official banking services in Iran had been monopolized by two banks,[26] one controlled by the British and the other by the Russians, after the Qajar rulers sold banking interests to foreign entities. These banks typically issued legal tender that was only valid in one city or province. Therefore, the legal tender issued by a bank in Kerman could not be readily used in Isfahan or other cities. This situation created an opportunity for informal banking services. Shahriar's business operation would offer such banking services. People in Bombay, India, who wished to remit funds to their family members in Kerman would transfer the funds through the trading houses in Bombay that were associated with them. This banking service proved to be an expanding opportunity for Shahriar's business.

Shahriar first acquired property, a parcel around Kerman, in 1870 when he was 14 and soon after his father died. A copy of the deed of sale officiated by a local Moslem clergy is still available. The fact that he was able to get a deed from a Moslem clergy is proof of his savviness, as usually the Moslem priests did not issue deeds to non-Moslems. However, the deed is written

---

26 https://en.wikipedia.org/wiki/Imperial_Bank_of_Persia

using derogatory terms referencing Shahriar's religion (as Gabr rather than Zoroastrian).[27] The terminology used to reference him in the deeds of subsequent property purchases was more respectful. This change in language was an indication of his perseverance and ability to win the hearts and minds of even the fanatical elements of society. In his case, the discriminatory rule that a Zoroastrian could not mount a horse or donkey while passing Moslems has been waived.

Shahriar acquired additional farming properties to the west of Kerman city around the villages of Baghin and Kabotarkhan. His sons joined and were actively involved in the business, and the business partners constructed aqueducts to deliver irrigation water and planted pistachio-growing farms. Much of this infrastructure exists to this day.

Shahriar's business demanded much of his time. He would nevertheless carve out time to attend to his siblings and mother. He made sure his younger brothers were getting the mentoring they needed to become self-sufficient in business. He was a role model to his siblings, inspired them, and set their aims high to work hard to achieve their goals.

Shahriar's three sisters also received the mentoring they needed to become self-sufficient. They learned the basics of knitting, cloth-making, and homemaking from their mother.

The details of Shahriar's marriage are covered in the next section of this chapter. Joining forces with his father-in-law enabled him to expand his trading business to other major cities in Iran and eventually internationally to India, England, Russia, and the US. Soon into his marriage, Shahriar purchased a stately home on the southern boundary of the Zoroastrian quarter. Zriesfe Avenue ran on the south side of his residence, and a number of other stately homes were eventually built on that street on what were once vacant lots.

As his sons, Soroush and Faridun, were growing up, Shahriar made sure they received the proper mentoring to be successful in business. He also wanted his two sons to be well-versed in the latest methods of doing international business, so he sent them overseas to expand their horizons. His oldest son, Soroush, spent some time in India and learned the latest in banking and financial services. His youngest son, Faridun, went to the UK in the early 20th century, where he learned the latest in actuary practices and financing. Both sons had departed for Bombay by ship. Faridun was likely the first Zoroastrian youth from Iran to be sent to Europe for studies.[28] After the two sons returned to Kerman, they rejoined their father in business. Upon the passage of Shahriar in 1919, his sons continued the family business that Shahriar had founded and

---

[27] The property deed identified the buyer as "Shahriar a Gabar and obedient to Islam, the son of Khodabux, a Gabr and Obedient to Islam". Gabr was meant as a demeaning and derogatory reference to Zoroastrians.

[28] Most of the Iranian population, especially religious minorities, were unable to travel to Europe during the Qajar period. First of all, there were no facilities to issue passports and official birth certificates. The Zoroastrian refugees who fled to India were typically issued an identity paper by the ship operators upon boarding the India-bound vessel from Iranian ports. That paperwork served as the only identification they had to facilitate their landing at Indian ports.

Faridun and Soroush boarded a steam ship in Bandar Abbas, which traversed the Persian Gulf for Bombay. They received identification papers from the ship operators. Upon arriving in Bombay, Faridun worked with the civil authorities in India who issued him temporary travel documentation to facilitate his trip to England. All of this was possible because Shahriar Khodabux could afford to pay the expenses for it, and he had the contacts that could facilitate the necessary course of action.

expanded it, given the improving conditions of Iran under Reza Shah Pahlavi. Copies of the telegraphs and communication issued by the Shahiar Khdobux & Sons Company of Kerman covering the early 20th century have been preserved and testify to the scope of the business it conducted. A dozen of the communications recorded in Shahriar Khodabux & Sons Company book are with Shahriar's nephews (Esfandiyar's sons) who were active in the trading business. The documents also include exchanges related to their inheritance after the passage of their father, Esfandiyar.

Shahriar's position as a leading Zoroastrian businessman of his generation in Kerman naturally led him to a leadership position in the newly established Zoroastrian Association of Kerman known as the Naseri Zoroastrian Anjuman of Kerman. The designation of Naseri is an acknowledgment of the fact that it was the Qajar king, Naser-ul Dinshah, who, in view of extensive lobbying by Maneckji Hataria, granted the charter for the establishment of the first Zoroastrian Association in Kerman and one in Yazd. Shahriar was involved with the Anjuman from the onset, and he served as its fifth President for several terms. During his tenure, he donated funds and real property to the Association for various community projects. A number of the communications and telegraphs recorded in his company books relate to the affairs of the community.

The Moslems in the commercial center of Kerman (the bazaar) and elsewhere had come to recognize Shahriar as a leading figure, as exemplified by their tolerance of Shahriar riding a horse in public.[29]

Shahriar brought the same degree of boldness and forward-looking vision to the conduct of his community service as he had demonstrated in building up his business operation. One example is when the late Kaikhosrow Shahrokh[30] returned to Kerman from India and brought with him the clothing he wore in India (jacket and pants). Within three days of returning to Kerman from Bombay, Kaikhosrow Shahrokh was summoned by Kerman's Governor Farmanfarma to appear at his court. On that day, Shahriar and some others, including Shahriar's father-in-law and leading Mobeds, appeared at Kaikhosrow Shahrokh's doorstep to accompany him. Once Kaikhosrow Shahrokh advised he was planning to appear in public in the clothing he had brought from Bombay rather than the color-coded clothing Zoroastrians were forced to wear, Shahriar and others embraced the idea. This plan would, in effect, be an act of civil disobedience in rebuking the unjust dress code rule imposed on Zoroastrians. A few of the elders, including Shahriar, walked in front of Kaikhosrow Shahrokh, and a few walked behind him. With

---

29 In general, Zoroastrians were barred from mounting a horse or a donkey in the Moslem public view, and anyone who violated that unjust imposition risked physical assaults and bodily harm. Shahriar was the only exception. This unjust limitation came to a natural end in early part of the 20th century.

30 Kaikhosrow Shahrokh was a Zoroastrian who hailed from Kerman and went to India at a young age. He returned to Kerman and was a teacher at the Zoroastrian school for a number of years. In early 20th century, he moved to Tehran and was affiliated with the trading house of Arbab Jamshid Jamshidian. Shortly, he got involved with the constitution movement of Iran that came to fruition in early 20th century, and he served as the Zoroastrian representative in the Iranian Majlis (Parliament) for several terms. Kaikhosrow Shahrokh was the founding president of the Zoroastrian Association of Tehran and helped establish community facilities including Tehran's fire temple, the Zoroastrian schools and the Zoroastrian cemetery in Tehran.

Echoes of Survival

Kaikhosrow Shahrokh dressed in pants and a jacket, the group set off from the Zoroastrian quarter and headed towards the city bazaar. They marched from one end of the bazaar path without any of the bazaaris interfering or challenging them. Then, the party headed to the Governor's mansion. Once they arrived at the Governor's mansion, they moved to the front of the line and appeared in front of the governor, where Kaikhosrow Shahrokh shook the Governor's hand and introduced himself.[31] That move did not draw any negative reaction from the Governor or his officials.[32] In fact, Governor Farmanfarma enlisted Kaikhosrow Shahrokh's services to tutor him and his son in English.

Shahriar, who never had an opportunity for formal schooling as a child, had nonetheless learned the basics of reading, writing, accounting, and record-keeping. He turned out to be a strong advocate for establishing schools to educate the youth of the community. The new campus for the Zoroastrian boys' school was endowed from the estate of Banu's father, Gushtasp Dinyar. Shahriar and his wife, Banu, were instrumental in the school's establishment on the new campus.[33]

It is not clear how extensively Shahriar interacted with Maneckji Hataria in person during Maneckji's trips to Kerman. However, Shahriar benefited from the reforms and improvements that Maneckji ushered in and that Maneckji managed to get Nasser-ul-Dinshah to agree to.

In the 1910s, Shahriar was more focused on his community service while his sons, Soroush and Faridun, effectively assumed the day-to-day running of the business. However, the events unfolding in southern Iran as a direct consequence of WWI necessitated Shahriar's intervention. In late 1916, Colonel Percy Sykes[34] returned to Kerman as the head of an armed force of British and Indian infantry and Persian recruits financed by the government of British India. They instituted the SPR force (Southern Persian Rifle).

Prior to Colonel Sykes' arrival, Soroush and Faridun, Mr. Kaikhosrow Kianian, and Mr. Jahangir Fravahar had sold grain from their stockpiles to the Austro-German and Ottoman forces that were in eastern Iran. Sardar Nosrat, the strongman of Kerman, was in hiding. Sykes was instrumental in dislodging the Austro-Ottoman forces from Kerman. Upon re-entering Kerman,

---

31 "The Memoirs of Keikhosrow Shahrokh", edited and translated by Shahrokh Shahrokh and Rashna Writer, The Edwin Mellon Press, 1994, Pg. 34.

32 Until that time, the Zoroastrians who visited the governor's office were expected to stand in the back of the hall until they were called upon. If there ever was a Rosa Park's moment for the Zoroastrians of Iran, this event was it.

33 "The Memoirs of Keikhosrow Shahrokh", edited and translated by Shahrokh Shahrokh and Rashna Writer, The Edwin Mellon Press, 1994, Pg. 19.

34 Brigadier Percy Sykes was appointed as Britain's first Consul general in Kerman by the government of British India, and he established the British consulate in Kerman. He had a distinguished record in Kerman and was in contact with the Zoroastrians of Kerman at the bequest of prominent Parsis in Bombay, including Sir Dinshah Petit. During the early years of World War I, he was reassigned to a post in Burma. Following the fall of the British and the Russian consulates in Kerman and Yazd to the relatively small army of Ottomans and Austrians who had penetrated the eastern parts of Iran, Percy Sykes was brought back with the aim of displacing the Ottoman-Austrians from Kerman and southern Iran. He was able to accomplish that task. Sykes was in charge of organizing the "Southern Persian Rifles" (SPR) meant as a security force in Southern Persia with the blessing of Ahmed Shah Qajar's officials. More information about Sykes' activities can be found in 'Persia in the Great Game – Sir Percy Sykes, Explorer, Consul, Soldier, Spy", by Anthony Wynn, John Murray Publication, 2003.

Sykes aimed to set an example for the merchants who had done business with the Austro-Ottomans. He threatened to execute the Soroushian brothers, Mr. Kaikhosrow Kianian and Mr. Fravahar. Shahriar, who had met Colonel Sykes years before when he was the head of the Zoroastrian Anjuman, and Sykes was serving as the British counsel in Kerman, appealed to Sykes for leniency. It seems that after paying proceeds from the sale of grain to the Austro-Ottomans as a penalty to the British, the Zoroastrians were spared. By contrast, the merchants in Shiraz who were in the same situation as the Soroushian brothers were not spared.

Shahriar's ascendency in wealth and social stature, all accomplished within the span of one generation, was a hallmark of the Zoroastrian revival that came about towards the end of the 19th century. It was a culmination of the convergence of several factors and a ringing validation of all the sacrifices the earlier generations had made toward the preservation of their faith and identity. A report generated by the British Council in Kerman, Sir Percy Sykes, and transmitted to his superiors in British India in 1904 bears witness to that reality.

No. 52, dated the 10th February 1904.

From—MAJOR P. M. SYKES, C.M.G., His Britannic Majesty's Consul, Kerman,

To—LIEUTENANT-COLONEL C. A. KEMBALL, C.I.E., Officiating Political Resident in the Persian Gulf and His Britannic Majesty's Acting Consul-General for Fars, Khuzistan, etc., Bushire.

I have the honour to offer a few observations on the Parsis of Kerman. By way of preface I would mention that their number is between 2,000 and 8,000, whereas the Yezd colony numbers 7,000. For the whole of Persia the total is about 10,000; Shiraz, Kashan and Tehran each having a tiny community. When I first visited Kerman, the condition of the Zoroastrians was deplorable as, not only the officials but even the populace constantly illtreated them and murders were not uncommon. Now, however, their position is infinitely better, especially since they were permitted to form an *Anjuman*, and they are steadily, if slowly, pursuing the path of progress.

You are perhaps aware that there is a society for the Amelioration of Persian Zoroastrians, the president of which is Sir Dinshaw Petit. This society administers funds and remits Rs. 620 to Kerman, Rs. 500 of which sum are devoted to education and the remainder to ceremonies and the marriage of orphans.

I have been in correspondence with Sir Dinshaw Petit, who called on me at Bombay in 1902, and with other Parsis, with a view to increasing their interest in Kerman and my efforts have, to a certain extent, borne fruit. But I have been more successful with the Parsis of Kerman who have made most creditable efforts in the direction of self-help. In this connection, Mr. Ardeshir Edulji, the capable agent of the Amelioration Society, has induced the community to subscribe about Rs. 11,000 for the erection of a new fire temple and for education.

In consequence, the school attendance now numbers nearly 100 boys and 60 girls, and the English class has risen from 4 to 23. I generally attend their examinations and present books, etc., as prizes, which are highly appreciated.

I have also ordered a large wall map of the world showing the British Empire in red, to present to the *Anjuman*. Before quitting this portion of my subject I would mention that the Russian Legation has recently sent the Anjuman a gift of one hundred Russian books and two maps. They will not, however, be used, all the children learning from the English primers, a large consignment of which I recently induced the committee to supply. It is gratifying to know that three of the pupils of the English class have obtained good posts at Tehran and three more posts are now being offered, as these boys have proved satisfactory.

I would represent that, in the Parsi community which is rapidly monopolising the wealth of Kerman, we have a powerful political instrument which should be turned to good account.

In this connection I have three suggestions to make : (a) The Parsi capitalists and philanthropists might be encouraged to turn their attention to their ancient home in Persia. (b) Sir Dinshaw Petit and the committee of the

Figure 10: Extract from a Telegram sent from Percy Sykey, the British Consul in Kerman, to his superiors regarding the Zoroastrians of Kerman

Towards the end, thinking about his life journey, Shahriar might have been wondering what else he could have done.

2.6.2 Banu Gushtasp Dinyar Bahram Klantar
1863 -1944 (Yazd, Kerman)

Gushtasp Dinyar Bahram was born in 1863 in the city of Yazd. His father, Dinyar Bahram, had been given the title of Klantar (Sharif) by the local government officials as it related to the internal affairs of the Zoroastrians in Yazd.[35] As such, the family was relatively influential. They were also successful merchants. One of Gushtasp's older brothers, Bahram, did not take any interest in pursuing the family business. He had an altruistic outlook and left Yazd for Isfahan and Tehran to study astrology at age 20. The family did not hear from him until years later when he came back to Yazd to visit. It turned out Bahram had traveled to Tehran, the capital city, whose sparse population at the time was mostly members of the Qajar clan. Shortly after his arrival in Tehran, Bahram was introduced to Mohamed Shah Qajar, the third Qajar ruler (ruled from October 1834 to September 1848). The Qajar king was impressed with Bahram due to his straightforwardness and entrusted him with palace storage control. In the meantime, Bahram's younger brother Gushtasp had expanded his trading business to Kerman. Gushtasp and his wife Katayun Jamshid sired four children: two girls by the names of Morwarid and Banu and two sons by the names of Borzu and Bahram, all born in Yazd. Unfortunately, both sons, one 21 years old and the other 19 years old, died during a cholera outbreak. The loss of her two sons was a heavy emotional burden on Katayun, and she passed away a short time later.

Back in Tehran, it turned out that in the late 1830s, a prominent Kermani, Nour-Ulla Ibrahimi, had a falling out with the Qajar court and was in open defiance of the Qajar ruler. Mohamed Shah arranged for his arrest. Subsequently, Ibrahimi was brought to Tehran, where he was found guilty of disobedience and sentenced to death. Nour-Ulla's relatives, desperate to save his life, sought to identify anyone who could intervene and get a reprieve on his death sentence. The family was advised by the insiders in Tehran to seek the help of Bahram, who had a good rapport with the Qajar ruler. Bahram's appeal to the ruler was effective, and the governor's life was spared.

When Nour-Ulla's contact in Tehran tried to pay Bahram for his help, Bahram refused and pointed out that his younger brother Gushtasp was engaged in business in Kerman and that the Ibrahimi's relatives could provide assistance to Gushtasp instead.

Gushtasp's business in Kerman was doing well, and he was able to secure a storefront with storage rooms in the main Kerman bazar. He had also purchased farmlands in the villages near Kerman and Yazd, like Jupar. Another Zoroastrian in Kerman who was able to secure a storefront in the Kerman Bazar was the young Shahriar Khodabux, whose business was also prospering but on a smaller scale.

---

[35] The story of Dinyar Bahram Klantar and his descendants are part of the family legend and were narrated by two of his descendants, Mr. Jamshid Soroush Soroushian in his memoirs and by Mr. Jamshid Pishdadi, an educator who narrated his recollection on January 7, 2008.

Echoes of Survival

Gushtasp's two daughters were engaged to two Zoroastrian men in Yazd. The marriage of her daughter Morwarid to a relative went off as scheduled. However, in the case of Banu, her fiancé[36] succumbed to cholera and passed away before they could get married. Banu was heartbroken over the loss of her fiancé, mother, and brothers, and so her father decided to take her with him to Kerman to give her a fresh start. Once in Kerman, Gushtasp was looking for a suitable match for her daughter and asked the elders of the Zoroastrian community who they would recommend. The name of the young Shahriar Khodabux was suggested. Shahriar's hard work and success in business from a young age gained him respect and acknowledgment from members of the community. His ability to support his mother and younger siblings was especially noteworthy.

Shahriar was about twenty-four years old when he got to know Gushtasp Dinyar. Although his sister, Daulat, and his brother, Esfandiyar, were already married, getting married was not on Shahriar's mind. So, when Gushtasp approached him about joint business and also tried to introduce him to his daughter Banu, Shahriar was ambivalent. Gushtasp Dinyar was impressed with Shahriar and saw much potential in him, so he insisted. Within a short while, Banu was married to Shahriar. The marriage was a lasting one. In total, Banu became pregnant eleven times. Unfortunately, there were miscarriages, one stillborn, and some of the newborns died of disease. When Banu became pregnant for the fourth time, she was duly worried if her child would survive childbirth. At the same time, Sultan Khosrow, the wife of Shahriar's brother Esfandiyar, had no trouble conceiving and carrying babies to full term and delivering them. One day when the pregnant Banu was stressed in view of her upcoming delivery, Sultan comforted her and encouraged her to think positively and focus on delivering a healthy baby. The two sisters-in-law then made a promise that should Banu's baby survive childbirth and grow up to adulthood, he or she would marry one of Sultan's children of the opposite sex. Banu went on to deliver a healthy boy who was named Soroush(yar). Several years later, Sultan gave birth to her first daughter, Iran Banu. Based on the pact the two mothers had made, Soroush and her cousin IranBanu were already considered engaged by their parents.

Banu went on to give birth to a daughter, Gohar, followed by a son, Faridun. Another daughter, Simin, was born and made it to her third birthday. She fell into the family's shallow pool and drowned. The older daughter grew up and was engaged to a Zoroastrian man. However, before her marriage, she became a victim of another cholera outbreak in Kerman. So, only the two sons, Soroush and Faridun, made it to adulthood. They both married and formed their own family. In the case of Faridun, Banu had made a pact with her sister Morwarid, which meant Faridun would marry Morwarid's daughter Gohar Banu.

Banu outlived her husband, Shahriar, by 26 years. Upon her passage in 1945, she was survived by her younger son, Faridun. Her older son, Soroush, passed away 4 years before her due to cardiac failure.

Banu's remains were buried in the Zoroastrian cemetery of Kerman that her two sons had endowed to the community. Her husband's remains were committed to the tower of silence

---

36 Her fiancé was Mr. Ardeshir Yeganegi the older brother of Bahram Yeganegi.

situated on a mountaintop on the northern outskirts of the city. Soon after the establishment of the cemetery, the Tower of Silence went out of use.

Banu had great leadership skills and was a daring person. She cared about the welfare of others and always reached out to help those in need.

After the passage of her father, Banu endowed some of the land that was part of her father's residence for the construction of a Zoroastrian school in 1904[37], as well as Kerman's current fire temple. Shahriar, whose residence bordered on the southeast of the fire temple complex, also donated some land.

Banu was a daring lady. Her father had endowed farmland away from the city for charitable use, including the upkeep of the Zoroastrian School for Boys erected on the land endowed for that purpose. The campus that eventually became the Iranshahr High School for Boys was endowed by the estate of Gushtasp Dinyar. Banu and her husband Shahriar were instrumental in that donation. Kaikhosrow Shahrokh was involved with that initiative. Banu took an active interest in the management of the properties endowed for charitable purposes from her father's estate. Given the distance from the city to some of the farmlands endowed, it would take almost two days of traveling from the city to reach them. After the passage of her husband, Banu would do the supervision herself. Traveling on donkey or horse with one of her trusted workers, she would make the trip and usually camp out in the open field en route to the farmland or back to the city after a few days of staying at the distance farm. Resting by a fire in the open space, she would use a long stick to ward off any wild animals that posed a danger to them. She made several such inspection trips.

Despite her husband's and father's success in business, Banu never lost sight of the need to reach out and help the families in need. Given her acts of kindness, everyone who knew her came to call her *Memas Banu* (Grandma Banu).

---

[37] The Zoroastrian School for Boys built on the land endowed by Banu Gushtasp was a large campus. In the beginning, it offered 6 grades of schooling and was named the Zoroastrian School for Boys. The school was managed by the Zoroastrian Association of Kerman that provided funding for its operation. After few years, the schooling was expanded to nineth grade. During the presidency of the Anjuman by Banu's son, Soroush, the federal minister in charge of Education visited Kerman, and met with the Zoroastrian Anjuman officials. He pointed out that Reza Shah Pahlavi was keen to increase the number of schools across the nation and make secular education accessible to all Iranians. At that time, the federal budget was very limited. As such, his request to the Zoroastrians of Kerman was to
1. Expand the scope of school to include higher grades,
2. Expand the capacity of the classes so non-Zoroastrians could also attend and be educated, and
3. To rename the school from Zoroastrian School for Boys to Iranshahr Highschool for Boys. The minister's logic was that non-Zoroastrian parents who may otherwise have hesitated to send their children to a non-Islamic religious school would be reassured.

The expectation was that the Zoroastrian community would bear the added cost.

Banu's son and other members of the board of Kerman Anjuman agreed to all the terms proposed to them. In time, the school became a full-fledged high school with up-to 12 grades of schooling. Capacity of the higher grades was increased by up to 300%. In the long term, this investment by the Zoroastrians of Kerman in the education of their fellow Kermanis paid dividends. Many of the Moslems who were educated at the Zoroastrian schools and went on to lead productive lives became sympathizers to the Zoroastrian community and to the heritage of ancient Persia.

Echoes of Survival

One example of what she did in the last years of her life bears testimony to her caring nature. After the passage of her husband and the passage of her eldest son, Banu turned inwards. Despite being surrounded by her remaining family and never being solitary, she seemed to be on a mission of her own. It turned out the harsh conditions that had been imposed on the population during the WWII occupation of Iran by Allied forces were exacting a heavy toll on the populace. Her sons, whose houses were adjoined to each other, had large storage facilities where grains from the farms they owned would be stored. Unknown to other members of the household, during the day, Banu would go to those storage places and prepare about 15 or so care packages that contained grain as well as other food items. Then, at past midnight, when everyone was asleep, she would slip away carrying the care packages hanging from her back. Banu would also carry a stick. She would head to neighborhoods whose residents were in need of help, leave a care package by the door of each house, and quietly return home before anyone got up. In the morning, when the residents would first emerge from their houses, they would find the packages on the outside. Her clandestine charitable work was going on for some time, and every house in the neighborhood she had targeted would receive one care package every month. The residents had come to depend on these care packages and had typically theorized that *Khazer*[38] was bringing it to them. As such, they never tried to find out the identity of their benefactor.[39]

Within a few months of her passage, Banu had fallen seriously sick and was homebound. She could no longer leave the house. From that point, all the care packages stopped. The recipients of her acts of generosity who were clamoring to find out what had happened for the care packages to stop arriving, heard that Memas Banu had fallen sick, and ever since then, the care packages had stopped coming. Finally, the identity of *Khazer* was revealed. On the day of her funeral, the people she had helped were accompanying her remains to the cemetery. The last shirt she had worn was hoisted on top of a poll and carried behind her casket as a flag. The chant from the crowd was, "Now that Memas Banu is gone, we are all orphans."

Banu's life was filled with tragedies that could have easily broken many others. But she seems to have come back and made the best of the situation. She never forgot to reach out and help others. Years later, after the death of Banu's mother, her father, while advanced in age, married a younger girl from one of the villages around Yazd. The young wife gave birth to two sons. The first one died of carbon monoxide poisoning. The younger son, Hormuzdyar, was born soon after the death of his father, and he grew up in his father's residence in Kerman. Banu played a critical role in raising her young stepbrother.

Banu was fondly remembered by one of her grandsons. When her grandson was very young and felt anxious about going to school, Banu would accompany him to school and stay around until her grandson felt at ease.

---

38 This means "a holy person."

39 The relief missions undertaken by Banu were independent of whatever relief her grandson, Jamshid, and daughter-in-law, Iran-Banu, were providing to the needy.

Shahriar Khodabux	*Banu Gushtasp Dinyar*
1856 – 1919 (Kerman)	1863 -1944 (Yazd, Kerman)

Soroush(yar)	*Gohar*	*Faridun*	*Simin*
1885-1940	1887-1904	1889 – 1951	1893-1895
Kerman	Kerman	Kerman	Kerman

Figure 11: Descendants of Shahriar Khodabux and Banu Gushtasp

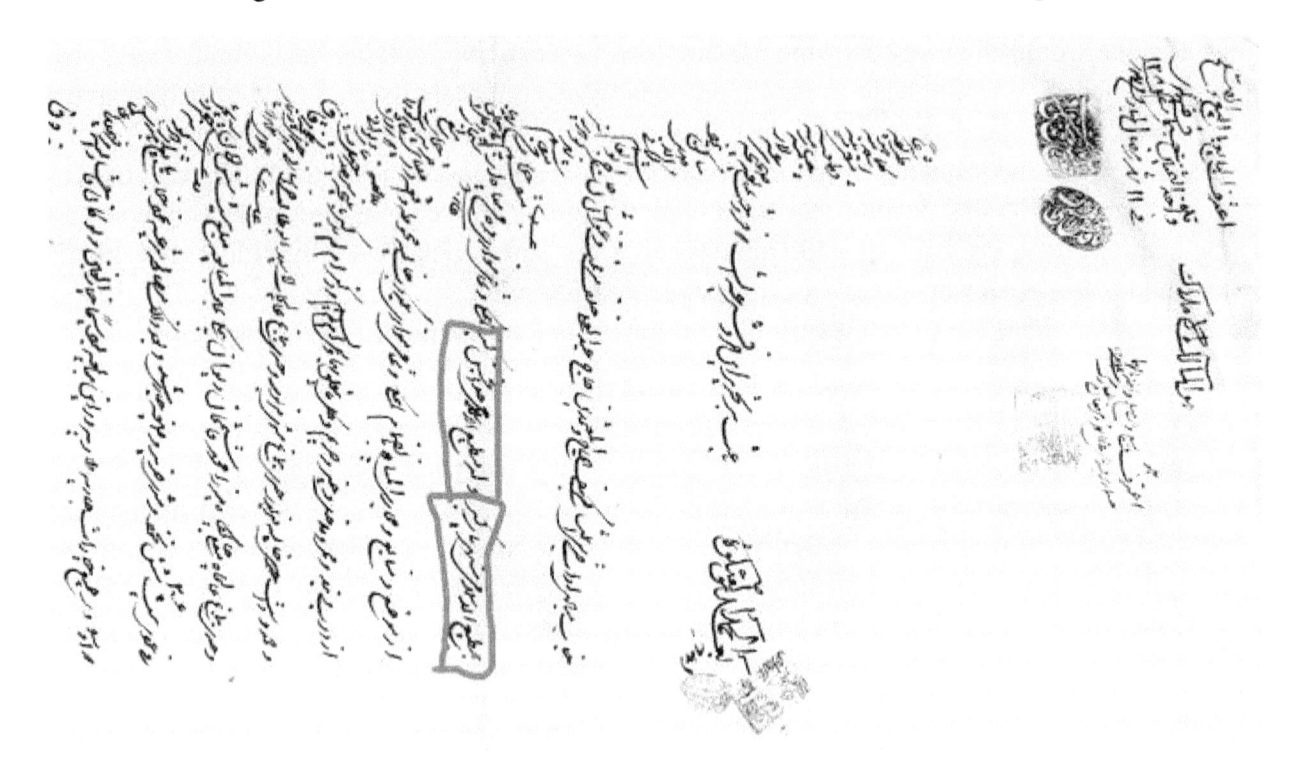

Figure 12: Deed of Purchase for a real property in 1868 issued to Shahriar by a local Islamic Clergy, where Shahriar is identified as "Obedient to Islam, Shahriar a Gaber[40], son of Obedient to Islam, Khodabux a Gaber"

---

40 Gaber is a derogatory term used by fanatical Moslems to refer to Zoroastrians.

Figure 13: 1894, Kerman: Leaders of the Naseri Zoroastrian Anjuman of Kerman, is 2nd sited from right Shahriar Khodabux, 3rd one is Kaikhosorow Shahrokh, 4th one is Dastur Rustom Jahangir, 6th one is Arbab Gushtasp Dinyar

*Figure 14: 1894, **K**erman: Governor of Kerman, FarmanFarmayan, and the British Counsel, Percy Sykes, sited in the middle of the First row. Shahriar Khodabux (4th from right)) and Kaikhosorow Shahrokh (5th from right) in the second row*

Figure 15: 1896, Kerman: Front row (right to left) Percy Sykes (British Counsel in Kerman), Shahriar Khodabux (5th president of the Zoroastrian Association), Dastur Rustom Jahangir (3rd president), Gushtasp Dinyar (4th president)

Figure 16: 1904, Kerman: (from Left to Right) Gohar Shahriar, IranBanu Esfandiyar, GoharBanu Bahram Dinyar, Banu Gushtasp Dinyar, Morwarid Gushtasp Dinyar

Figure 17: 1905 Kerman, Shahriar Khodabux (sited 5th from the left) at his Commercial office with the rest of his staff. His youngest brother, Kaikhsorow, is sited 4th from the right.

Figure 18:1944 Kerman, Banu Gushtasp, sat in the front a month before her passage. Her family and members of the household have assembled for the memorial photo.

2.7 Soroush Shahriar Khodabux and IranBanu Esfandiyar Khodabux
2.7.1 Soroush Shahriar Khodabux Shahriar Jamshid
1885-1940 (Kerman)

Soroush and his younger brother Faridun (1888-1950) maintained a close working relationship throughout their lives and were business partners. They were the only surviving offspring of Shahriar and Banu, who made it to adulthood and started their own families. Their residences in Kerman were located next to each other. Upon the passage of their father, Shahriar, Faridun, as the younger son with his wife, GoharBanu (1899 – 1988), and their children occupied their father's stately home. Their mother, Banu Gushtasp, continued to live in that house through the rest of her life.

To the east of that mansion, additional residential quarters with their own bedrooms, living room, family room, kitchen, and other facilities were built. Those living quarters were occupied by Soroush Shahriar, his wife IranBanu (1893 -1982), their children, and their household. The courtyard of their house, around which rooms had been erected, was centered by a large and shallow pool.

Soroush and Faridun attended the Zoroastrian Boys' School and were taught by the late Kaikhosrow Shahrokh who had returned from Bombay and was very dedicated to the cause of education of young Zoroastrians.[41]

As they were growing up, Shahriar mentored his two sons to become effective at running and expanding the family business. The two brothers were also sent to India in the early years of the 1900s for further education. Soroush stayed in Bombay, and Faridun sailed to London,[42] where he learned the fundamentals of modern financing and actuary. Soroush was focused on furthering his knowledge of modern banking and trade. Upon their return to Kerman, they joined their father's firm, "Shahriar Khodabux and Sons," which was involved in trade with other major cities such as Tehran, Yazd, Bandar Abbas, Shiraz, Mashhad, Bombay, Odessa, London, Manchester, Moscow, and New York.

Soroush and later his brother Faridun followed in the footsteps of their father and were elected to leadership positions of the Kerman Zoroastrian Anjuman.[43]

Soroush and Faridun travelled outside Iran in the late Qajar era for studies. They both returned to Kerman, and both passed away in Kerman. Some of their cousins moved away from Kerman in search of better opportunities presented to Iranians during the Pahlavi dynasty era. Khodabux Esfandiyar Khodabux moved to India in search of better opportunities. Rustam Kaikhosrow Khodabux moved to the US and later brought two of his younger brothers, Khodamorad and Khodarahm, to the US. Another cousin, Jamshid Kaikhosrow-Khodabux,[44] moved to Tehran and Qazvin in northwestern Iran. Khosrow Esfandiar established a business operation in Tehran. His younger brother Sohrab also ventured to Tehran but returned to Kerman. Khosrow's two older brothers, Mehraban and Darab, went to the Persian Gulf port of Bandar Abbas to represent their uncle Shahriar's trading business. Unfortunately, both of them died young of contagious diseases.

In the earlier years at the helm of the firm, Soroush and Faridun had a close call that was a result of the wider implications of WWI that unfolded in Kerman and almost cost them their lives. This topic was covered in the previous chapter. However, it was during their tenure at the helm of the family business that major reforms and improvements in Iran were ushered in upon the elevation of Reza Khan Sapanj to the peacock thrown and the abolishment of the Qajar dynasty as an act of the Iranian Parliament (Majlis). Going forward, the new monarch adopted the last

---

41 After staying in Kerman for several years, Kaikhosrow Shahrokh moved to the capital city where he became the second Zoroastrian representative in the Majlis (parliament).

42 In effect, Faridun was the first Iranian Zoroastrian of the Qajar era to go to Europe for educational purposes. Some years later, young Zoroastrians (Jahanian and Jamshidian families) from Yazd and Tehran were sent to France and Switzerland to study business and commerce.

43 *Anjuman* is the Farsi rendition of Association.

44 During the Soviet invasion of northern Iran that happened as a result of the Red Army and the British Army occupation of Iran in the years of WWII, Jamshid, who resided in Qazvin and had knowledge of the Russian language, acted as the de-facto mayor of the city. He was able to liaise between the Soviet occupiers and the people of Qazvin and to help protect the Iranians resident in Qazvin. The older generation of Qazvinis were generally very appreciative of his efforts.

name of *Pahlavi* and became known as Reza Shah Pahlavi.[45] Eager to remake his country into a modern and progressive nation, countless reforms were introduced. Soroush, as the president of the Zoroastrian Association, Kerman and his brother were eager to see those reforms take hold. They became active advocate for those reforms not solely for their potential for the betterment of the nation but also for the opportunities they presented for the Zoroastrian community and other Iranians. The brothers fully embraced those progressive reforms and actively showcased successful examples of implementing the same at a community level. Specifics of some of those reforms are described below.

1. Calendar reform: Until the time of the Pahlavi dynasty, the official calendar used in Iran was the Islamic lunar calendar. In pre-Islamic Iran, the solar calendar was used. The Pahlavis restored the solar calendar for official use. The first day of spring was celebrated as the start of each new year. The purely Iranian month names were brought back to be used in reference to the twelve months of the year instead of the Islamic names that were used until that time. The main push was on widespread adaption and use of the solar calendar by the populace. As was to be expected, the Islamic Mullahs were opposed to this change. The Zoroastrians were using their own solar calendar. But the start of the new year had shifted away from the beginning of spring since no official adjustments had been made to account for leap years in the intervening 12 centuries since the last time it had been done by the Sasanians. Soroush, under the leadership of the Zoroastrian Association, worked with the members of the community and encouraged them to adopt the new calendar ushered in by Reza Shah's government.

2. Vital Statistics: Until the reign of Reza Shah, there was no governmental record keeping of the birth, marriage, and death of the Iranians. Zoroastrian families would typically record the birth and passage of a family member in their family book of Vendidad[46] with an indication of the date of the event. In some cases, those family records would be lost or abandoned. A federal ministry of Vital Statistics (*Sabto Ahval*) was established during the tenure of Reza Shah with offices in all major cities. Each local office would maintain records of births and deaths happening within their jurisdiction. For every birth, an official birth certificate would be issued for the newborn. This process required every registrant to have a first name and a last name. Last names were not yet common in Iran, and everyone would be referred to using their first name followed by their father's first name. That was the way of the Moslem Arabs. From that point of time onwards, every Iranian was required to adapt a last name that would become the birthright of the subsequent generations of the family. For the Iranians who had been born before this ministry was established, the requirement was for them to go to the local office and provide their best estimate of their birth date, their chosen last name, and their marital status. Soroush was eager to see 100% compliance by the Zoroastrian community in

---

45 https://en.wikipedia.org/wiki/Reza_Shah

46 A Zoroastrian religious book

Kerman. He adapted Soroushian (Sorooshian)[47] as his own last name. The rest of the larger family followed suit.[48] The Zoroastrian Anjuman worked with the rank and file of the community to figure out their dates of birth and adapted last names, and to get it registered with the ministry. The compliance rate of 100% was accomplished in the Zoroastrian community much to Soroush's delight.

3. Establishment of Schools: Soroush and his brother, Faridun, had the opportunity to attend a formal school at a young age. An iconic photo was taken in mid mid-1890s showing the two brothers and other Zoroastrian pupils sitting on the ground next to their teacher, the legendary Kaikhosrow Shahrokh, who had returned from Bombay and was a teacher in Kerman for several years. As the photo would indicate, the school had minimal facilities and instructors. Students of varying ages were taught by a single instructor. Those were the Qajar era days when secular schooling was frowned upon by the Islamic clergy. The Zoroastrians, realizing the importance of secular education, had secured permission from Nasser-ul-Dinshah[49] for the establishment of their own schools for both girls and boys subject to the condition of operating their schools with a low profile and out of sight of the Moslem populace so those schools would not draw any attention. As Soroush and his brother were growing up, they had the opportunity to go overseas to further their education. When Soroush was at the head of the Anjuman, the Anjuman board championed establishing new school campuses[50] with better facilities, including a multitude of classrooms and multiple instructors to teach the different grades. Towards that end, a large parcel of land that was part of Soroush's maternal grandfather's (Gushtasp Dinyar Klantar) residence had been partitioned off to be used for the building of a middle school (and eventually high school) for boys. Additionally, a new fire temple was to be built on the same parcel of land. The construction of the new facilities had

---

47 There is only one Farsi language rendition of the last name. When the name was transcribed using latin alphabets by the Iranian Passport officials, in some cases they inserted "ou" and in other cases "oo".

48 The descendants of Khodabux's five sons adapted "Soroushian" as the last name that Soroush Shahrior Khodabux had adapted. There were a few exceptions. Rustom Kaikhosrow Khodabux who had left Iran adapted the last name of Kermani on his US immigration papers. His first and middle name had remained as Rustom Kaikhosrow according to his 1927 landing records at NYC harbor. His younger brother Khodamorad, who came to the US in 1933, also adapted last name of Kermani, and his first and middle name were recorded as Khodamorad Soroushian according to his landing paper. The other exception was Rustom, the youngest son of Esfandiyar Khodabux, and Sultan who had been kidnapped from Kerman at age 6 and taken to the southwest port of Khoramshahr and sold as a slave. The kidnapping of minority children happened often during the Qajar and prior era, and the kidnappers were never punished. It turned out that Rustom grew up in the Khuzestan province when Reza Shah came to power and united all of Iran. Reza Shah's government required all Iranians to adapt last names and to get official birth certificates. Rustom had no contact with the rest of his family in Kerman to be aware of their approach. When it came to adapting a last name, remembering his mother's name (Sultan), he adapted the last name of Sultani. One other family group, the male descendants of Sohrab Esfandiyar Khodabux later decided to modify their last name to Soroushiani. At least two of the descendants of Khodabux born in the US and UK in the course of the 21st century have been given the middle name of Soroushian.

49 Thanks to the ceaseless efforts of Maneckji Limji Hataria, who secured Nasser-ul-Dinshah's consent for Zoroastrian schools to be established and operated in Kerman and Yazd.

50 A new campus for a girls' middle school and high school was started. The school was named after Kaikhosrow Shahrokh.

started during the tenure of his father Shahriar. During Soroush's tenure, additional halls and classrooms were added with support from various donors, including himself. His mother, Banu Gushtasp, was fully committed to this project. The new school was operating under the name of Zoroastrian School for Boys. This school expansion was happening at an opportune time for Iran, and with the rise of the Pahlavi dynasty that came to power in 1924, there was increased emphasis on establishing secular schools all over the country with the aim of elevating the national literacy rate and educating the next generation of Iranians. Towards that end, one of the cabinet ministers, Ali-Asgar Hekmat, visited Kerman and met with the board of the Zoroastrian Anjuman. He had a set of requests to the Zoroastrians of Kerman from the central government. He pointed out that the Zoroastrians had already established a school for boys on a relatively large size campus with an adequate number of classes and instructors, all paid by the Zoroastrians. His request was for the capacity of each grade to be increased and higher grades to be added so it would become a full-fledged high school. He also requested the school name be changed from "Zoroastrian School for Boys" to "Iranshahr High School."[51] Further, the request was that enrollment be open to all Iranians (Moslems and other minorities). Once again, the bulk of the operational cost of the school had to be borne by the Zoroastrian community.[52] The Anjuman board, led by Soroush, agreed, and the enrollment capacity for each grade was almost doubled.

4. Dressing code reform: In the late 1920s through the 1930s, reforms aimed at a more practical clothing style for the Iranians were championed through the Majlis (parliament). Until that time, Iranian men would typically wear the one-piece rob similar to the way Arabs dressed. The Iranian women wore a full-body veil (hijab) in public that concealed their faces and identity. The starting point for this national reform was men's clothing, with the aim of implementing two-piece clothing (pants and jacket-like outfits).[53] [54] The reform started with government employees. A sufficient quantity of men's clothing was procured by the central government and made available to the governors in various provincial capitals to hand out to the male workers and to require that the bureaucrats and government workers show up for work in the two-piece clothing. In Kerman City, the governor's office contacted Soroush Shahriar Soroushian with a request. They

---

51 The reason cited for dropping reference to the Zoroastrian religion in the name of the school was that some hard-core Moslem families would be reluctant to send their kids to non-Moslem schools, thereby denying them the opportunity to get an education.

52 This was with minimal tuition paid by students whose families could not afford it.

53 The first time in recorded history when men were dressed in two-piece clothing (pants and a jacket-like outfit) was at the time of Parthian dynasty of Iran (247 B.C. – 224 A.D.). At that time, the Romans, Egyptians, Arabs, Israelites, Indians, Chinese all wore a one-piece cover. The Persian men (ambassadors, soldiers, etc.) wore two-piece clothing. Wearing pants was common in Persia going back to the time of Achaemenides. Reza Shah was in effect restoring the style of clothing for men that had been invented in Iran for first time in history and subsequently adapted elsewhere.

54 For the Zoroastrians, this measure must have felt God-sent. If was only years earlier when the Zoroastrian men were forced to wear the one piece robe, color-coded to identify them as Zoroastrians and thus subject to harassment and physical abuse at the hands of zealot Moslems who would have full immunity in abusing minorities.

requested Soroush to make his father's stately mansion available for afternoon receptions[55] in which workers from various government offices in Kerman would be invited for a meal, followed by a speech by a governor's representative during which he would inform the government employees of the new clothing requirement. Every worker would be issued a new two-piece of clothing and shown how to use it and be asked to start wearing the new two-piece clothing from the next day onwards. Soroush was more than happy to accommodate this request, which came at a cost to him. The receptions went on for about a week. Every afternoon, workers from two or three of the ministries (Health, Transportation, Education, Treasury, Vital Statistics, Agriculture, etc.) were invited to hear the governor's address.

In time, many local tailor shops were opened in Kerman, and a new style of clothing for men (pants and jackets) was produced locally. Zoroastrians were amongst the first tailors to set up shops.

Soon afterward, the directive banning Iranian women from covering themselves in the Chador (head-to-toe veil) was issued. Whereas for Moslems, this measure was generally met with resistance, for the Zoroastrians it was a time to celebrate. Celebrations were held in Kerman, Yazd and other localities with considerable Zoroastrian concentration. Soroush and the other Anjuman board of directors were instrumental in arranging a community celebratory gathering, where many of the ladies who had managed to source the new style of women's dressing showed up wearing their new dresses. Pictures of the gathering were recorded by the Zoroastrian photographer, Mr. Bahram Sohrabi, who had started one of the first photography shops in Kerman.

5. Abolishment of community subsidies: Since its inception in the late 19th century, the Zoroastrian Association of Kerman (Anjuman Naseri Kerman) has provided material assistance to families in the community who were in need of help. A precedent had been set whereby families donated a portion of their annual income (money, grains, or other goods) to the Anjuman. Once the annual collection was complete, the Anjuman would distribute the proceeds amongst the needy families. Given the opportunities for Zoroastrians and Iranians ushered in by Reza Shah's reforms, Soroush, as the head of the Anjuman, proposed that the annual collection would continue. However, the redistribution amongst the families would cease, as every family would need to try and stand on their own.[56] In the meantime, the proceeds of the collections would be applied towards meeting the operating costs of the Zoroastrian schools, which until that time were dependent on subsidies coming from the Zoroastrians in India. There was a backlash against this proposal. Around the year 1922, this matter came to a head. A group

---

[55] There were not too many large halls in Kerman at the time. Shahriar's residence was one of the few houses that had a large hall and other essential facilities.

[56] The needy families were supported through direct donations from wealthier families.

of Zoroastrians led by Faridun Sohrab Sohrabi formed another informal Anjuman[57] and took control of the Zoroastrian schools. Members of the old Anjuman withdrew their children from the school and stopped paying tuition.[58] A Zoroastrian Youth Organization that had come into existence and started organizing education classes for the youth. Members of the old Anjuman sent their children to these newly organized classes. This conflict did not last long. There was local mediation by a lady by the name of Firozeh Mulla,[59] a stalwart of the community. Also, the Zoroastrian representative to the Majlis, Arbab Kaikhosrow Shahrokh, sent his son from Tehran to mediate. An iconic picture of the next Anjuman election was captured by the famed photographer Bahram Sohrabi. In this photo, the election observer from Tehran, holding the ballot box, stands next to Soroush Shahriar Soroushian, and they are flanked by a large number of the rank and file of the community who had come out to cast their vote. The old Anjuman board received the most votes. Members of the splinter group were invited to join in. Some members of the opposition decided to work with the board. The original proposal went into effect, and the subsidies for the schools from India were no longer needed.

6. Aramgah: The Zoroastrian community in Kerman city had used the Towers of Silence that was located on two hilltops to the northeast of the city, for the disposal of their dead.[60] That is where the remains of Shahriar and his parents and their ancestors had been committed. Carrying the corpses from the Gaber Mahala to the towers of silence had been fraught with trouble due to fanatical Moslems assaulting the precessions at will. At first, Soroush at the helm of the Anjuman, arranged for a metallic carrier from Bombay to be used for transportation of corpses on their last journey. The availability of this carrier made the conditions more bearable for the grieving families accompanying their dearly departed on their final trip to the Towers of Silences.[61] The opening of the Medical School of Tehran University provided incentives for those who would snatch corpses and transport them to Tehran and sell them to the medical school. A combination of factors brought the community to the point of accepting the use of cemeteries. Soroush and the Anjuman board decided to proceed with establishing a Cemetery (Aramgah).[62]

---

[57] The Naseri Zoroastrian Anjuman of Kerman had originally been charted to operate under direct edict of Nasser Ul-Dinshah Qajar. The original charter had been renewed once more by Nasser Ul-Dinshah and a third time by his successor Muzafar Ul-Dinshah. The informal Anjuman that was set up did not have any official charter.

[58] Tuition was based on family's ability to pay. Wealthier families had to pay higher tuition for the schooling of their children.

[59] Firozeh Mulla was a descendant of Khodabux Shahriar.

[60] Historically Zoroastrians did not use burial as a means of disposal of the remains of their dead. Use of fertile land for purposes other than agriculture was frowned upon by the nature-preservation-centric Zoroastrian belief system. Also, the fact that decaying flesh was considered to be a source of pollution of the earth was another factor. Dead bodies were left in a walled enclosure on hill tops or mountain tops, where vultures would descend and eat the decaying flesh. Once the flesh was gone, a mixture of sulfur would be sprayed on the remaining skeleton to melt it away.

[61] The two walled Tower of Silences that were in use in Kerman through the early part of the 20th century still stand a century later and are considered historical sites.

[62] *Aramgah* literally translates as "abode of quite"

Towards that end, Soroush and his brother donated a large plot of land that they possessed from their ownership of the village of Saedi to the northeast of the city. The land was elevated and surrounded by scenic and soaring mountains. It was uniquely suited for cemetery use, as it would provide a peaceful venue for the families of the departed. A wall was constructed around the plot, and trees and shrubs were planted. To make sure there would always be water supplied to the cemetery, Soroush also donated a portion of his water rights based on his own ownership of Saedi. This cemetery has continued to meet the needs of the Zoroastrian community of Kerman to this time and has plenty of unused space for future burials.[63] The management and administration of the cemetery have been entrusted to the Zoroastrian Anjuman of Kerman. In recognition of the endowment of the cemetery real estate by the two brothers, the first row of grave plots has been set aside for the exclusive use of the family. Soroush and his wife, Iran Banu, and his oldest son, Jamshid, are buried next to each other at one end. At the other end, the graves of Faridun, his wife GoharBanu, and two of their sons, Shahriar and Manuchehr, can be found. Soroush and Faridun's mother, Banu Gushtasp remains, are also buried in the same cemetery in the second row.[64]

7. Expansion of business into farming: The "Shahriar Khodabux and Sons" company had a modest start as mainly a trading and informal banking enterprise under the stewardship of its founder, Shahriar Khodabux. Their business office was located in the ChaharSue portion of Kerman's main bazar. They traded in products sourced locally, such as carpets, wool, garments, durable agricultural products, and grains, as well as imported consumer goods from overseas. The business also expanded into the acquirement of farm and agricultural lands around the province of Kerman that were available for purchase. This trend accelerated with Soroush and Faridun becoming more involved in the decision-making. One major factor driving this trend was that under the Pahlavi dynasty, all farmlands were subjected to taxation by the central government. The farms were evaluated for taxation based on their potential for productivity. The owners were required to pay annual taxes. A good portion of the farmlands at the time were considered Crown properties and in possession of members of the Qajar clan, many of whom lived in Tehran and were absentee landlords. Due to a lack of proper management by the absentee owners, the productivity of the farms was typically very low. Faced with high farm tax liabilities, many of the absentee owners decided to sell their holdings. These families were looking to sell to the highest bidders and those who could definitely make the payments. The Soroushian brothers formed a partnership with the Kianian brothers (Kaikhosrow in Kerman and Sohrab based in Yazd). They also invited a prominent Moslem family of

---

[63] Prior to the establishment of the Soroushian Cemetery of Kerman, a Zoroastrian businessman by the name of Sohrabi had made the use of his backyard available for burial of the dead. A few graves can be found in the grounds of that house. Once the Soroushian Cemetery became available, the Zoroastrians of Kerman exclusively used that facility, and the Towers of Silence went out of commission.

[64] Banu would have preferred to be buried between the graves of the other community member who had passed away just before she did and the one who passed away right after her passage.

Sardar Mojalall (Aamary)[65] into an equal partnership.[66] Pulling their own financial resources as well as raising additional capital, the partners were able to make attractive offers to the sellers. The Qajar families in Tehran were acquainted with Arbab Kaikhosrow Shahrokh[67], who was vouching for the Zoroastrian partners. The Qajar families seemed to prefer to sell to Zoroastrian buyers as well. Prime farms around the province of Kerman in Zarand County, Sirjan County, Kerman County, and Jiroft County were acquired by the partners, who proportioned them among themselves and started working to develop these farms. One of the challenges the partners faced was securing waterway rights for these farms. In most cases, the irrigation water would come from underground aqueducts (Qanats) that would originate at the basin of mountains located long distances away. To get to the final destination, the underground Qanats had to traverse lands that were part of other villages. Soroush, realizing the potential risk presented by this arrangement, determined it was best to buy minority ownership in the farming lands that were part of these other villages. One other challenge that Soroush faced was that many of the villagers had been indoctrinated by the Mullahs (Islamic clergy) to be hateful of non-Moslems (kaffirs). The news had got to the villages that kaffirs[68] were new owners, and as such, some villagers were hostile and insulting to the new owners. Soroush knew he had his work cut out to win the hearts and minds of the villagers, something his father had successfully accomplished as well. At the villages that were located far away from the city and the brothers and their families or their foremen would need to stay for several days and night at a time, Soroush realized residential facilities were needed to be built. Soroush typically chose one of the walled orchard gardens that had a running stream of water passing through it. He would then enlist local construction workers to build a residential facility that included bedrooms, a living room, a kitchen, a bathroom, and a storage facility. In addition, he was intent on using the latest construction materials, such as bricks. In many cases, a small-scale brick-making facility would be constructed close to the building site to produce the required building material for the residence in that village as well as other villages the brothers had acquired. The brother's dedication to the betterment of the village went a long way toward winning over the villagers. The partners worked hard to develop the farms they had acquired to reach the farms' full potential. Pistachio, citrus, dates, and fruit crops were planted and grew depending on the village climate. Grains were also grown based on water availability. All of these development activities progressed and were made possible by Reza Shah's central government initiatives in building/improving roads between cities and villages. Making the roads safe and secure for traveling by instituting

---

65 Adapted the last name of Aamary

66 1/3 for the Soroushian brothers, 1/3 for the Kianian brothers and 1/3 for the Aamarys

67 Zoroastrian representative in the Iranian parliament (Majlis) at that time

68 "Kaffir" is an ignominious term used to refer to non-Moslems

the Gendarmerie security forces in the interior of the country[69] was another step that helped spur economic activities in the country and expand agriculture.

The Soroushian-Kianian-Aamary partners did their share in developing the agricultural base of Kerman province. Soroush had developed a unique skill in planning and engineering new Qanat systems. He was responsible for the development of five new Qanat systems around the province. In some cases, it would take up to seven months of continuous work to construct one of the qanats. Soroush would stay with the construction crew and manage all facets of the construction except for short absences, where his presence was needed in Kerman City to attend to other matters, including Anjuman's affairs. The brothers also acquired agricultural holdings outside the partnership.[70] Relative to Soroush's expertise in planning and managing the construction of major underground irrigation systems, one of his grandsons named after him, Soroosh Jamshid Sorooshian, is recognized as a foremost expert in hydrology.[71]

Ability to raise capital from the Moslem Bazaris: For their business expansion plans, the brothers were looking at all sources of financing that could be leveraged. Kerman's bazar had its share of merchants with large-scale operations. They were mostly Moslems and had typically been indoctrinated to have prejudicial views of non-Moslems or at least pretend to do so.[72] Some

---

[69] By contrast in the Qajar era, the safety of travelers and goods on the roads was not a sure thing. Parviz Soroush Soroushian related an event that happened in the pre-Pahlavi era in late 1910s. His father, uncle, and Mr. Kaikhosrow Kianian were importing merchandize from England shipped to Bandar Abbas on the Persian Gulf. From there, the goods were to be transported on camel to Kerman. The shipment was expected in Kerman and was already overdue. Days later news arrived that highway robbers had attacked and stolen all the containers on route to the city.

On hearing the news, the three of them early next day rushed to Governor Sardar Bakhtiary to seek his help to recover their stolen goods. As they were walking in the courtyard of the governor's headquarter towards his office, they noticed dusty container boxes placed next to the walls. On close looking, they found the marking on the boxes addressed to their businesses in Kerman, and realized the governors must have been in on the heist. By that time, they had reached the governor's office, and when they were ushered in, the governor in a stern tune asked them the purpose of their visit. Realizing if they complained, there was a chance their lives could be in jeopardy, they told the governor they had come to wish him well and left immediately afterwards.

[70] One example was when the trading house of Jamshidian in Tehran became in possession of citrus and date growing farms in AzzizAbad, a village in the county of Bam, they approached the Soroushian brothers to sell to. The Soroushian brothers proceeded with the purchase without getting anyone else involved. Another example predating the Pahlavis was during the ending of the Qajar rule and governorship of Farmanfarmian. At the time Kaikhosrow Shahrokh was a teacher in Kerman before relocating to Tehran. He was also an English language instructor to the children of Farmanfarmian. One day when teaching the children, he overheard that the governor was planning to sell his ownership in the village of Saedi to the northeast of Kerman. Kaikhosrow Shahrokh informed the Soroushian brother and Mr. Kianian as to what he heard. The three Zoroastrians approached the governor who agreed to sell to them. The Soroushian brothers also partnered with the Kianian brother and two other Zoroastrians families from Tehran (Firouzgar and Yeganegi) to purchase agricultural farmland in the villages of Saeed-Abad and Firoz-Abad in the southwest of Tehran from one of the Qajars. The sale to the Zoroastrian partners was facilitated by the late Arbab Kaikhosrow Shahrokh who was acquainted with the seller. Firoz-Abad had the unique distinction of being the first village in Iran to have a telephone line extended to it. The Zoroastrian owners had paid for the extension of the telephone line from Tehran to the owners' residence in the village.

[71] https://en.wikipedia.org/wiki/Soroosh_Sorooshian

[72] The typical sentiment expressed by these merchants to Zoroastrians or other minorities as to the reason for their reluctance to do business with them was of the following nature: "Although you are a trustworthy person, you are destined to go to hell. Why don't you salvage your soul by embracing Islam. Otherwise, I cannot engage in business with you."

would confide that their parents or grandparents were Zoroastrians who had converted to Islam. Soroush was eager to interest them in profitable joint ventures. He also realized the Moslem merchants were typically very conservative and not likely to expand into other businesses or partner with Zoroastrians. His work was cut out for him to change his mind and to make headways. Soroush would typically approach these merchants with his business proposals and invite them to participate. His own track record of having done well in business was a factor in his favor. By sheer persistence and determination, he was able to win over some of those merchants who became eager to partner with him whenever Soroush called upon them.[73] This way, Soroush was able to improve the working environment in the city's commercial center.

Another example of Soroush and Faridun's business dealings with the merchants in Kerman was their interaction with the Russian traders in Kerman. There was a colony of Russians in Kerman who were engaged in business. They were involved with sourcing local agro-farming products such as regular wool, specialty wool, and tragacanth for export to Russia and importing granulated sugar as well as sugar cubes,[74] footwear, clothing, and petroleum products from Russia for retail marketing in Kerman. For a while, the Russians were occupying the larger multi-level buildings that were eventually purchased by Shahriar Khodabux and Sons. The Czarist Russian Consulate was right across the street from that residence. The Russians also started the first electricity generation operation in Kerman with limited coverage. With the Bolshevik revolution engulfing Russia and the nationalistic Reza Shah taking charge in Iran, the Czarist Russians felt vulnerable and were looking to liquidate their holding in Kerman, including their electricity generation company. They approached Soroush Soroushian and his associates with the intent of selling them the electricity generator they had brought in from Russia and were operating. Soroush did not see a fit in procuring the electricity generation operation. There was an Isfahani merchant named AbulGhasem Harandi who had come to Kerman from Isfahan and Yazd to engage in business. He had established a working relationship with Soroush and Faridun and had proved to be dependable. So, when the Russians heard from Soroush that he was not interested in pursuing the electricity generation operation himself, they asked if he could recommend someone reliable and vouch for them. Soroush suggested Mr. Harrandi. Mr. Harrandi accepted the challenge and eventually paid the price he had agreed with the Russians. Over the year, he expanded his electricity generation network throughout the city.

8. Carpet export business to the US: In the mid-1910s, a carpet merchant from Tabriz in North Western Iran arrived in Kerman. Mehdi Dilmaghani, the Tabrizi carpet merchant, was planning to establish a carpet dealership and showrooms in New York City. His

---

[73] In 1995, an aged Moslem merchant by the name of Haji Asghar Rustomi residing in his birth city of Kerman reminisced that when he was a young man working in his father's store in the bazar, at times Soroush would stop by and discuss a new business venture with his father. His father, if he had the liquidity at the time, would typically tell Soroush that he would participate on a 50% basis, provided Soroush would hold the other 50%. His willingness to do joint ventures with Soroush and his brother had increased over time due to positive experience he had. Interestingly, this merchant was very religious and would not even eat foods prepared by Zoroastrians.

[74] Specially sized solid sugar blocks were referred to as Russian Sugar. Zoroastrian would typically wrap them in green decorative paper and gift each other on happy occasions such as weddings, NovRuz, etc.

initial plan was to market the hand-woven carpets produced in the province of Kerman as well as carpets woven around Tabriz. In Kerman, he approached the Soroushian brothers as well as their business partner, Mr. Kaikhosrow Rustom Kianian, to become his supplier and export large quantities of carpet to New York City for him to sell.[75] Dilmaghani's business in New York City proved to be successful[76], and his dealings with the Soroushian brothers[77] and Mr. Kianian were very profitable and durable. They were only interrupted by WW II when commercial shipments across the Atlantic were not safe anymore. Prior to this carpet exporting business, Shahriar had already established a limited operation with a gallery in New York City and had exported a limited number of carpets to New York. However, the dealing with Mr. Dilmaghani's New York operation was at a much higher volume.

9. Supporting other initiatives of Reza Shah and raising their families: The brothers were fully vested in the progressive initiatives the central government was launching and did whatever they could to encourage adaptation and implementation by community members and Kermanis that they could influence. Reza Shah's initiative to launch a national defense force was initially based on volunteers signing up and being compensated by wealthy Iranians who could contribute towards national defense. However, soon, the government implemented a conscription system in which all Iranian boys at the age of 18 would sign up and serve in the army for two years. Finding the conscripts was not always easy as the Department of Vital Statistics was of recent vintage, and their records were not complete yet. Soroush's four sons served their conscription in the army. His second son, Parviz, enrolled in the Military College[78] and graduated as an officer. He was stationed in the southwest province of Khuzestan and saw action during the Allied invasion of Iran.

During his inspection tour of southeast Iran, Reza Shah came to Kerman city. Arbab Kaikhosrow Shahrokh, who represented the Zoroastrians in the Iranian Majlis, had arrived in Kerman the day before to be present to welcome Reza Shah to Kerman. Soroush Shahriar

---

[75] Mr. Dilmaghani also establish his own company in Kerman to source locally produced carpets. He hired employees to run the company after his departure. Upon his relocation to NYC, his nephew visited Kerman to oversee the operation of his uncle's company on several occasions. However, due to long absence of the Dilmaghanis from Kerman, a local man by the name of Ahmad Yazdanpanah pretended he was a Dilmaghani and took over the business operation in Kerman.

[76] https://www.dilmaghani.com/

[77] Shahriar Khodabux and Sons company was already engaged in exporting Kermani carpets to a retail store in New York City starting in 1910. Their export business to the Dilmaghani Co. in NYC was in addition to their other carpet export business to the US.

[78] The Officers' College was established by Reza Shah Pahlavi in 1921 before he ascended the throne.

Soroushian led the Zoroastrian delegation welcoming Reza Shah.[79] The other members included Kaikhosrow Rustom Kianian, Soroush Ardeshir Kaboli, and Hormuzd Hematti.[80]

Soroush Shahriar and his brother, Faridun Shahriar, inherited their father's business and vastly expanded it during the period of the Pahlavi dynasty by forming effective partnerships with two other families and buying farmlands around the province of Kerman as well as in Tehran. The brothers focused on developing the agro-farming business they had acquired. That meant constructing new irrigation systems and procuring a right-of-way for the construction of underground tunnels used for channeling water from a mountain basin to the villages that were far from the mountains. With the availability of pure water sourced from mountain basins, pistachio or fruit or citrus orchards were cultivated in several locations around the Province of Kerman. Soroush was mostly on the move attending to their joint business, while Faridun primarily worked out of their bazar headquarters or home office and attended to the actuarial and administrative aspects of the business. The constant business demand and oversight needed kept Soroush away from his family for a considerable amount of time. Also, the demand for his time to promote the interest of the Zoroastrian community as the head of the Anjuman was another factor that kept him busy. Soroush's oldest children, daughter Katayun and son Jamshid, spent more time with him than their younger siblings. Hormuzd, his youngest son, remembered that at times when his father returned home from an extended stay on the farms, he would be in town for a few days before departing to manage a different farm. As part of the preparation for the next trip, the car would be loaded with provisions to sustain him and his driver for the duration of the stay at the next farm. On occasions, Hormuzd and his older brother Esfandiyar would sneak in the back of the car and hide under the provisions. Once the car was well on its way, they would surface. On some trips of shorter duration, they would be allowed to go along.[81] On the longer trips, their father would have the driver turn back to the city and drop off his two sons.

Soroush, Faridun, and their families would often have dinner together. Soroush's niece Banu recalls that every time his uncle came home from the bazaar with necessities for his children (such as toothbrushes, etc.), he would also purchase them for Faridun's children.

---

[79] In anticipation of Reza Shah's visit to Kerman, Soroush Soroushian and Kaikhosrow Kianian had ordered two pairs of formal men attire (Edwardian vintage fashion) from Tehran to be shipped to Kerman. The pair arrived the morning of Reza Shah's arrival. The pair had been tailored to the same exact size, and there was no time to do any alternation, as Soroush Soroushian and Kaikhosrow Kianian had to depart to reach Mahan in time for the royal arrival. It happened that Soroush was short and heavy-set, and Kaikhosrow was tall and slim. When they put on their formals, in the case of Soroush the pants were longer than he was, and in the case of Kaikhosrow his pants came short of his full height. When Reza Shah in the reception line reached the Zoroastrian delegation, Arbab Kaikhorow Shahrokh introduced the group. Reza Shah looked at Soroush and Kaikhosrow and quipped, "Gentlemen, it seems your wives mixed up your pants."

[80] Hormuzd Hematti was the head of the Telephone Office in Kerman and was responsible for expanding the telephone number in the city and good portion of the Kerman province.

[81] On such occasions, arrangements would have been made to inform IranBanou and other members of the household that the two young boys are safe and in the company of their father.

Mehrborzin Jamshid Soroushian

Soroush's busy life and the pressures of his business and community work took a toll on his health and resulted in a cardiovascular ailment that was progressively deteriorating. In the mid-1930s, accompanied by his daughter Katayun and her husband, Mr. Jamshid Farvahar,[82] Soroush traveled to Germany to be seen by a famed heart specialist. After a short stay, they returned to Kerman. In the summer of 1939, with his heart condition worsening, Soroush decided to make another trip to Germany for additional treatment. This time, his oldest son, Jamshid, accompanied him. They left Kerman for Tehran in early August of 1939 to make travel arrangements for the outbound and return.[83] The outbound trip took them to the Port of Baku by sea and by train over the Soviet Territory into Ukraine, Poland, and Berlin. Their trip coincided with the opening days of WWII, something they had not anticipated. By the time they were ready to return to Iran, traveling through Poland and the Soviet Union was no longer an option. They had to scramble their return passage. *Intourist*,[84] the international travel agency they were using, suggested taking the Berlin to Baghdad railway that had recently come into operation all the way South. The return trip proved to be very perilous, the full details of which will be covered in the next chapter.

The arduous trip to Germany exacted a heavy toll on Soroush, whose health continued to deteriorate. He tried to immerse himself in his agro-farming business, but his health was limiting his ability to move around. He was homebound more than before, and that limitation also took a toll on him. Soroush lived for another year and passed away in December 1940. In early July 1940, the news was received that Arbab Kaikhosrow Shahrokh had been found dead on a Tehran street. Soroush's youngest son, Hormuzd, remembers his father was at home, and on hearing the news, he became very emotional and kept saying that the late arbab had done so much for the Zoroastrians and for the nation and that his loss was a real tragedy. Hormuzd recalls that was the only time he saw his father tearing up. Soon afterward, Soroush asked his brother and their business partner, Kaikhosrow Kianian, to come to see him. Once they arrived, Soroush informed them that Arbab Kaikhosrow Shahrokh, in support of his community activities and official duties, had taken out personal loans to pay for the expenses associated with entertaining officials and for community-related travels. The debtors were willing to wait for the repayment

---

82 Mr. Jamshid Farvahar was the oldest son of Jahangir Jamshid Farvahar. Jahangir Farvahar was amongst the leading Zoroastrians of Kerman and worked closely with Soroush Shahriar Soroushian on community projects. Jamshid had good business acumen and had travelled to Europe (Germany, France) from a young age. He spoke German and English and had some fluency in French as well. Once he travelled back from Germany riding a motorcycle. He was constantly looking for business opportunities, and since getting engaged to Katayun, he was homebound in Kerman until his five daughters were born. He was keen on sending them to England for medical training. While in Kerman and married to Katayun, he shadowed his father-in-law and learnt from him.

83 While waiting for the issuance of their visas in Tehran, Soroush asked to visit the Officers' College that Reza Shah had instituted for training Iranian army officers. He wanted to pay a visit to an army general who had served in Kerman and now was teaching at the Officers' College. Once there, he informed the general that his second son Parviz was enrolled in that college. On hearing that news, the general immediately asked his assistant to go and find Parviz and bring him back with him. 20 minutes later, Parviz in uniform entered the general's room and was surprised to find his father and older brother Jamshid waiting for him.

84 This was a Soviet travel agency with offices in the USSR, Tehran, Berlin, near east, and some other major cities.

of his debts as long as he was alive. But now that he was gone, they would likely go after his material possessions, including the house in which his family lives in Tehran. His family would be at risk of becoming homeless, and that would not reflect well on the Zoroastrian community. Soroush asked his two partners to join him in paying off the late Kaikhosrow Shahrokh's debts. Unfortunately, the two partners did not show any interest, and Soroush ended up arranging for payments from his own holdings. That was the least he could do for the community and national leader who had been one of his first teachers. Soroush passed away in December 1940 just in time to be spared another set of crushing news that would have devastated him even more: the invasion of Iran in August of 1941 by Britain and the Soviet Union and the forced abdication of Reza Shah and his exile to South Africa.

The news of Soroush's death sent a shock wave through the Zoroastrian community of Kerman, many of whom rushed to his house to express their sympathy.

Soroush and Faridun each had four sons and two daughters. Soroush and IranBanou's firstborn was a girl named Katayun, followed by four sons, Jamshid, Parviz, Esfandiar, and Hormuzd. Their last child was a girl they named MahinDokht. Their offspring received their education in Kerman at the Zoroastrian schools, which was up to the highest level available at the time. Katayun attended the Zoroastrian girl school in Kerman.

Katayun had the distinction of being among the first females in Iran and likely in the Middle East to drive a car. Her father, Soroush, had purchased a vintage model of the Oakland[85] automobile manufactured in Detroit and exported to Iran in the early 1920s. Soroush insisted that his eldest daughter and son learn to operate the car and drive him around to attend to his business. At a young age, both Katayun (14) and Jamshid (12) learned to drive the car. Katayun, along with a few other Zoroastrian girls[86] of her age, had the distinction of being the first group of girls to ride bicycles to school in Kerman. Bicycles were introduced in Iran at about that time, mostly imported from England and India. Conservative Moslems would not allow their daughters to ride bicycles.

After graduating from the Zoroastrian School for Boys, Jamshid attended the school set up by the British missionaries in Kerman and then in Isfahan to receive a higher levels of secular education. More about Jamshid's life will be covered in the next section.[87]

By the time the other sons were school-bound, the Zoroastrian Boy School in Kerman had added higher grades. So, they continued their education at the Zoroastrian schools and at the school where missionaries taught secular subjects. Then they were sent to Tehran. Esfandiar

---

[85] A few of the Oakland cars (forerunner of Cadillac) were brought to Iran. One was used to drive Reza Shah Pahlavi around Tehran. The first US President who was driven in a car from the White House to the Capitol for taking his Oath of Office was Woodrow Wilson, and he was driven in an Oakland. Prior to that, US Presidents rode in horse-driven carriages.

[86] The other girls were Farangis Kaikhosrow Kianian and the daughters of Hormuzd Hematti.

[87] From his experience at the Missionary School in Isfahan, he developed a keen interest in studying Zoroastrian literature and history. He was self-taught and through communication with leading scholars in the subject in Iran and overseas he became well versed in the subject and published many books. More about his accomplishments will be covered in the next section.

got admitted to the Tehran University's Law School. Parviz decided to attend the military college in Tehran and became a commissioned army officer. After graduation, he was posted to the southwestern province of Khuzestan and saw action during the August 1941 British naval surprise attack on Iranian southwestern ports. Parviz's unit was overwhelmed due to the sheer size of the invading force. Parviz and his unit were captured as prisoners of war and kept in captivity in southern Mesopotamia.[88] Upon the abdication of Reza Shah (September 16, 1941) and Iran's declaration of war on the Axis nations, the Iranian POWs were returned to Iran, and Parviz was reunited with his family in Kerman. By then, his father had passed. Upon return to Kerman, Parviz engaged in the family agro-farming business.

Esfandiar completed his law school education and returned to Kerman to engage in the family agro-farming business.

Hormuzd attended the American College (Alborz) in Tehran but had to drop off to complete his conscription service in Kerman. He then accompanied his ailing uncle Faridun to America in 1948, where his uncle received medical care at the Mayo Clinic for his cardiovascular condition. The uncle returned to Kerman. Hormuzd stayed on and moved to the US west coast, where he attended California Polytechnic at San Luis Obispo and attended the agricultural college in Davis, where he received his bachelor's degree. Before moving to the West Coast and while still in New York, Hormuzd had to secure the funds that were owed to his father by the Dilmighani Carpet Business in New York City. Due to the disruption in cross-Atlantic trade during WWII, the amounts owed to the Soroushian brothers and Mr. Kaikhosrow Kianian were invested on their behalf. Now, Hormuzd was requesting the transfer of the investments to the heirs of Soroush Soroushian. After verifying his identity and informing the investment company that his father had passed away and that he had been deputized by his siblings to collect the amount, he was advised the total sum had been invested in his father's name. Hormuzd secured the services of an estate and tax attorney, who was able to clear the investment amount after paying estate tax and transferring the remainder to six accounts opened in the name of Hormuzd and his five siblings.[89] Hormuzd returned to Kerman in the latter part of the 1950s and engaged in the family agro-farming.

MahinDokht studied at the Zoroastrian schools and the missionary school in Kerman. In late 1849, accompanied by his brother Esfandiar and a British missionary nun who had served at the missionary school in Kerman, he headed to the port city of Bandar Shahpur in the southwest of Iran. From there, MahinDokht and the British nun boarded a ship headed for England. Mahindokht learned English and studied Home Economics in London. She was the first female in the family to go overseas to study. Two years into her arrival, Katayun's two oldest daughters, IranBanu and Mahin (twelve and thirteen years old at the time), flew to London to go to school and eventually to attend medical schools in England. In time, they became

---

[88] This is present day Iraq.

[89] Since Faridun Soroushian and Kaikhosrow Kianian were still alive, their shares were transferred to their two sons Kaikhosrow Soroushian and Shahrokh Kianian without any estate taxes being deducted.

medical doctors. MahinDokht was there to receive them, find housing for them, and act as their guardian. In 1952, two more of Katayun's daughters, Morwarid and Shirin, 12 and 11 years old at the time, arrived in London. Once again, MahinDokht helped them settle into their new environment. Morwarid and Shirin continued their studies in England, and years later, Morwarid was admitted to the Manchester University Medical School and became a medical doctor. Katayun's youngest daughter, Parvin, joined her sisters in England a few years later. In late 1952, due to the great smog of London, MahinDokht fell severely ill and was hospitalized. Due to the gravity of her condition, her brother Parviz was deputized by the rest of the family to go to London and help her sister.[90] Parviz left immediately for Tehran to make travel arrangements when he received news from London that MahinDokht's condition had improved and she would be released from the hospital. Consequently, he canceled his trip to London. The following year, Esfandiar accompanied his mother on a trip to London to visit with MahinDokht and Katayun's daughters. Hormuzd also traveled from the US to England by sea during his summer break and in time to visit with his mother, brother, and nieces.

Soroush and his wife IranBanou were both born in Kerman and died in Kerman. They were buried at the Soroushian Zoroastrian cemetery in Kerman. Soroush died in 1941 while Reza Shah Pahlavi was on the throne of Iran. His wife and their offspring all passed away in the aftermath of the 1979 Islamic Revolution. All six of his offspring were born in Kerman, but only one of them, his oldest son Jamshid, died in Iran. The others passed away in North America or in the UK.

Their oldest son, Jamshid, passed away in Tehran, but as per Jamshid's last wish, his remains were taken back to Kerman and buried at the Soroushian Zoroastrian cemetery between the burial plots of his father and mother. The remains of Jamshid's wife, Homayun Sohrab Kianian, who passed away in 2006 in Tehran, were also taken back to Kerman and buried close to the grave of her husband.

Katayun and Parviz died in London (1986 and 2011, respectively) and were buried at the Zoroastrian cemetery of London. Esfandiar passed away in the San Francisco Bay area in 2012 and was buried in Northern California. Hormuzd died in San Clemente, Southern California, in 2016, and his remain was cremated as per his wish.

MahinDokht, the youngest child of Soroush and IranBanou, was the first of the siblings to die[91] in 1983 at the age of 58 in Vancouver, Canada, and was buried at the Zoroastrian cemetery of British Columbia.

---

90 No direct commercial air travel service between Iran and the UK was established in the early 1950. Getting to London required flying to Beirut, then to Cairo, and onto Rome before reaching London. Such a journey would have taken several days. There were limited number of flights and seats available.

91 Due to breast cancer

Mehrborzin Jamshid Soroushian

As for the grandchildren of Soroush and IranBanou, all but one of them were born in Iran,[92] mostly in Kerman and a few in Tehran. Most of them were born during the reign of Mohamed Reza Shah Pahlavi,[93] a rare period in Iran's recent history that qualifies as the golden years of Iran. The grandchildren received their education in Kerman, Tehran, or overseas. Most of them attended college in Europe or in the US. In the aftermath of the Islamic revolution of 1979, thirteen of the grandchildren of Soroush and IranBanou settled in North America. Seven settled in the UK, and one granddaughter, Mahvash, spends part of the year in Iran and the rest in Northern California.[94]

Faridun was born in Kerman in 1889. His wife, GoharBanou, was born in Yazd in 1899. They lived in Kerman, and both passed away in Kerman. Faridun died in 1951 during the reign of Mohamed Reza Shah Pahlavi. His wife, GoharBanou, and their siblings all passed away post-1979. The remains of Faridun and GoharBanou were interred at the Soroushian Zoroastrian Cemetery of Kerman in the row of plots reserved for Soroush and Faridun Soroushian, their spouses, and their descendants. The remains of two of their sons, Shahriar and Manuchehr, were also interred close to the graves of their parents. The remains of their second son, Kaikhosrow, were buried in 1991 at the Zoroastrian Cemetery of Southern California.[95] The remains of their two daughters, Banu and IranDokht, and their youngest son, Iraj, are entombed at Tehran's Zoroastrian cemetery.[96]

Their eldest son, Shahriar, studied in Kerman and Tehran and remained in Kerman to assist his father in the family business. The other three sons studied at the Zoroastrian school in Kerman and attended college in the US.[97] The three sons returned to Iran. Kaikhosrow and Manuchehr returned to Kerman and joined the family business. The youngest son, Iraj, who had studied as a pharmacy doctor, went to Shiraz upon his return and finally settled in Tehran with

---

[92] MahinDokht and her husband, Dr. Manuchehr Shahriari, resided in Gottingen, Germany at the time their daughter MahDokht was born. After completion of Dr. Shahriari's Medical School at Gottingen University, the family relocated to Iran. During the Pahlavi era, many of the Zoroastrian who could afford sending their children to England or Germany or the US did so. Most of the students returned to Iran upon completion of their studies and helped in rebuilding Iran.

[93] Katayun's first two daughters, IranBanou and Mahin, were born while Reza Shah was still in power.

[94] Of Katayun's five daughters, two of them who are still alive as of the time of this writing and are settled in London. Jamshid's five children (3 daughters and 2 sons) have all settled in California. The three daughters live in the San Francisco Bay area. The oldest daughter, Mahvash, and her husband Goodarz spend part of the year in California and the rest in Kerman and Tehran attending to the family business in Iran. Jamshid's two sons reside in Southern California. Parviz's one son and two daughters live in the UK, and his oldest daughter, Tira, resides in the greater Chicago area with her family. Esfandiyar's four daughters and their families have settled in the San Francisco Bay Area of California. Hormuzd's only surviving son lives in Southern California. MahinDokht's only daughter and her family live in North Vancouver, Canada.

[95] As a US military veteran of WWII, upon his passage, a letter of appreciation from the US President George H. Bush was sent to his widow.

[96] Known as Qasar Firozeh, the site of the Zoroastrian cemetery of Tehran came about as a result of the efforts of Arbab Kaikhosrow Shahrokh.

[97] Their second son, Kaikhosrow also attended the American college of Alborz, a reputed highschool in Tehran, before traveling by ship from the east coast of India to New York. The ship he was on was within half an hour of reaching the Panama Canal (enroute to NYC Harbor) when the captain informed the passengers that Pearl Harbor had been attacked by the Japanese forces.

his family. In the aftermath of the 1979 revolution, Kaikhosrow[98] moved to the US, where his wife, his two sons, and daughter had settled.

Banu, the eldest daughter, studied in Kerman and was sent to the American boarding school for girls in Tehran. The younger daughter studied in Kerman. Banu and her husband, Dr. Mehraban Hormuzdi, lived in Kermanshah for several years, where Dr. Hormuzdi[99] was an official of the Iranian National Oil Company. Some of their children were born in Kermanshah. The youngest daughter, Irandokht, was born in Kerman in 1924, completed her education in Kerman, and married Mr. Parviz Rastegary. Both sisters, Banu Hormuzdi and IranDokht Rastegary, eventually settled in Tehran with their husbands and families.

In the wake of the Islamic Revolution of 1979, ten of Faridun and GoharBanou's grandchildren settled in the US. Two settled in Europe, and nine remained in Iran.[100]

Soroush, like Reza Shah, had limited time to make his contributions to the advancement of his nation and his Zoroastrian community (in the case of Soroush). But they both accomplished a great deal in their own rights despite the shortness of the time they had.

Soroush and Faridun turned the focus of their family business from trade to agriculture and farm ownership, similar to what Kaikhosrow Hormuzd, their 6th ancestor before them, had done in the mid-18th century.

2.7.2 IranBanu Esfandiyar Khodabux
1892 -1981 (Kerman)

As the oldest daughter of Sultan and Esfandiyar, IranBanu (or simply Banu) was a great help to her mother in caring for her seven siblings. The demands of taking care of her siblings at a young age meant she did not have the opportunity to receive much formal education. However, learning to read, write, and be literate was a lifelong pursuit. Tragedy struck the family with the loss of two of her brothers, Hormuzdyar and Darab, due to outbreaks of diseases and the kidnapping of her youngest brother, Rustom, at a young age. One of her other brothers, Khodabux, left for India but did not fare too well.

Her marriage to her first cousin, Soroush-Shahriar-Khodabux-Shahriar-Jamshid, had been prearranged by her mother and Soroush's mother. She was 19 years old when the marriage to her 25-year-old fiancé was consummated, and within a year, her first daughter, Katayun, was

---

[98] While as a student in the US during the years of WWII, Kaikhosrow enlisted in the US armed forces and was scheduled to be deployed to the Pacific. However, when president Truman decided to nuke Japan, the war was cut short and Kaikhosrow was not deployed.

[99] Mehraban Hormuzdi hailed from Kerman was among the first group of young Iranians high-accomplishers who were sent to Europe to complete advanced studies and to return to Iran and contribute to the modernization of Iran. This was an initiative championed by Reza Shah Pahlavi. Dr. Hormuzdi attended University of Manchester in England and was amongst the first Iranians to receive a Ph.D. in engineering. His return happened during the opening years of WWII, and the ship on which he was traveling from the port of South Hampton to Bombay was almost torpedoed by a German U-2.

[100] Other than the grandchildren of Faridun and GoharBanou, who stayed in Iran to attend to the farms they have inherited, most others arranged to send their children to the US or other countries.

born. Two years later, she gave birth to her first son, Jamshid, who was named after the first generation of the family, who had arrived in Kerman in the 1790s. She gave birth to her second son, Parviz, and her third son, who was named Esfandiyar in honor of her late father. Then came the fourth son, Hormuzd, followed by her last daughter, Mahindokht.

At her parents' house, she and her seven siblings lived modestly. On marrying her cousin, she entered a more affluent life. However, she never forgot her humble beginning and was always mindful of those who needed support.

IranBanou did not have much material attachment and routinely sent care packages to the needy families of the community whom she knew. Descendents of some of these families testify to how their grandparents and parents were looking for this assistance. On occasions when their need was dire, they would send for it and request IranBanou's help, which always came through.

During WWII, soon after the Allied forces occupied Iran, much of the grain production of Iran was subject to confiscation by the occupying forces for the consumption of their military. Mass starvation set in among the Iranian populace. IranBanou's oldest son Jamshid was arranging for the delivery of grains and other farm products from their farmlands across the province to be safely brought to the city and stored in their silos. IranBanou was active in managing the distribution of grain access to families in need.

One of her nieces recalls that in the pre-WWII years, many of the older residential units in Kerman lacked a bathing facility. Her aunt IranBanou's house had a bathing facility with hot water heated over a burning furnace, the heat of which was also directed to the inside of the bathing room to warm it up. Every Friday, her aunt's bathing facility was open to her extended family members.

When she visited her son's household, she was always looking to help out and could be found in the kitchen helping out. Through the end of her life, she kept herself busy with housework to maintain her mental sharpness despite her physical limitations. In the years after the Islamic revolution of 1979, only two of her sons stayed in Kerman.[101] Her other offspring and her grandchildren had all left Kerman. Only one of her offspring was buried in Kerman. All the others passed away in North America and the UK. She had inherited a small farm from her father that she turned bequeathed to her two daughters while she was still alive.

Over a life span of 89 years, she witnessed monumental changes and improvements in her city of birth, her community, and her country. With her husband and her two oldest sons active in Zoroastrian community affairs, she observed the tremendous improvements in the condition of the Zoroastrians and Iranians that came about during the progressive reign of the Pahlavis (1925-1979). She witnessed the invasion of Iran by Allied forces during WWII and the devastation caused by a man-made famine of that period that claimed countless Iranian lives, as well as the epidemics unleashed on Iranians by occupying forces and the refugees fleeing from

---

[101] After IranBanou's demise, her second son, Parviz, and his wife, Parvaneh, also relocated to Tehran and London.

the Soviet Union. These epidemics almost claimed the life of her oldest son, Jamshid. She witnessed the fall of Iran from grace by the Islamic revolution of 1979 and the exodus of all but one of her 21 grandchildren to the West.

She outlived all her siblings, her husband, and two of her granddaughters. It was in her birth city of Kerman that she passed away at age 89 and was buried at the Soroushian Zoroastrian Cemetery of Kerman, endowed to the community by her late husband and his brother. Between her grave and that of her husband, the remains of her oldest son, Jamshid, are interred. Her eldest daughter and second son are buried in the Zoroastrian cemetery of London. Her other two sons died in California, and her youngest daughter[102] died one year after her in Vancouver, Canada, and was buried at the Zoroastrian Cemetery of British Columbia.

---

102 Before her passage from breast cancer, IranBanou's youngest daughter, Mahindokht, made one last trip from Vancouver, Canada to Kerman. Before her departure she asked her daughter Mahdokht what memento from her grandmother she desired. Mahdokht asked for the packet size Avesta Book that her grandmother always used for praying. Her mother was able to retrieve that book. Mahdokht treasures it to this day.

Mehrborzin Jamshid Soroushian

<u>Soroush(yar) Shahiar</u>[103]   <u>IranBanu Esfandiar (1892 – 1981)</u>

1885 -1940, *Kerman*   1892-1981, *Kerman*

Katayun

1912- 1986 (Kerman–London)

(married to) *Jamshid Farvahar*

Jamshid

1914–1999, (Kerman, Tehran-Kerman)

Homayun Kianian

Parviz

1917-2011 (Kerman, London)

Parvaneb Falazadeh

Esfandiar

1919 – 2012 (Kerman–N.CA)

Katayun Shahriari

Hormuzd

1923- 2015 (Kerman-S.CA)

Mehrikh Mazdaie

Mahindokht

1927, 1983 (Kerman-Vancouver)

Manutchehr Shahriari

Figure 19: Descendants of Soroush Shahriar and IranBanu Esfandiyar

---

[103] Last name of Soroushian (Sorooshian) was adapted in 1926, after the government mandated that all Iranians adapt last names and to be issued birth certificates.

Figure 20: 1895 Kerman: Soroush (*), his younger brother Faridun (**) at school with their teacher, Kaikhosrow Shahrokh (+) and other Zoroastrian pupil.

Figure 21: 1905, Bombay: Soroush (seated to the right), his brother Faridun (standing behind him), and two other Zoroastrians posing for this photo in Bombay.

Figure 22: 1920, Kerman: Family photo taken a year after the passage of Shahriar Khodabux. His two sons, Faridun (seated, first from left) and Soroush, seated to the left of their mother, Banu Gushtasp. The three children to the left are Faridun's oldest son, Shahriar, his oldest daughter, Banu, and his second son, Kaikhosrow, cuddled in the back row. The four children are shown to the left.

Figure 23:1922, Kerman: Special election of the Anjuman witnessed by an inspector from Tehran holding the ballot box – center stage. Soroush Soroushian is standing to his left.

1924, Bombay: Photo taken during a trip to India, L-R: Kaykhosrow Rustom Kianian, Jahangir Rustom Fravahar (standing), Soroush Shahriar Soroushian

Figure 24:1929, Kerman: Katayun Soroush Soroushian with her fiancé, Jamshid Jahangir Fravahar, featured with the Oakland car imported from America; she learned to drive the car from a young age and was amongst the first females in Iran to operate an automobile.

Figure 25:1930, Kerman: Commemorative photo taken on the occasion of the visit of Mr. Petit (a Parsi Philanthropist) from Bombay (sited 6th from right). Soroush Soroushian, the president of Kerman Anjuman, is seated between Mr. and Mrs. Petit. Other dignitaries and community members are in attendance.

Echoes of Survival

Figure 26:1936, Kerman: Zoroastrian Community Celebration of the National unveiling of Iranian Women (Hijab-baradari)

Figure 27: 1959, Kerman: Wedding of Esfandiyar, the third son of IranBanu to Ms. Katayun Shahriari

2.8 Jamshid Soroush Shahriar and Homayun Sohrab Rustom
2.8.1 Jamshid Soroush Shahriar Khodabux Shahriar Jamshid Soroushian
1914-1999 (Kerman, Tehran-Kerman)

As the oldest offspring of Soroush Shahriar and IranBanu Esfandiar, Jamshid and his elder sister, Katayun, spent more time with their father than did their other four siblings. Their father, Soroush, was a force of nature and was always on the move, running and expanding his business. At the same time, Soroush was active in Zoroastrian community advocacy and stewardship.

Jamshid followed in his father's footsteps, especially when it came to community stewardship and advocacy. The times were different, and the Zoroastrian community and the nation had entered a new and promising phase in the years following WW II.[104] Jamshid added a new dimension to the scope of his forebearers' contributions, specifically scholarship in the field of Zoroastrian and ancient Iranian studies.[105]

Jamshid was born in 1914 and grew up in a busy household. From a young age, his father, Soroush, had high expectations of his eldest son and pushed Jamshid to take on greater responsibility beyond his age.[106]

School Years: Jamshid completed his schooling at the Zoroastrian school in Kerman up to the sixth grade. Jamshid recalled that the overtly disciplinarian approach of the boys' school turned him off. In earlier years and for a short while, his grandmother accompanied him to school and sat with him for a while until he felt reassured and willing to resume schooling. It was also during Jamshid's elementary schooling in early 1922 that an internal conflict broke out in the community. A group of younger Zoroastrians incensed by the pending suspension of annual subsidies to needy families formed a parallel association and took control of the schools. The old guard and many of the traditional families withdrew their children from the schools. A youth organization that had come into existence took the lead in organizing schooling at alternative venues. Jamshid and his cousins were among the youth attending the alternative school.[107]

Upon completion of his elementary schooling, Jamshid attended a British Missionary school in Kerman[108] for a few years, where he was taught English and science. Finally, his father sent him to Isfahan to attend the British missionary boarding school that had higher levels of instruction focused on secular subjects such as science and mathematics. The missionary school

---

[104] The year of 1940 marked an era of transition for the family. Until the year before his demise, Soroush was dominating the scene. Past his demise in December of 1940, his sons had to take over. As the eldest son, Jamshid took a leading role until his brothers were able to return to Kerman and to participate.

[105] https://www.iranicaonline.org/articles/sorushian

[106] This was a reflection of Soroush's own experience of growing up.

[107] Fortunately, this internal conflict was soon resolved and the unified schooling resumed. This event happening during the Anjuman presidency of Soroush Soroushian and was covered in the previous chapter.

[108] The school was known as Morsalin. Later, the school was renamed Pahlavi High School and became a public school.

had a student body mostly from Christian and Moslem families who were seeking higher education for their children based on the British educational system. Jamshid was the only Zoroastrian student in that school. At times, school officials would make derogatory comments about his religious beliefs, which irked him enormously. Jamshid felt especially stressed since he had no in-depth knowledge of the Zoroastrian religion to challenge the negative assertions made against his religion. Jamshid funneled all those negative comments directed against his religious beliefs into a lifelong passion to become more knowledgeable about Zoroastrianism, history, culture, and the literary legacy of ancient Iran. From a young age, Jamshid gained a keen familiarity with Ferdowsi's ShahNameh.[109] He could recite some of the poetry from memory and used his knowledge to maximum effect in dealing with bureaucrats by citing Ferdowsi in support of the moral arguments he was making.

By the early 1930s, Jamshid had returned to Kerman from Isfahan and was helping his father manage the family farm business. By the mid-1930s, Jamshid's father, Soroush, accompanied by his sister Katayun and her fiancé Jamshid Farvahar, left for Germany for his father to seek medical care for his worsening heart condition. During his father's absence, Jamshid managed the family farm business with his uncle, Faridun.

Soon after his father's return from Germany, Jamshid reported for his mandatory two-year military service in Kerman. The head of the military unit in Kerman, Brigadier General Maymand, who was also in charge of the draftees, would abuse his position of power to extort the draftees and their families. As such, his conduct made the young army draftees' experience very unpleasant. Jamshid, who became aware of Brigadier General Maymand's[110] corruption, informed his father. Soroush left for Tehran and appealed to the Army headquarters. Soon afterward, Maymand was relieved of his command and replaced by Brigadier General Siyapush, who proved to be a dedicated and honorable commander.

After completing his military service, Jamshid resumed helping his father manage his family's farming business. By that time, his sister Katayun married her finance, Jamshid Jahangir Faravahar, and they had their first daughter, IranBanou, within a year.

Trip to Germany and WWII: By the Summer of 1939, Soroush's worsening heart condition necessitated a second trip to Germany for additional treatment. This time, Jamshid accompanied his ailing father. In mid-July 1939, Jamshid and Soroush departed for Tehran to

---

109 ShahNameh (Epic of Kings) was composed by the legendary poet Ferdowsi of Tous, Khorasan between 977-1010 C.E, and consists of about 50,000 couplets (distiches) of poetry in the Persian language. The history of pre-Islamic Iran as documented in the Pahlavi text Khodaie-Nameh was the source of information for Ferdowsi's monumental poetic composition in Farsi (Persian). It helped preserve the recorded history from an authentic source and also helped preserve the Farsi language against the Arabs' aggressive attempt to replace Farsi with Arabic in the Iranian homeland. Arab rules actively sought and destroyed the Pahlavi texts to suppress literature and knowledge of ancient Iran.

110 Brigadier General Maymand was also implicated in cooperating with smugglers from Afghanistan.

arrange their round trip to Germany.[111] They made their travel arrangement through *Intourist*,[112] a Soviet travel agency with offices in many countries in Europe and the Near East, including Iran and Germany.

In early August 1939, the father and the son headed to the Caspian port of Enzeli (Bandar Pahlavi) in Northern Iran and boarded a Soviet ship that sailed to the port of Baku. Other passengers boarding were mostly Russians, and there also were two Danish nationals. Jamshid recognized the name of Westergaard, a famed 19th-century Danish scholar[113] of Iranian Studies. Jamshid made the acquaintance of Westergaard, who had come to Iran to work on the railroad project in the Khuzestan province and was indeed the grandson of the 19th-century scholar.[114] The other Danish traveler was a diplomat returning to Copenhagen. Making the acquaintance of these two Danes proved to be helpful in the later phase of their trip to Germany.

Traversing the Caspian Sea, they encountered high swells and stormy waters, but the ship made it to Baku. The passengers coming from Iran had to be quarantined to make sure they were not inflicted with cholera. As such, they were taken to a remote island in the Caspian Sea off Baku and had to stay there for a few days. There was minimal facility on that island, with few rooms with broken windows for the passengers to stay in.

At the Russian embassy in Tehran, the passengers seeking visas were advised to take with them a sufficient amount of food to sustain themselves during the phase of their trip from Poland to Germany, as there would be no food to purchase. As such, the Soroushians had purchased preservable foods and fruits at the port of Enzeli to take with them. As part of the quarantine, the passengers' baggage was sprayed and disinfected. As a result, all the food and fruits they had brought with them had to be thrown away. After the quarantine period had passed, the travelers were allowed to land at the port of Baku[115]. During the day, they would be taken to tourist sites in and around Baku. The two Danes had also booked an identical travel arrangement

---

[111] While waiting for the issuance of their visas in Tehran, Soroush asked to visit the Officers' College that Reza Shah had instituted for training Iranian Army officers. He wanted to pay a visit to an army general who had served in Kerman and now then teaching at the Officers' College. Once there, he informed the general that his second son Parviz was enrolled in that college. On hearing that news, the general immediately asked his assistant to go and find Parviz and bring him back with him. Twenty minutes later, Parviz entered the general's room in uniform and was surprised to find his father and older brother Jamshid sitting there.

[112] Intourist established in 1929 in the Soviet union specialized in assisting travel through the Soviet Union and beyond.

[113] 19th century Danish scholar, Niel Ludvig Westergaard, who spent time in Persia (Iran) and India between 1841 and 1844. He engaged in the study of the Behistun inscriptions in western Iran and Persepolis in the Fars province of Iran. While passing through Yazd and Kerman enroute to Bombay, he convinced some Zoroastrians to part with their family religious texts (handwritten Pahlavi or Avestan texts) promising to take them to Copenhagen for safekeeping. On his return to Denmark in 1845 he was appointed as professor of Indo-Oriental philology at the University of Copenhagen. One of his pupils was Arthur Christensen, who visited Iran in early 20th century and made notable contributions to the study of history of Sassanians.

[114] He had also married an Iranian girl while he was working in Iran.

[115] The intourist had arranged for them to stay at a comfortable hotel in Baku for two nights, including meals

as the Soroushians through *Intourist*. Finally, on the third night of their stay in Baku, the four boarded a steam engine train for the next leg of their trip.

The train took them through Soviet territory and then west towards Ukraine, passing through Kharkiv, Kiev towards Poland. Jamshid and his father were carrying two small handmade rugs with them to Germany.[116] The Polish Customs inspectors confiscated the rugs and issued Jamshid a receipt, telling him to claim his rugs at the last train station before entering Germany.

Upon arrival at the Warsaw main train station, Jamshid and Soroush bade farewell to the two Danish passengers and boarded the next train heading towards Berlin. At the last train station, before reaching German territory, the father and the son disembarked so Jamshid could claim their two rugs. The station officials told them that the rugs had not been received at their station yet and that they had to return to Warsaw station to claim them. At that point, Jamshid asked his father to stay at the station and wait while he took the next train to Warsaw to claim their rugs.

Jamshid recalls that the Warsaw station had a tense feeling. He immediately approached the Customs office at the station and showed his receipt. Suddenly, two Polish guards picked Jamshid up and dragged him to a makeshift holding room into which they threw him. Every five minutes or so, the guards opened the door to throw additional people into the room. Jamshid, determined to leave and rejoin his father, gathered his focus and positioned himself for the next opening of the door. As soon as the guards opened the door, he darted out and ran towards the terminal from which German-bound trains would depart. Fortunately, a train was about to depart and was closing its doors. Jamshid darted towards the train door. Luckily, at that time, the two Danish travelers who had already boarded that train noticed Jamshid in distress and rushed to the door from the inside. They kept it open and pulled in Jamshid. Soon, Jamshid reunited with his father, and they both were on the train as it rolled into Germany and headed towards Berlin.

Jamshid recalls once the train crossed into Germany headed in the direction of Berlin, he saw German military vehicles and tanks on the roadway heading in the opposite direction towards the Polish border.

Finally, Jamshid and Soroush arrived at the Berlin train station. This was Jamshid's first trip outside Iran, and he had no familiarity with the German language. As such, this experience was very taxing for him. Fortunately, they came across an Iranian national at the station who was very helpful. He accompanied them to a guesthouse in Berlin managed by another Iranian named Ahmad Akbari. They stayed at the guesthouse while making arrangements for their doctor's visit. Berlin at the time had a sizeable Iranian diaspora that included businessmen and

---

116 There was not much foreign currency that the Iranian central bank and other banks could sell to Iranian civilians planning to travel outside Iran. Instead, passengers could take with them merchandise and sell or barter them overseas subject to import regulations of the destination country. In this case, besides taking the two rugs with them and also paying for their trip expenses in Iran to the international travel agency, Jamshid and Soroush also relied on the two Zoroastrian carpet merchants in London and Albany, New York to send them German currency. The two merchants were Mr. Khodadad Mehrabi in London and Mr. Rustom Soroushian Kermani in New York. Jamshid and Soroush had managed to ship them a supply of carpets from Kerman to pay for their German currency needs.

the students who Reza Shah's government sent to receive higher education. The guesthouse was a gathering place for many of the Iranians in Berlin. Jamshid and Soroush came to know a number of Iranian students,[117] and eventually, they met ShahBahram Shahrokh, the son of Arbab Kaikhosrow Shahrokh. ShahBahram's superb oratory skills landed him the position of head of Radio Berlin's Farsi language broadcast. His pro-German, anti-British broadcasts in Farsi, which were carried on shortwave radio, captured an audience in Iran. The Soroushians had a letter of introduction from Kaikhosrow Shahrokh asking his son to provide assistance to them during their stay in Germany. They informed ShahBahram of their treatment by the customs agents in Poland. ShahBahram asked for their receipt and promised to follow up. He also persuaded the Soroushians to buy a bulky shortwave radio (Telefunken)[118] and have it shipped to Iran, which they did.

After a short stay in Berlin, Soroush was able to secure an appointment at a famed sanitorium in the city of Bodenheim, which was south of Frankfurt and on the river Rhine. The sanitorium had access to natural mineral hot springs for therapeutic use. A famed medical doctor, Professor Fulhurd, who had treated Soroush on his first trip, was going to treat Soroush again. As soon as the availability of a room was confirmed, the Soroushians left for Bodenheim. By this time, the German army had launched a full-scale invasion of Poland. Consequently, night curfews were imposed in German cities and villages, and the lights at night were turned off. Given the circumstances, Soroush's treatment the second time around was not as effective as the first time.

While in Bodenheim, the German command in Poland had located their rugs at the Warsaw customs office and sent them to Germany to be given to the Soroushians. Upon receiving the rugs, Jamshid was able to sell them for a considerable amount.

In less than two weeks, Soroush checked out of the sanitorium, and the Soroushians headed back to Berlin to plan their return to Iran. Returning through Poland was no longer an option, and the Soroushians found their way to the Berlin office of *Intourist* travel agency to plan their return. The agency came up with an itinerary for them to travel by the Berlin-Baghdad railway through the Balkans into Turkey, then to Syria, and then to Baghdad. From Baghdad, they would travel by car to Tehran. Based on the recommendation of the travel agency and with the help of ShahBahram, they secured visas for former Czechoslovakia, Hungary, the former Yugoslavia, Bulgaria, Turkey, Syria, and Iraq. Unfortunately, they were not advised to secure a visa from the French embassy, as France was administrating Syria.

---

117 Jamshid recalls meeting the following individuals in Berlin: Abbas Mazda, Akhundzadeh (later changed his name to Kaikhosrow Mitra), Akbari, Mustafah Sarkhosh, Kaykhosrow Zareh (Zoroastrian), Eisa Shahabi Bami, Esmael Khoshan, and Akhavi.

118 German-made Telefunken short wave radios were a popular brand. Few of them had reached Iran at that time. Within a decade or sok, Telefunkens and other brands would be more readily available in Iran.

Echoes of Survival

ShahBahram also convinced Jamshid and Soroush to buy a small electricity generator to take with them to Iran and use it to operate their shortwave radio to listen to broadcasts.[119] This was an expensive purchase, and since carrying it with them was not an easy task, ShahBahram promised to ship it to Baghdad to a merchant of Armenian descent. He gave them a signed letter addressed to the merchant in Baghdad so they could claim their generator from him and take it with them to Iran.

On the day of departure from Berlin, ShahBahram helped with tagging their luggage and inscribed SS[120] on the outside for Soroush Soroushian. Furthermore, ShahBahram and another Iranian by the name of Esmael Koshan accompanied them to the train station, and before boarding, Koshan gave Jamshid a copy of the book Mein Kampf,[121] translated into English and asked Jamshid to deliver it to the Olympic bookstore in Tehran's LalehZar Avenue. Jamshid packed the book in his briefcase and did not give it a second thought.

The trip through the Balkans was rather uneventful. At the German-Czechoslovakia border crossing, they were informed that they could not carry more than 200 German Marks with them into Czechoslovakia. They were told that the rest of their money (1,800 Marks} could not be taken with them to Czechoslovakia and had to be left in Germany. Jamshid had no choice but to send the additional currency to ShahBahram Shahrokh and asked him to keep it safe and return it to him at a later time.[122]

The train took them to southern Turkey and onto Northern Syria.[123] When Jamshid and Soroush arrived at the border crossing with Syria from Turkey, the Syrian border agents refused admission since the Soroushians did not have a French issued visa on their passports for entering Syria. The Syrian customs agent, a person of Assyrian descent, advised them to go back to the nearby Turkish city of Adana and apply for visas at the French Consulate. Further, he advised them that it would be a short trip, as the visas would be readily issued, and he offered to hold their luggage for safekeeping until they returned. The Soroushians trusted the agent and left the heavier luggage with him, and they boarded the next train heading north to Adana. The interaction was anything but cordial at the French consulate. The French official rudely informed them that he required instruction from Paris. The Soroushians had to wait in Adana for two weeks, and they made daily stops at the consulate only to be turned away each time. Fortunately, they came across an Iraqi national of Iranian descent in Adana who spoke Farsi, Arabic, and Turkish. He helped arrange for them to stay in one of his acquaintance's guest houses and arranged for their food. Further, this Iraqi national, who had befriended a telegraph office employee, managed to send a telegraph to the attention of Arbab Kaikhosrow Shahrokh in

---

119 At that time, limited electricity generation was available in Kerman, for few hours a day at best.

120 Abbreviation for Soroush Soroushian

121 "Mein Kampf, or "My Struggle," was written by Alolph Hitler before he reached the pinnacle of power.

122 The German authorities at the border crossing took the money and ShahBahram's address in Berlin to send it to him. A receipt was given to Jamshid. The money was never recovered.

123 Syria at the time was controlled by the French.

Tehran, informing him of the plight of the stranded father and son. He would also accompany the father and the son to the French consulate for their daily inquiry.

On receiving the telegram in Tehran, Arbab Kaikhosrow Shahrokh, who was the Zoroastrian representative in the Iranian parliament as well as the president of the Tehran Zoroastrian Association, immediately called on the French ambassador requesting him to intervene on behalf of the Soroushians. The French ambassador sent an urgent telegram to Paris requesting that the Soroushians be issued visas at the Adana Consulate and then be admitted into Syria for travel to Iran. The next day, when the Soroushians and their Iraqi helper stopped at the French consulate, the French Consul received them cordially and apologized for their past behavior. With their French visas secured, Jamshid and Soroush bade farewell to their Iraqi friend and to their local host, and they took the next train towards the border crossing.

At the Syrian customs office, they asked the Assyrian customs agent to return their luggage, and he became very agitated. He summoned the border guards in Arabic. Before long, two border guards appeared and led the Soroushians to a makeshift holding cell with minimal facilities in the relatively remote outpost of *Medina Akbar*. The prison door was locked. With winter approaching, it was getting cold. The Soroushians pleaded with the prison guards for food and drink. There was a sparse Kurdish population living in Medina Akbar, and when hearing about the plight of the father and the son, they brought them dry bread and a teapot with cups. At that point, Jamshid suddenly remembered the book he was carrying in his briefcase, which had a photo of Hitler on its cover. Past midnight, Jamshid pleaded with the prison guard to let him out to relieve himself. Fortunately, the guard relented and let him out and pointed him in the direction of a stream nearby and close to railroad tracks. Further, the guard allowed Jamshid to take his briefcase with him without inspecting it. Under the cover of moonlight, Jamshid rushed towards the stream. Once out of sight, he reached for the book and tore pages from it, and shoved the cover and the pages of the book into the bottom of the water bed, and covered it. Soon, he returned to the holding cell and avoided raising any suspicion.

A restless, cold night passed, and early the next morning, a French officer accompanied by two soldiers entered and angrily led the father and the son to a train cabin. They carried whatever possession they had with them. Shortly, the train left for the nearby city of Aleppo in northern Syria, which was home to a major French garrison. Jamshid and Soroush were taken inside the military base to a holding room. Shortly afterward, inspectors came in and subjected them to a body search followed by a search of their possessions. Since no incriminating evidence was found that would implicate them as German spies, the presiding French officer, through a translator, told them a report had been received that two skillful German spies with SS markings on their luggage had crossed the border into Syria. As such, the two of them had been picked up on that suspicion and sent to this military base for further investigation. The officer expressed his regret and said there was no recourse but to proceed with an official inquiry.

Soon afterward, the father and the son were separated and escorted by armed guards to different inspection rooms that, in effect, were military courts. Seated inside were a number of high-ranking French officers and one junior officer who could speak Farsi. Jamshid was asked to sit on a chair across from the officers. The junior officer started by asking Jamshid about the number of Nazi military units, tanks, and planes. This line of questioning brought a puzzled and confused look to Jamshid's face since he could not relate to any of it. Jamshid explained that the purpose of their trip to Germany was for his father to seek medical care and that the timing of their trip, which overlapped with the breakout of the war, was a mere coincidence. He pulled out all the medicine, medical prescriptions, and notes relating to his father's medical care from his briefcase, and he presented them to the panel as evidence of the purpose of their trip. Jamshid complained about the mistreatment that he and his father had received from the officials and about the theft of the luggage they had entrusted to the customs agent. Further questioning was pursued, and their responses were recorded. Jamshid was asked to sign the document that was put in front of him. The junior officer whispered to Jamshid that he and his father had been sent to the military base to be executed, but now that they had established their innocence, they were free to leave the military base and go to Aleppo City. Jamshid informed them that, besides their suitcase being stolen, their money was running low due to all the delays they encountered and that they did not have the means to travel further. The young officer took pity and asked what travel agency had booked their trip in Berlin. Jamshid responded, "*Intourist.*"[124] the French officer's face opened up, and he told Jamshid that there was an *Intourist* office in Aleppo. He called the *Intourist* office and asked them to come and pick up Jamshid and his father from the base. Shortly afterward, Soroush was escorted to join his son. He was utterly exhausted but happy to be reunited with his son, and he told of a similar ordeal to which he had been subjected.

Shortly afterward, a local *Intourist* agent arrived at the military base in his car and took Jamshid and Soroush back to his office. Once acquainted with their situation through an interpreter, he put them up at a local guesthouse for a few days to recover, providing for their meals as well.[125] Then, he bought them train tickets to resume their trip to Baghdad[126] and also gifted them with food provisions to sustain them on the way to Baghdad. He also arranged for their short stay in Baghdad.[127] Then, the agent took them to the train station for their departure to Baghdad. The Soroushians expressed their appreciation to the travel agent for all his help and boarded the train that was part of the famed Berlin-Baghdad railway.[128]

---

[124] https://en.wikipedia.org/wiki/Intourist#:~:text=On%20November%2015%2C%202019%2C%20Ne%C5%9Fet,Intourist%20from%20Thomas%20Cook's%20liquidators.

[125] *Intourist* in-country agents realized their office in Berlin had failed to advise the Soroushians to secure French visa before their departure. That failure had been the cause of all the problem the Soroushians experienced in trying to cross the border into Syria. As such, he was willing to assume responsibility for getting the father and the son to their destination.

[126] Train service was widely available in former Ottoman territories in the Middle East. Ottomans understood the importance of reliable transport, something the Qajars had neglected to develop in Iran. The first major railroad line construction project connecting the Caspian region in the north to a major Persian Gulf port in the south of Iran was undertaken during Reza Shah's reign.

[127] The travel agency did assume responsibility for some of the problems Soroush and Jamshid had encountered, such as for not informing them about the need to secure French visas in Berlin as well the currency limitation in Czechoslovakia.

[128] The Ottomans, with German financing and engineering, started construction of the Berlin to Baghdad railway in 1903. The final leg was completed in 1939. By contrast, any such railway construction considered a modernizing project would have been

Upon arriving in Baghdad, the Soroushians checked into the hotel for a short stay. Their first task was to make arrangements for their return trip to their homeland. Jamshid was able to locate the merchant from who ShahBahram Shahrokh had directed him to collect his electricity generator. On showing the merchant the receipt from ShahBahram, the merchant became agitated and told Jamshid that he had not received any unit from Berlin to give to him, so he turned him away. Once again disappointed at the course of events, Jamshid and Soroush booked passage on a passenger car leaving for Tehran. Besides them, two Greek actresses were also traveling to Tehran. As the car approached the Iranian border crossing, the tri-color flag of Iran adorned with the image of a lion and a rising sun came into view, and Jamshid and Soroush felt a sense of joy and relief.

The coldness of the winter and lack of warm clothing while passing through the Zagros Mountains in Western Iran proved too much for Jamshid's gall bladder. This caused him excruciating pain. He was rushed to the American hospital in Hamadan on the way to Tehran, where he was hospitalized for two weeks with his father staying with him. During their stay in Hamadan, they were visited daily by the late Ardeshir Yeganegi and his wife, Farangis Shahrokh,[129] the eldest daughter of Arbab Kaikhosrow Shahrokh. The Yeganegis had established the first modern leather processing factory in Hamadan.

After Jamshid had sufficiently recuperated, the father and son continued on the next leg of their journey and reached Tehran. It was almost two months earlier that they left Tehran for a trip to seek medical care. Instead, their travels had turned into a horrid experience due to the outbreak of WWII. Soroush's and Jamshid's stay in Tehran was short, and they soon departed for Shiraz. There was a lawsuit being litigated in the Shiraz Court involving a foreman for the Soroushian brothers and Kaikhsorow Kianian, who was managing their farm holdings in Sirjan County. After arriving in Shiraz, Soroush, in consultation with the other two partners, decided to settle the matter out of court, and he withdrew the complaint.

With their legal matter in Shiraz resolved, the father and the son left for Kerman via Sirjan using commercial transport vehicles, and they reached home a few days later.

Events of 1940

After they recovered from their trip ordeal, Jamshid and Soroush resumed their business activities in Kerman. Although the small electricity generator they bought in Germany never arrived, the Telefunken radio they had purchased and shipped to Iran did arrive.[130] This Telefunken short-wave radio was among the first ones in Kerman.

---

fiercely opposed by the mullahs in Iran, as was the case with the first locomotive line between Tehran and the Islamic shrine of Shah Abdul Azim el Rey (Shahr-e-Rey). Due to their opposition, that construction plan had to be abandoned.

129 https://en.wikipedia.org/wiki/Farangis_Yeganegi

130 They had shipped the radio in a container from Berlin though *Intourist*. *Intourist* managed to get the shipment to Baghdad and had arranged for it to be delivered to the Khosravi customs location at the border crossing to Iran. When Jamshid and

Echoes of Survival

During the hours that electricity was available from the Harandi Electric Generation Company of Kerman, the radio could be operated. The radio broadcasts were heard from Berlin in the afternoons. The news of Soroush Soroushian having brought a short-wave radio to Kerman spread in the community. Given the Zoroastrian community's tendency to embrace new technology, community members would stop by and ask if they could listen to ShahBahram Shahrokh's broadcasts from Berlin. Given the interest from the community, the radio was placed next to the window in the living room overlooking the courtyard. Chairs were placed in the courtyard for visitors to sit and listen to the daily broadcasts in the afternoon. These afternoon gatherings became popular. Attendance was ever-increasing, and there was much talk about what the broadcaster was saying.

The broadcasts from Berlin had a distinctly anti-British flavor, and sometimes, they criticized Reza Shah for Iran staying neutral in that worldwide conflict. Jamshid recalls that one of the Parsis residing in Kerman, a medical doctor by the name of Dr. Kayghobad Fariduni,[131] informed him that the British Counsel General in Kerman would like to have a conversation with Soroush Soroushian. He invited Soroush to the British consulate in Kerman. One afternoon, Jamshid, accompanying Soroush and a few other close family members, drove to the British consulate at the end of a long street that was a cul-de-sac. At the entrance to the street, the car was stopped by the Iranian police.[132] The occupants were asked the purpose of their visit. The officer informed them that no Iranian subject could enter a foreign consulate without prior authorization from the police headquarters or from the Ministry of Internal Affairs. It happened that Soroush Soroushian owned a walled orchard adjacent to the British consulate complex. The Soroushians informed the officer that they wanted to inspect their orchard and were accompanied by a police car that followed them to make sure they were going inside their property. It turned out there was a water channel that ran between the British consulate compound and the property next to it owned by the Soroushians. This opening in the lower part of the wall between the two properties was not meant for humans to pass through. However, given the circumstances, Soroush, Jamshid, and the other two family members accompanying

---

Soroush finally got to that border crossing, their boxed-up radio was waiting for them. They cleared it through the Iranian customs office and took it along with them.

131 Dr. Fariduni, a citizen of British-India, was the medical doctor for the British Consulate in Kerman and all those who worked at that Consulate. He had also set up a practice in the city and would treat Kermanis who sought his care. He was married to a Zoroastrian woman from Kerman.

132 During the rule of the Qajars, the British and the Russians operated freely across Iran and would interfere in the internal affair of the country through enlisting corrupt bureaucrats. The British operated up to 64 consular offices or interest sections in strategic locations in Iran. Their fortress-like consulate in Kerman came in existence in late 19th century. The expense for operating these consular sections was borne by the government of India. Once Reza Shah came to power, and realizing the scope of British influence, he ordered Iranian security posts be established outside each of these British consulates, and any Iranian subject trying to enter a facility to be stopped, unless they had pre-clearance from the Iranian officials. As result of these limitations, the British closed down some of their offices. The Kerman consulate stayed in operation until 1952, when premier Mosadeq severed diplomatic relation with the British and expelled all British diplomats. Post-Mosadeq, when diplomatic relations between Iran and Britain were restored, only a few consulates were allowed to reopen. The Consulate in Kerman was not one of them. The British sold their large consulate facility to the Iranian National Oil Company.

them managed to squeeze through and get to the other side. The British were expecting them, and once inside the compound, they were immediately led to the main building where the Consul General was. After greeting them, the British representative made a tacit threat. He pointed out that the British and Zoroastrians of India were getting along well. He then pointed to the afternoon gatherings at the Soroushian family home and the anti-British propaganda from Berlin in the Farsi language being broadcasted for the large gathering in their courtyard. The Consul General demanded an immediate cessation of the afternoon gatherings. He went on to point out that while Reza Shah had curtailed the British's scope of operations in Iran, they still had influence. In the event the Soroushians continued with the afternoon gatherings, they should expect serious retribution. The Soroushians left shortly afterward and returned to their own orchard, where they returned home. The daily radio gatherings were suspended. This was not the last acrimonious encounter with the British Consul General that Jamshid experienced.

Passage of His Father

The heart-wrenching events the father and son experienced on their trip to Berlin for the purpose of medical treatment had left Soroush in worse physical shape than before the trip. Given Soroush's worsening condition, his mobility was reduced, and Jamshid had to carry on the job of looking after the family holdings. Soroush passed away in December of 1940 and was buried at the Soroushian Aramgah in the row of graves reserved for Soroush, Faridun, and their families. On the day of Soroush's burial, a large crowd of Zoroastrians and Moslems who had known Soroush gathered at Soroush's house, and many accompanied his remains on its last trip. After the passage of his father and with his two younger brothers who were in Tehran, Parviz, and Esfandiar, Jamshid had to carry on with the management of his father's estate.

WWII-Related Events in Iran and Kerman

In the meantime, the war in Europe was raging, and in June 1941, after Germany launched an attack on the Soviet Union, a sense of unease pervaded all over Iran, given the World War was getting closer to Iranian territory. Two months later, the British and Russian armies launched a full-scale surprise invasion of Iran.[133] This act was an unprovoked invasion without prior warning. In the early hours of August 25, 1941, British naval forces anchored off the port of Basra (present-day Iraq) sailed towards the Iranian port of Abadan, and they bombarded the Iranian naval ships that were anchored at the Iranian naval base. After sinking the Iranian naval ships, a flood of sepoys came ashore. Iranian ground forces, including Parviz Soroush Soroushian, mounted a defense but were simply outgunned and outnumbered. The Russian tanks and air force launched a full-scale invasion from the northwest and northeast of Iran. By August 30, 1941, a ceasefire was reached. On September 16, 1941, as a condition imposed by the Allied forces, Reza Shah abdicated in favor of the Crown Prince, Mohamed Reza

---

[133] https://en.wikipedia.org/wiki/Anglo-Soviet_invasion_of_Iran

Shah. Reza Shah was forced into exile and ended up in Johannesburg, South Africa, where he died on July 24, 1944.[134]

The invasion of Iran and the abdication of Reza Shah were very unsettling for Zoroastrians and other minorities, who were generally fearful that law and order would break down. The news that Reza Shah and members of his family were departing Tehran by a motorcade towards Isfahan, Yazd, and Kerman en route to Bandar Abbas on the Persian Gulf was followed very closely by the Zoroastrians. Within several days of departing Tehran, Reza Shah's entourage had left Isfahan and was heading to Yazd en route to Kerman. The day Reza Shah's motorcade was expected in Yazd, the majority of the Zoroastrians of Yazd, filled with heavy hearts, started gathering at the Markar Circle on the Road to Kerman. The two sides of the highway were filled to capacity with Zoroastrians eager to catch a last glimpse of the great Shah, who had done so much for the country and its people. When the motorcade arrived, the onlookers were filled with emotions.[135] The day after passing through Yazd, Reza Shah's motorcade was expected in Kerman.[136] That morning, Jamshid Soroush Soroushian got in the family automobile and drove Westwards on the highway to Yazd. Within forty minutes of driving distance from the city, Jamshid pulled his car to the right side of the road, drove a short distance up a hilly incline, and then turned his car around and parked it. He had a commanding view of the roadway in both directions. On the other side of the road, within a distance, was one of the pistachio farms that his father had developed and owned. Jamshid waited patiently for hours. About 2 hours later, he recognized a Rolls-Royce belonging to the British Consul General in Kerman approaching. As the car passed where Jamshid was parked, it slowed down, and the occupants, who had likely recognized Jamshid's car, glanced at him. At this point, Jamshid was trying to control his emotions. The Rolls-Royce continued a short distance, and then it pulled off to the right side of the road and parked. About 30 minutes later, the dust rising from the Western direction was an indication of cars approaching. Some 15 minutes later, Reza Shah's motorcade slowly made its way and passed the vantage point of Jamshid, who was looking to get a glimpse of the Shah. After Reza Shah's motorcade passed in the direction of Kerman,[137] Jamshid hesitated to leave and noticed the British Consul was in no hurry to leave either. Some 5 minutes later, another Rolls-Royce that had followed Reza Shah's motorcade arrived and

---

134 His remains were sent to Egypt for safe keeping, and in 1951, the remains were flown to Iran via Saudi Arabia and were buried at a mausoleum erected for him at Rey, South of Tehran.

135 This narrative was based on reporting by two witnesses, Mrs. Homayun Sohrab Kianian, and Mrs. Paridokht Rustom Mavandad who were present that day and stayed in line for hours to catch a glimpse of Reza Shah as his motorcade passed through.

136 All the roads on which Reza Shah's motorcade was traveling were indeed constructed and improved during his rule. The roadways were a legacy of his years on the throne, and was part of the infrastructure building projects undertaken in Iran during the Pahlavi period.

137 Mr. Iraj Sepaheri at the time a student at Iranshahr Zoroastrian High-School for boys, recalled, on the day Reza Shah was to arrive in Kerman, the headmaster had asked all older boys to come to school early wearing their Boy Scout uniforms. Then the assembled Boy School troop with the headmaster leading them marched from Eastern part of the city to the Western part and the house of Mr. Harandy, where Reza Shah was expected. The Cup Scouts were positioned on both sides of the road leading to Mr. Harandy's residence. When the motorcade arrived hours later, the Cup Scouts saluted Reza Shah.

pulled off the road to meet with the occupants of the Rolls-Royce that was parked. Jamshid gathered the arriving Rolls-Royce that belonged to the British Consul General in Isfahan, who had followed Reza Shah's motorcade. A few minutes later, the two Rolls-Royces started moving. The newly arrived one turned back towards Yazd and Isfahan. The Kerman-based British Consul's car started moving speedily towards Kerman to stay close to the motorcade. After the British departed the scene, Jamshid also left for Kerman.

All these WWII events were happening rapidly. Reza Shah stayed in Kerman for a few days before departing for Bandar Abbas. In the meantime, the family was concerned about the well-being and the whereabouts of Parviz, who had been stationed in Abadan when the British had launched their surprise attack. The Iranian army had no specific information to share with the family but reassured them that Parviz had not been reported as a casualty. Finally, two weeks later, the British consulate in Kerman contacted the family and informed them that Parviz was in captivity as a prisoner of war (POW) and that he was safe in a POW camp in Southern Iraq. Parviz and other Iranian POWs were released once the terms of the ceasefire between Iran and the invading forces were signed, and Iran formally declared war on the Axis nations (which was a condition of the ceasefire).

In the meantime, the floodgate of occupying allied forces entering Iran was wide open. Their focus was to secure the oil production facilities in southern Iran and the transport routes from the Persian Gulf to the Russian border so that US-made arms could be supplied to the Red Army. Additional British ground forces, mostly Indian sepoys, entered Iran from the east and set up camps outside major cities in southern Iran. A regiment of British forces was stationed in a makeshift camp in the proximity of the British consulate in Kerman. A notorious Capitan, Hassan, a native of Western India[138] embedded with the colonial British army, was sent to Kerman. The British and the Russian forces commandeered agricultural production in Iran that was meant to feed the Iranian populace. Instead, they directed the seized grains to feed the occupying forces inside Iran and send the excess grain to their bases elsewhere.[139] Iranians faced mass famine and hunger. Capitan Hassan's forces guarding main roads coming into the city of Kerman would immediately seize the grains and the produce being transported to Kerman city.[140] Soroush Soroushian's estate, managed by Jamshid, arranged to bring in products from their own farms through routes that were not guarded. The grains would be stored in the storage

---

138 In 1947, that part of west India was partitioned into West Pakistan.

139 Although the dominance of foreign forces in Kerman were from the British army, units of Red Army would at times roam the countryside of Kerman. Mr. Hormuzd Soroushian, Jamshid's youngest brother, remembered that large Red Army trucks could be seen roaming the countryside of Kerman looking for herds of sheep grazing the land. Once they spotted a herd, they would drive to the shepherd and offer to buy the herd. If he refused, they would seize the herd by force, and if the shepherd put up a resistance, he would have likely become a casualty.

140 Mr. Dinyar Parsi, at the time a young Zoroastrian employee at Bank-e-Melli in Kerman (previously Imperial Bank, that was nationalized by Reza Shah's government), testified to the following recollection of the events he witnessed: The Bank operated a large storage facility (operated as a silo) and that the British forces had commandeered it. The seized grain was sent to that storage. At times there was more grains coming in than being shipped out. When the silo was filled to capacity, the British operative would destroy the excess grain rather than distribute it amongst the starving population.

silos the Soroushians had built on their estate in Kerman city. The excess grain and produce would be quietly distributed amongst the needy Zoroastrians and other Kermanis. Understandably, they had to operate clandestinely and make sure the recipients would not divulge the information to reach the British agents.

Events Leading to an Assault on the Zoroastrian Quarter

During the allied occupation of Iran, there was yet another event that impacted the Soroushian family. As covered in the previous chapter on Soroush Shahriar Soroushian's life, a rug merchant from Tabriz by the name of Dilmaghani had come to Kerman in the mid-1910s. He had concluded business arrangements with Soroush and Faridun Soroushian, Kaikhosrow Kianian, and some other Zoroastrian merchants. Dilmaghani was looking to them to source handwoven carpets from Kerman and villages to be shipped to his dealership in New York City. Independent of these sourcing arrangements, he had also set up his own carpet company and employed locals, including a few Zoroastrians. The Dilmaghani Carpet Company of Kerman was also in the business of sourcing carpets for export to New York City. The head of the office ran the business according to instructions from the owner. Since his initial visit to Kerman, when he set up the Dilmaghani Carpet company, Mr. Mehdi Dilmaghani has never visited Kerman again. His nephew, based in Tabriz, made a few trips to Kerman on his uncle's behalf and provided supervision. However, after his third trip, the nephew did not come back, and it almost appeared as though the business had been abandoned by the founder and his family. At this point, a shrewd Kermani by the name of Ahmad Yazdanpanah, who seemed to have been aware of the long absence of the Dilmaghanis, showed up at the business and introduced himself as a representative of the Dilmaghanis and referred to himself as a Dilmaghani instead of using his real name. He managed to convince the office manager that he was in charge. Leveraging the reputation of Dilmaghani, he starts to make headways. He was a populist and acted in a "Robinhood manner," which meant that he saw his calling in taking wealth away from the wealthy and distributing it among the needy. In time, he became somewhat of a folk hero. His actions resulted in run-ins with most of the well-established and wealthy businessmen in Kerman.[141] Yazdanapanah was also buying agricultural lands in the northern part of Kerman province towards Zarand. That is the context in which he approached the Soroushian and Kianian brothers. He was interested in a village in northern Kerman (Karim Abad) that the Soroushian and Kianian brothers owned. Although he was not successful in convincing the owners to sell the property to him, he managed to get the partners to trust him to manage the agricultural land and village. The arrangement did not work, and the owners decided to terminate their contract with Mr. Yazdanpanah and his nephew. Finally, in early 1943, Mr. Yazdanpanah indicated he was willing to relinquish control and asked the owners to go to the village and officially resume management of their farms. On the date that had been agreed on, a party

---

141 He also had run-ins with the government officials. It is reported that when a new governor who had been assigned to Kerman had arrived, the governor's office invited most city leaders to meet the new governor. Yazdanpanah was not invited. Hearing of that get-together, Ahmad Yazdanpanah burst into the meeting and made a scene. A day later he sent two rugs to the governor to apologize for behavior. If his intention was to impress the populous, he likely succeeded.

consisting of Faridun Soroushian, Sohrab Kianian,[142] Mr. Shahpur Kianian representing his father, Jamshid Soroushian, and his brother Parviz, as well as their uncle Faridun and cousin Shahriar Faridun Soroushian, traveled to the village to meet with Mr. Yazdanpanah. Soon after the owners arrived, they were surrounded by a gang that had been brought in by Mr. Yazdanpanah. Without explanation, the gang, some of who were armed, turned on the owners and pushed them inside a stable in the village. The owners were told they had to stay there until the next morning, when Mr. Yazdanpanah would come to negotiate with them. No amount of protestation was effective. Soon, the night arrived, and it seemed the guards assigned to watch the stable were sleeping. Parviz Soroushian (recently returned from POW captivity) put his military training to use. In the middle of the night, with the help of the other young people amongst them, he scaled the wall of the stable and quietly lowered himself on the other side. Under the moonlight, he quietly made his way towards the nearby highway. After running for a few hours, he reached the nearest Gendarmerie station. He explained the hostage situation in the village to the duty officer. The first station telephoned the next station and asked for support. By the early hours of the morning, several gendarmerie jeeps with armed gendarmes arrived at the village. Parviz was riding in one of the jeeps. The armed gangs were disarmed and arrested. The captives were freed from the stable and returned to Kerman. Faced with the aborted abduction he had arranged, Yazdanpanah finally relinquished control. As part of the settlement, some land was given to Yazdanpanah's nephew by the owners. The property was later sold.

The event that unfolded several months later was even more stressful to the owners and the Zoroastrian community of Kerman. As mentioned, Yazdanpanah caused distress to other land owners and business leaders and made powerful enemies. One late afternoon during the following summer, Soroush was planning to return to Kerman City from the northern part of the Kerman province. His loyal driver, a Zoroastrian by the name of Soroush,[143] told him it was getting late and advised him to wait until the next morning to depart. As they approached Kerman city, darkness was falling. Suddenly, a car appeared from the opposite direction, and a few people jumped out and blocked the road. As Dilmaghani's car came to a stop, the armed men forced the driver to drive off the road and stop. The assailants, who had covered their faces, first pulled Soroush from his seat, tied his hand behind him, and stuffed his mouth. Then, they pushed him into a nearby ditch. The next thing that Soroush recalls was hearing a few shots followed by the sound of the other car speeding away. The next day, a car coming from Kerman and driving north spotted the abandoned vehicle of Yazdanpanah. The driver pulled to the side. The occupants immediately spotted Soroush in the ditch. He was making noise to get attention. After untying him and hearing what had happened, they moved away from the car and spotted the body of Yazdanapanah. His body was taken to Kerman city, and news reverberated throughout the city. The fanatical mullahs blamed the Zoroastrians and pointed out that a few months earlier, Yazdanapanah had a falling out with the Soroushian and the Kianian brothers. The situation got

---

142 Sohrab Kianian was domiciled in Yazd. His brother Kaikhosrow, domiciled in Kerman, represented him. During that period, he happened to be in Kerman.

143 Soroush Rahnamon, known as Soroush Shoufar, later became a driver for the "4 Points" operation in Kerman.

very tense as the mullahs called on the believers at the mosques to avenge the killing of Yazdanpanah by attacking the Zoroastrians.[144] In view of the rising tension, the Soroushians sent out a call to other Zoroastrians to stay indoors and not to venture outside until the mobs dispersed. With tensions rising, the Soroushians and Kaikhosrow Kianian had male workers with guns on the roof of their houses with a commanding view of the main street. Their brandishing of rifles was meant as a warning to the would-be assailants. The mobs continued to assemble on the south side of Zriesfe Avenue, the main street to the south of the Soroushians' and Kianian's residence. The mob chanted in unison verses to the effect of, "The innocent Dilmghani has been murdered at the hand of non-believers and foreigners." Mrs. Kiandokht Kianian, who was a young girl at the time, recalls the parents getting all the kids ready with backpacks full of food and drinks and telling them they may need to be sent to hide in secret places in the basements of the houses. They were further warned that if their hiding becomes necessary, they should be prepared to stay quiet and in place for several days and only come out when all the noise has subsided and the assailants have moved away. Mrs. Kiandokht further recalled that British military vehicles stationed in Kerman started to drive up and down the Zriesfe Avenue and that every time they passed the Soroushians and Kianian's residences, the drivers would honk the horns of their vehicles. Finally, the calls to city officials asking them to appeal to the mullahs to call off the mobs were effective, and the mobs dispersed without any major injury. A few Zoroastrians who had ventured onto the streets had been roughened up, but they survived. Many years later, a Baluchi man confessed to being the ring leader of the assault team that killed Dilmaghani. He implicated a Moslem businessman who had grievances against Yazdanpanah as well as the fact that a female member of his own family had been sexually assaulted by Yazdanpanah.[145]

Epidemics brought in by the Refugees

In the aftermath of the occupation of Iran by the British and Soviet forces, some 116,000 Polish refugees were sent to Iran by land and over the Caspian Sea to northern Iran[146] in the latter part of 1942. They were part of the much larger group of Polish citizens who Stalin had forced from their homes in eastern Poland and sent to the Soviet forced labor camps in Siberia and elsewhere. Many of them had perished en route to or in the Soviet labor camps due to harsh conditions. The survivors came down to Iran from the north. A group of them came from the northeast through Khorasan province and headed south to Bandar Abbas through Kerman. Some of the refugees were infected with contagious diseases such as typhus. Soon after their arrival in Kerman, an epidemic of typhus broke out in Kerman city that claimed many lives, including a number of young Zoroastrians. Jamshid also contracted this disease, and despite the care he was getting from several of the doctors in town, his prognosis was not very promising. Colonel

---

144 Similar situations like this had not happened during the reign of Reza Shah when the security forces were under strict order to protect all citizens. As a result of the occupation of Iran by allied forces, the security forces had been disarmed, and the allied forces were in charge. However, events like this were more common during the Qajar period.

145 On one of Yazdanpanah's properties in Kerman, an orphanage for boys was erected and named "Dilmaghani Orphanage." It was still in operation in 2020.

146 https://rarehistoricalphotos.com/polish-refugees-iran-1942/

Mehrborzin Jamshid Soroushian

Jahangir Oshidari, who was stationed at the Iranian Army base in Kerman at the time, has documented his memories of the events of that epidemic in Kerman. Colonel Oshidari was an ordained Zoroastrian priest (Mobed) who had also trained as a veterinarian and joined the Iranian army. He was a historian as well. Colonel Oshidari had made the acquaintance of Jamshid Soroushian at school in Kerman. In an article he submitted for publication in "Jamshid Soroush Soroushian Commemorative Volume I,[147] Dr. Oshidari recounted that typhus was unknown in Iran before this outbreak, and most physicians had no familiarity with treating it. Worse yet, its symptoms were often mistaken for those of malaria or typhoid,[148] and the prescribed medication to treat the latter conditions was actually harmful to a patient suffering from typhus. The casualty rate amongst the population of Kerman was considerable, although some who were infected survived. Mobed Oshidari further reports that every afternoon, upon returning from the army base to go to his parental house, he would pass by a number of funeral corteges following caskets of victims.[149] Some afternoons, upon returning from the base, he would visit Jamshid, whose condition was vacillating between being breathless and alert. He reports Jamshid was somehow holding on. On the occasions that Jamshid was alert, he would request Dr. Oshidari to recite from the ShahNameh. As the poems of Ferdowsi illuminating the actions of heroes of ancient Iran were recited, Jamshid would become alert and resolute.[150] Jamshid recalled that once, while Medical Dr. Mehraban Shahriari was visiting, he was running a high fever and had become delirious and on the verge of passage. He recalls vividly that Dr. Shahriari, as a last resort, started to recite the Kushti prayer from the Avesta (Zoroastrian prayer book) loudly. Jamshid's hallucination was that a demon-like creature with a mace in his hand was coming to knock him out, and as the Avestan words were chanted, the demon figure started to phase out. Soon afterward, Jamshid's fever broke, and he was on his way to recovery. The epidemic subsided after another month, but it left many Kermanis dead in its wake.[151]

With his siblings back in Kerman, their father's estate was subdivided among the four sons and the two daughters. A considerable estate tax had to be settled. Each of the inheritors focused on managing their inheritance from the farm holdings they had received.

---

[147] "Soroush Peer Mughan: Jamshid Soroushian Commemorative Volume I" Sorraya Publisher, Tehran, 2003, pages 45-48 in Farsi

[148] Both Typhus and Typhoid are contagious and can be deadly. The former is spread by mosquitos and flies carrying the disease from infected animals of person to a healthy person. The latter is spread by eating food or drinking bacteria-contaminated water.

[149] Dr. Dawdson, a much-liked British medical doctor who had served in Kerman for many years, was bitten on his neck by a fly after visiting a patient in the Jewish quarter of Kerman. Immediately, he turned to his nurse and told her my funeral will come up shortly. A few days later his remains were carried to the Christian cemetery of Kerman.

[150] Hormuzd, Jamshid's younger brother in Kerman at the time, recalls that they would drive up Jupar Mountain and carve out frozen ice in big containers and rush them home so Jamshid's legs could be cooled down to bring down his temperature.

[151] Many of the Polish refugees who survived their ordeal were shipped off to India and elsewhere after few years in Iran. A small group stayed in Iran and some married Iranians. The young men among them were given further training by the British and sent off to fight the Germans in north Africa. The survivors were generally grateful to the Iranians for their generosity in providing them shelter in their hours of need.

Echoes of Survival

Marriage: In 1945, as WWII was winding down, Jamshid married Homayun, the third daughter of Sohrab and Simin Kianian. Until then, Homayun was domiciled in Yazd. Sohrab was the business partner of the Soroushian brothers, and on several occasions, when the Soroushians were traveling to Tehran and passing through Yazd, they had stayed at the stately home of Sohrab Kianian.[152]

Homayun and Jamshid had met on previous occasions when Jamshid passed through Yazd and stayed at Sohrab Kianian's house or when Homayun, her parents, and siblings came to Kerman to visit with their uncle Kaikhosrow and his family.

Homayun and Jamshid married in Yazd a few days after Homayun's older sister, Azar (also known as Morwarid), married her cousin Shahpur Kaikhosrow Kianian, who lived in Kerman as well. Soon after their marriages, the two sisters, accompanying their husbands, left for Kerman, where they resided for the rest of their lives.[153]

Jamshid and Homayun moved to a newly constructed home with a good-sized garden on the north side of Zriefe Avenue. Jamshid's cousin Shahriar Faridun Soroushian also built a home two doors away from him. Besides Shahriar, other siblings and cousins also established spacious homes on Zriesfe Avenue[154] in the distance between Jamshid's and his parents' houses.

This was a reflection of the great confidence the family and the community had in Kerman and in their nation during the prosperous years of Mohamed Reza Shah Pahlavi, a period marked by peace, security, and tranquility. During this period, state protection for all Iranians, including minorities, was the rule of the land.

Jamshid and Homayun raised five children (three daughters and two sons). Their first offspring was a daughter by the name of Mahvash, who was born in 1946. Then came the two sons, Soroush (1948) and Mehrborzin (1952). Twin daughters, Armity and Anahita, followed in 1956. All five children were born at home in Kerman.

Jamshid's main focus was on managing and expanding the farmlands he had inherited, as well as attending to his growing family. As far as agricultural expansion was concerned, Jamshid's emphasis was on developing additional fruit orchards and pistachio gardens. At the same time, he took an active interest in leading the Zoroastrian Association of Kerman. The Soroushians have always been involved with community advocacy for generations. In fact, Jamshid was following in the footsteps of his uncle (Faridun Soroushian, 7th president), his father (Soroush Soroushian, 6th president)), his grandfather (Shahriar Khodabux, 5th president), and his great grandfather (Gushtasp Dinyar Klantar, 4th president), who had been in community

---

[152] There were not many hotels at that time.

[153] Homayun and her sister Azar are buried next to each other at the Soroushian cemetery of Kerman.

[154] They included Manuchehr Faridun Soroushian, Khosrow Sohrab Kianian, Katyun Soroush Soroushian, Parviz Soroush Soroushian, Shahpur Kaikhosrow Kianian, and Shahrokh Kaikhosrow Kianian.

leadership since the inception of the Naseri Zoroastrian Anjuman of Kerman.[155] Jamshid served as the tenth president of the Anjuman for several terms from the 1950s through the mid-1960s.[156] The times were different, and the community prospered considerably compared to a century earlier when the community was on the brink of extinction. Improved health and educational opportunities benefited the community. Afflictions of the past, such as epidemics, famine, mass starvation, and insecurity in the cities and in the countryside, were events of the past. Minorities received full protection from the state like never before in the past 1300 years. The population of Zoroastrians had increased considerably, and many families were migrating to Tehran to take advantage of the opportunities available in the capital. A percentage of the youth were going overseas (primarily Germany, the UK, and the USA) to pursue higher education or specialization in their fields. A number of the Kermani Zoroastrians who had established themselves in Tehran were endowing their parents' homes in Kerman that they had inherited to the Kerman Anjuman to be put to good use worthy of their parents' memory. Some of the Kermani Zoroastrians who had migrated to North America and the UK and had become successful were donating substantial funds to be used for establishing additional facilities for the community and the city. Such donations were used to build a hostel, a medical clinic, and a community hall. All these transactions kept the Anjuman management team very busy. At the same time, situations would arise that impacted the community and needed to be dealt with.

Jamshid's Community Advocacy Activities:

In the early 1950s, a constitutional crisis came about during the premiership of Mohammad Mosaddegh.[157] He was the 35th premier since Iran had adopted a constitutional monarchy in 1908. As a part of his initiatives, Iran's natural resources were nationalized. The nationalization of Iranian oil, which until then was controlled by a British oil company, brought about a major showdown with the British government. The ensuing constitutional crisis saw the young Mohamed Reza Shah and his queen Sorraya leave Iran on August 16, 1953. Major demonstrations broke out in the capital.[158] The news of Shah's departure and the fear of a breakdown of law and order was unsettling for many Zoroastrians residing in the capital and provinces, including Kerman. Adding to the anxiety felt by many was the fact that the Tudeh

---

[155] In recognition for his essential efforts that led to procuring a royal decree for the establishment of the Naseri Anjuman of Kerman, Maneckji Hataria is considered the first president of that Association, and his successor Ardeshir Reporter as the second president. Neither actually served in that official capacity. The third president was Mobed Rustom Jahangir (Hormuzdi), a contemporary of Gushtasp Dinyar and Shahriar Khodabux. During the reign of Naser-ul-Dinshah and his son Muzafar-ul-Dinshah, the presidents of the Naseri Anjuman were appointed by the local governors. The governmors would nominate a prominent member of the Zoroastrian community known to them. Subsequently (past 1910s), the community would elect the president and the board members of the Zoroastrian Association.

[156] Jamshid's brother, Parviz served as the 12th president of association.

[157] https://en.wikipedia.org/wiki/Mohammad_Mosaddegh

[158] https://en.wikipedia.org/wiki/1953_Iranian_coup_d%27%C3%A9tat

Party[159] (communist party) was becoming more active and visible.[160] Due to the political uncertainties that had manifested itself, most Zoroastrians were keeping a low profile. Some were quietly burying precious metals and their important documents in the courtyards of their homes or in other places they felt would be safe.[161] Although much of the political drama was unfolding on the streets of the capital, there were rioters and mobs on the move in other cities. In Kerman, mobs of leftists and Islamists did break into the homes of some Zoroastrians and stole whatever they could. Notably, one family, the Kasravis, hosted a wedding at their house in Kerman just before the Shah's departure. Relatives had come from Yazd, and gifts were given to the newlyweds. The family had borrowed carpets from friends and neighbors so guests could be hosted in their courtyard. Then, a huge mob gathered in front of the Kasravi's home in the Kerman Zoroastrian quarter and started banging on the door of their house. The matriarch of the family stepped to the door. As soon as the door was opened, the mob surged in and threw the lady to the side with a severity that resulted in her arm fracturing. Sensing danger, the guests rushed onto the roof. A few younger members of the family were able to jump onto the roofs of the neighbors' houses. From there, calls for help went out. Jamshid and others, on hearing of the riots going on, reached out to a Zoroastrian-commissioned commander at the Kerman military base by the name of Arastu Khosrow Soroushian. He was a cousin of Jamshid.

The Iranian military in the provinces had adopted a neutral stance in the political conflict between the monarch and those opposing him and were staying in their barracks. In this case, Arastu would be taking a risk. Given the severity of the situation, he led his men to the Zoroastrian quarter. By the time the army arrived at the home of the Kasravi family, the mobs had cleared out the contents of the house, including all the carpets and other significant household goods. On hearing that the army was approaching, the mob fled the scene and dispersed. Arastu kept his men on guard around the Zoroastrian quarter for several hours before withdrawing them to the barracks. The situation stayed tense for a few days. Once Radio Kerman announced that the Shah had returned to Tehran and a new premier was in charge, law and order were restored.

There were no other notable incidents impacting the Zoroastrian quarter from 1954 to the end of the Pahlavi dynasty in 1979. There was a steady stream of Zoroastrians from Kerman migrating to Tehran, lured by the opportunities that the capital city offered them. Youth of the community moved away from Kerman to attend universities in Tehran and other cities, as well as overseas. Of the remaining Zoroastrians, some also ventured outside the traditional

---

159 https://en.wikipedia.org/wiki/Tudeh_Party_of_Iran

160 Soon after a new prime minister was appointed, the Majlis voted to outlaw the Tudeh Party. Many of the former members had to take an oath of loyalty to the Constitutional Monarchy. Some time later, a former Tudeh Party activist, who was a Zoroastrian, stated that the Tudeh party's plan in Kerman had been to seize Shahriar Khodabux Soroushian's house and use it as its headquater. It was not to be.

161 Burying documents or precious metals and coins was a defensive measure the Zoroastrians had come to rely on. On many past occasions (Qajar era and prior) when the mobs broke into vulnerable Zoroastrians' homes, they would typically ransack the place and carry away all that they could. Hiding coins and documents was critical to the Zoroastrians' ability to try and recover and move forward.

Zoroastrian quarter and bought homes in more affluent and upcoming areas to the West of the sprawling city.

By contrast, Moslem residents of Kerman were increasingly interested in buying family homes in the Zoroastrian quarters that were being vacated by the inheritors. It turned out that one such buyer while digging in the courtyard of the house he had bought, had unearthed precious metals and silver coins that had been hidden for emergency use over 80 years earlier.[162]

The news of this treasure being found results in others becoming interested in buying properties in the Zoroastrian quarter of the city.

Another event that occurred during Jamshid's tenure as the president of the Kerman Zoroastrian Association was notable for a different reason. Under the civil codes of Iran, all marriages had to be registered. Administering marriages was considered to be the duty of religious authorities. The Moslems could have their marriages registered at the official registrar offices in various cities. The Zoroastrians and other minorities would register their marriages with their associations (Anjumans), which were officially recognized by the government. Anjumans would only register the marriage when the bride and the groom were both Zoroastrians. In the late 1950s, a young Zoroastrian from a prominent Yazdi family who had returned from studying in the US was planning to marry a girl from a northern province of Iran who was born a Moslem. Their plan was to have a Zoroastrian marriage. The official Registrar's office would not register such a marriage and required that both bride and groom be Moslems.

Out of an abundance of caution, the Tehran Zoroastrian Anjuman turned down the couple's request to issue a marriage license and register their marital status. The couples' appeals to the Yazd and Shiraz Anjumans were also futile. As a last resort, the couple contacted Jamshid Soroushian about the Kerman Anjuman's position and received a positive reply. Soon, the wedding party arrived in Kerman and was hosted at Soroush Shahriar Soroushian's house for the duration of their stay. A wedding ceremony was held for the couple at the same venue. A Zoroastrian priest presided over their marriage ceremony. Their marriage was registered in the books of the Anjuman and transmitted to the official registration book at the Registrar's office in Kerman. In the aftermath of the Islamic revolution of 1979, this couple and their offspring, like many other Zoroastrian families, left Iran for the US. Jamshid, as the head of Anjuman, agreed to this bold move and followed in the footsteps of his father and grandfather, who championed groundbreaking initiatives in their own times.

Another event that happened on Jamshid's watch as the president of the Anjuman involved a young Zoroastrian female who was an accredited teacher and had been assigned to a school in Jiroft in the southern part of the province of Kerman. A male colleague of hers who realized she was a Zoroastrian had managed to get her to go to a mosque. Then, he claimed she

---

[162] In the uncertain period of the Qajar rule, Zoroastrians feeling vulnerable and subject to assault and raid of their properties would typically hide away coins and precious metals in their backyards. In the event of an assault on their homes, they could dig the coins and use them to buy food for survival. During the Pahlavi era there was no need for such precautions. However, in some cases, the new occupants of their parent's homes had forgotten about the hidden treasures.

had become a Moslem and threatened her with violence if she did not convert. Realizing she was no longer safe in Jiroft, she managed to leave as fast as she could and return to her parents in Kerman. Back in Jiroft, when her departure was noticed, her colleague from school got hold of her records at the school and found out her parents' address in Kerman. Then, this matter was referred to Shia authority in Kerman city, cleric Mohammad Javad Houjati Kermani,[163] who later became an Ayatollah. Houjati led the effort to claim the distressed Zoroastrian girl. The parents, realizing they could not be assured of their daughter's safety in their own home, quickly took her to Jamshid Soroushian's residence and informed him of what had transpired. Once Jamshid heard from the girl herself about the course of events, he assured them that they could stay until her safety was assured. Jamshid was aware of the past history that such matters rarely ended up in favor of the vulnerable Zoroastrians. Jamshid was well acquainted with the high-ranking officials locally, including the governor, and so he telephoned and informed them of the nature of the exigency and that if the situation got out of hand, the security forces needed to intervene promptly. In the late afternoon, the news came that a mob led by cleric Houjati was marching down Zriesfe Avenue toward Jamshid Soroushian's house. The mob was chanting as they marched. Soon, the crowd descended on the front door of Jamshid's house and started banging on it. They were chanting to the effect that they were reclaiming the new Moslem convert whom they considered to have been kidnapped. At that point, Jamshid asked everyone to stay calm. He went to the front door and opened it. In the crowd, he spotted Houjati, with whom he had a rapport from before, and motioned him to come close. The crowd, seeing that Houjati was engaging with Jamshid Soroushian, calmed down. Jamshid invited Houjati to step inside to discuss the situation. Houjati and a few of his close associates stepped in. Houjati asked the rest of his followers to stay calm and wait for his command. Behind the closed front door, Jamshid invited Houjati to make his case, and once he was done, he informed him that his narrative was inconsistent with the account he had heard from the girl herself. She had represented that she was tricked into going to the mosque and that she had no intention of converting to Islam. Jamshid suggested that Houjati and a few of his associates could talk to the girl and ask her about her intentions. The only condition Jamshid set was that if the girl informed them that she had no intention of converting, then Houjati and the crowd would peacefully disperse and consider the matter closed. Houjati eventually agreed. At that point, Houjati stepped outside, informed the crowd of the plan, and asked them to stay peaceful until he returned. Then he returned with his close associates. The front door was closed once again. Jamshid accompanied Houjati and his men to the room where the girl was staying. The girl was shaken to see the Islamic clergy and hostile-looking men accompanying him. Jamshid reassured her that she was safe and encouraged her to answer the questions that Houjati would ask her truthfully without fear of retribution. Then Houjati started questioning her as to the reason for changing her mind about accepting Islam. She answered that she had never expressed interest in converting to Islam. Despite extensive questioning and cross-examination, her responses

---

[163] Years later, he was elevated to the rank of Ayatollah and was very influential in the aftermath of the Islamic Revolution of 1979. His ancestors down to two generations earlier were all Zoroastrians.

remained consistent. Eventually, Houjati accepted her assertion that she was never interested in converting to Islam and left with the crowd that had accompanied him. Despite that peaceful conclusion, Jamshid informed the parents that their daughter's safety in Kerman could not be guaranteed and that she would be safer in Tehran. Quietly, arrangements were made for her to depart for Tehran the next day. Jamshid contacted Zoroastrian community advocates in Tehran and asked them to meet the girl and her family at the arrival gate of the bus terminal in Tehran and to help her get settled in Tehran.

In the early 1960s, the Shah of Iran championed several major reforms (referred to as white revolution). The initiatives were put to a national referendum and passed overwhelmingly. The initiatives included land Reform, women's suffrage, and the creation of a literacy corps. Every Iranian male, on reaching age 18, was expected to spend two years of national service[164] and get military training. With the creation of the literacy corps, the draftees who had to be high-school graduates would receive military training for six months. For the remaining 18 months, they would be assigned to teach in remote villages after getting basic training on how to teach. The aim of the program was to increase the literacy rate in the remote villages. In 1965, an 18-year-old Zoroastrian male from Kerman reported for his mandatory national service and volunteered to be part of the literacy corps for the second part of his service. He was assigned to a remote village in the northeastern province of Khorasan close to the city of Sabzavar. His service in the village started in 1966, and he was well-adjusted and established a good rapport with the villagers. However, months later, the villagers started to notice that the new Literary Corps volunteer assigned to their village was not attending the village mosque. His absence was notable during the periods of religious mourning when every villager would be in attendance. Finally, the villagers approached him and asked him why he was not showing up at the village mosque. The soldier informed them that he was a Zoroastrian, not a Moslem. Upon hearing that, the villagers turned on the soldier and stopped sending their children to his school. Furthermore, they threatened him that unless he accepted Islam, his safety could not be guaranteed. At that point, the soldier becomes concerned about his safety in the village, and he sends a letter of appeal to Jamshid Soroushian, the president of the Kerman Zoroastrian Association. Upon receiving the letter of appeal and confirming its authenticity, Jamshid took steps to contact the Royal Court. Mr. Alam, the court minister, brought the matter to the attention of the Shah. Within a week, a Royal Decree was issued that all Zoroastrian military draftees could only be assigned to villages in Yazd and Kerman close to the main cities. Upon issuance of that decree, the Zoroastrian soldier was reassigned from Khorasan to a village in Kerman to serve the rest of his term.

During his tenure as the president of the Kerman Zoroastrian Anjuman, a few controversial issues surfaced that threatened the harmony of the community. Jamshid and the board of the Anjuman dealt with each issue in a manner they felt made sense. In one case, an overseas Kermani Zoroastrian had donated funds to be used for the construction of a community

---

164 There were two exceptions: One was in the case of a young boy who was the sole male offspring of the family and the other was for Moslem priests who were exempted from national military service.

gathering hall and kitchen facility to be erected on the grounds of the main fire temple in Kerman. The donor had also indicated to some of his Moslem contacts that once the facility was built, it could also be used by others outside the community. Community members were concerned that allowing a large crowd of potentially hostile people on the grounds of the Zoroastrian temple could have unpleasant results. The objections were strong, and some argued that the donation should be returned unless the terms of use were changed. Jamshid took the matter up with the donor and informed him of the basis for the objections. The donor agreed that the use of the facility he was financing could be limited to the Zoroastrian community, and the issue was resolved.

Jamshid's Scholarly Activities: Since returning to Kerman from Isfahan in the early 1930s, Jamshid has shown a keen interest in engaging in advanced Iranian studies. Towards that end, he started procuring and reading all the scholarly literature that had been published by scholars of Zoroastrian and ancient Iranian studies. He also worked actively to establish contacts with scholars of ancient Iranian studies in Iran and abroad. His case is one of self-learning and self-educating rather than formal university education.[165]

From 1938 to 1939, Jamshid published a number of rebuttals to the Iranian scholar Saeed Nafisi[166] in the Mehr Publication, a national scholarly journal. Nafisi was promoting the idea that ancient Iranians tolerated the marriage of next of kin. Jamshid was presenting evidence to the contrary. The series of exchanges between Jamshid Soroushian and Saeed Nafisi received attention from other scholars as well.[167]

Amongst the first group of scholars with whom he established close working relationships was Professor Ibrahim Pour-Davoud,[168] a prominent scholar of ancient Iranian languages and the founding chairman of the Ancient Iranian Studies Department at Tehran University. The lifelong collaboration between the two resulted in multiple trips by Professor Pour-Davoud to Kerman as a guest of Jamshid. Jamshid's first scholarly production was a lexicon of the Darii dialect spoken by Zoroastrians of Iran.[169] Professor Pour-Davoud was a great influence and mentor to Jamshid in his undertaking of this significant work.

---

[165] Jamshid pursued his scholarly interest as a side hobby while focusing on the family business.

[166] https://en.wikipedia.org/wiki/Saeed_Nafisi

[167] Shahbazi, A. Shahpur, 2003: "Khvetudas", Soroush Peer Mughan - Jamshid Soroushian Commemorative volume I (Farsi), Sorraya Publisher, Tehran, Iran, pages 237-247

[168] https://enba.wikipedia.org/wiki/Ebrahim_Pourdavoud

[169] To shield themselves from harm, Zoroastrians of Iran going back to the 17th century started to use a new dialect, Darii, that was extracted from Farsi. Arabic terminologies that had crept into colloquial Farsi were replaced by pure Farsi words. The Darii spoken by Zoroastrians could not typically be comprehended by the Moslems. The use of this dialect was a measure of protection adapted by Zoroastrians against ill-meaning Moslems who could have otherwise eavesdropped on the conversions Zoroastrians had among themselves and brought harm to them.

The other notable early connection Jamshid made was with Wilhelm Eilers,[170] a German scholar of Ancient Near Eastern Studies who was in Iran from the mid-1930s.[171] At the invitation of Jamshid, Professor Eilers and his wife visited Kerman in the 1960s and were hosted by Jamshid and his wife, Homayun. Jamshid encouraged Professor Eilers to analyze the linguistic characters of the Darii language spoken by generations of Zoroastrians in Iran.

Otto Helmut Wolfgang Lenz was another professor specializing in ancient Near Eastern and Zoroastrian Studies who was in regular communication with Jamshid. He and his wife came to visit with Jamshid several times and were his guests during their stay in Kerman.

Professor Mary Boyce of the University of London SOAS (School of Oriental & African Studies), specializing in Zoroastrian and Manichian Studies, took half a year of sabbatical leave to go to Iran for research in 1963. At Jamshid Soroushian's invitation, she came to Kerman and stayed for a few months at his house. Afterward, she proceeded to Yazd, where she stayed at Sohrab Kianian's house. Finally, she proceeded to the village of Sharif Abad, where she stayed with the local Zoroastrians. Professor Boyce's six-month stay in Iran, which came about at the urging of Jamshid Soroushian, was very productive. She observed many of the local Zoroastrian ceremonies. After her return, she had gathered enough information to be used as source material for several of her insightful books and scholarly articles on Zoroastrianism. While in Kerman, Jamshid arranged for her to visit all sites of religious significance to Zoroastrians in Kerman. While visiting the site of the abandoned and partially-demolished fire temple in Mahalleh Shahr-Kerman that had been in use from the 19th century to the early 20th century, she was looking for the stone carving that bore details about the construction of the site and when it happened. It was soon determined that the stone carving was missing. Jamshid Soroushian and the Anjuman arranged for an excavation crew to dig under the rubles of the crumbled fire temple. Fortunately, the stone carving was found, and it was not damaged. It now hangs on the walls of the ShahVahram Izad building in Kerman. The stone carving indicated the fire temple had been erected in the 1860s during the reign of Nasser-ul Dinshah Qajar. Maneckji Limji Hataria was identified as the person who had championed the construction of the temple. Next to that fire temple, the living quarters of the high priest and a few rooms to be used at a school for boys had been erected as well.

While Professor Boyce was in Kerman, Professor Gilbert Lazar from Sorborne, a specialist in the Pahlavi language, also came to visit and stayed for a few days. There was a constant stream of international scholars of Zoroastrianism who would come to Kerman, and some were hosted by Jamshid and Homayun at their residence during their stay. These visits provided for extensive exchange of knowledge and ideas and proved to be very productive. Jamshid Soroushian went on to author seven books on various aspects of Zoroastrians and

---

170 https://www.iranicaonline.org/articles/eilers-

171 Wilhelm Eilers worked in Iran for years. In 1941 in the aftermath of the allied invasion of Iran, Eilers being a German nation was interned along with his wife and his two sons (who were born in Iran) and sent to Australia for 5 years. Upon his release from WWII internment, Eilers went back to Germany and got an appointment at Wurzburg University. In the decade of 1970s, one of Professor Eilers' sons served in Iran as a German diplomat.

Iranian history, popular culture, and traditions. He was invited to speak at various scholarly gatherings, such as universities in Kerman and the Kermanology Institute.

With a number of universities established in Kerman and an influx of students from other parts of Iran, some of the students who were interested in learning about ancient Iranian history, culture, and religion were led to contact Jamshid Soroushian, who was very receptive of the students' inquiries. At times, his living room would turn into an informal university classroom with numerous students attending to learn from him. He continued this practice every time he was in town.

Jamshid's Legacy: Jamshid's contribution to Kerman's cultural and intellectual growth cannot be underestimated. He was generally respected by the citizenry of Kerman and many Kermanis who came to know him. Former Chief Justice of Kerman, Mr. Foroughi, had of Jamshid, "He is a wonderful man, but he expects his audience in the span of a 15-minute conversation over a cup of tea to become a believer in the supremacy of Zarathushtra's message."

A recently published book on well-known families of Kerman[172] identifies Jamshid Soroushian as the second-best-known Zoroastrian of Kerman. The book identifies Kaikhosrow Shahrokh as the first.

Going from a withdrawn student at the missionary schools where his religion was ridiculed to becoming a well-recognized authority on the subject of Zoroastrian and Iranian studies is a legacy of Jamshid Soroushian.

In remembrance of Jamshid Soroushian, two of the graduates of Kerman's Iranshahr Zoroastrian Highschool made the following comments referring to their experience with him in the 1950s when they were attending school:

1. Dr. Ardeshid Kaikhosrow Anoushiravi recalls that Jamshid Soroushian held several classes for the students on Gathic teaching. He felt those lessons kindled a fire in him to learn more about the message of Zarathushtra, and, as a result, he took up that study along with his medical sciences education.

2. Dr. Kaikhosorw Harvasp, in a tribute he made to Jamshid Soroushian that was published in the first volume of Jamshid Soroushian Memorial set,[173] recalled the following experience: "Kaikhosrow and his brother Hooshang had first place ranking in their respective classes. During one of the annual NovRuz celebrations that the Anjuman hosted for the Zoroastrian community, all the high performers were acknowledged, and a gift was given to them. That year, Kaikhosrow and his brother Hooshang were called onto the stage to be recognized for their academic accomplishment. Shortly after the conclusion of the NovRuz celebration at the school and returning to their home, there

---

[172] "Kermani Families" (in Farsi – Khanehdanhayeh Kermani), by Mehdi Irani Kermani, Kermanology Publication, (ISBN# 978-622-7011-11-1), 2021, p. 222

[173] "Soroush Peer Mughan: Jamshid Soroushian Commemorative Volume I" editor, Dr. Katayun Mazdapour, Sorraya Publisher, Tehran, 2003, pp. 23-26 (in Farsi)

was a knock on the door. Jamshid Soroushian and his younger brother appeared at the door and were visiting to exchange NovRuz greetings with Kaikhosrow's parents. Soon after, the guest was led to a room where the NovRuz Table was set up, and after an exchange of greetings, Jamshid Soroushian complemented Mr. Mehraban & Mrs. Morvarid Harvesp on raising such well-accomplished sons and then encouraged them that given the high potential your sons have you should send them to Germany for advanced education. Both Kaikhosrow and his brother in the next room were hearing the conversation and were inspired by what they heard." Ultimately, they did not go to Germany.[174] Soon after graduating from Tehran Medical University, Kaikhosrow headed to the US for residency and specialization in Pediatrics, and he practiced medicine in Florida through the end of his life. His brother Hooshang joined him in Florida as well.

Following his passage in 1999, a two-volume Memorial book in his honor was produced with articles contributed by International and Iranian scholars of Zoroastrian and Iranian studies. The first volume in Farsi was published in Tehran, and the articles were contributed mostly by Iranian scholars. The second volume in English under the title of "The Fire Within – Jamshid Soroushian Memorial Volume II" was published in the US in 2004. Most of the contributors were scholars of Zoroastrian and Iranian studies in Europe and the US. The English volume was recommended reading material for students enrolled in Harvard University's Ancient Iranian Studies program.

Jamshid and Homayun spent most of their lives since marrying in 1945 in Kerman, and they were both buried in Kerman. They traveled extensively inside Iran and to India, Europe, North America, and throughout the Middle East and, at times, stayed for several months with their two sons and youngest daughter in America and with their daughter, Armity, in Germany,

In the aftermath of the 1979 Islamic revolution, Jamshid's three brothers and two sisters relocated to North America or England to be close to their sons and daughters.[175] Some of them traveled back to Kerman for short periods to attend to their agribusiness. Jamshid's five siblings all died outside of Iran.

2.8.2 Homayun Sohrab Rustom Kaikhosrow Viraf Kianian
1924 – 2006 (Yazd, Tehran-Kerman)

Homayun was the youngest daughter of Arbab[176] Sohrab Kianian and Mrs. Simin Khosrow ShahJahan. Along with her older siblings were KhorshidBanu and Azar (sisters) and Khosrow and Faridun (brothers: Her two younger brothers were Rustom and Shah Bahram. They

---

174 Iranian Zoroastrians of that decade favored Germany as a destination for higher education, in particular medicine and engineering. In subsequent decades, the US became the more preferred destination.

175 Jamshid and his siblings, like many other Zoroastrian families, had sent their children to North America or Europe during the prosperous years of the Pahlavis to pursue higher education. Their aim was to return to Iran upon completion of their studies. In view of 1979 Islamic Revolution, almost all of them decided to stay abroad and gave up on the idea of returning to the Islamic country.

176 Arbab is a title given to well-to-do Zoroastrian men.

were born in Yazd. Homayun was born in 1924, a period that coincided with the elevation of Reza Shah Pahlavi to the throne of Iran by the vote of the Iranian Majlis (Parliament). Homayun's father, Sohrab, was a leading figure in the Zoroastrian community of Yazd and served as the president of the Yazd Anjuman for consecutive terms through the end of his life. Sohrab and his younger brother, Kaikhosrow, had been reared by their father, Rustom-Khaikhosrow-Viraf, to be focused on building a business based on trade. Rustom had been a successful businessman operating from Yazd. With his wife, Mahasti, they reared three offspring: two sons and a daughter by the name of Firozeh. Rustom had asked his eldest son, Sohrab, to stay in Yazd and manage the family business, which was primarily focused on trade and agrobusiness. He then accompanied his younger son Kaikhosrow, Kaikhosrow's wife Homayun, and their first daughter Farangis to Kerman City. Until then, Rustom had a business representative in Kerman. With the arrival of Kaikhosrow and his family, Kaikhosrow was able to take over and lead the Kerman branch of the family trading business.

Sohrab married Simin, the sole daughter of another leading Zoroastrian businessman from Yazd, Khosrow ShahJahan. Khosrow Shah Jahan was involved in trade with India and Europe. Both Rustom, the father of Sohrab, and Khosrow, the father of Simin, served on the board of the Naseri Zoroastrian Anjuman of Yazd during the same period.

In time, Sohrab followed in his father's footsteps and became active with the Anjuman. His tenure at the Anjuman coincided with the reign of Reza Shah Pahlavi. Sohrab proved to be a dedicated and effective head of the Anjuman.[177] He was well respected by the community members as well as the government bureaucrats. His stately home in Yazd had a courtyard with residential units on three sides of the courtyard. Many Zoroastrians passing through Yazd and visitors to Yazd would stay as his house guests. His wife, Simin, was used to seeing visiting guests hosted at her own father's house.

Simin's father, Khosrow, was a leading community figure and a successful businessman who had founded his family's trading business. Along with his younger brothers (Parviz, Goodarz, Rustom, and Bahram), he expanded it to major cities in Iran (Shiraz, Isfahan, Tehran, Bandar Abbas), India, Europe, and the US. One of his lasting legacies was the creation of two

---

177 Sohrab's tenure as the head of Yazd Anjuman was a period of rapid change and progress for the Zoroastrians. An increasing number of Zoroastrians from Yazd, the nearby villages, and Kerman were relocating to the capital of Tehran that was fast-growing and providing opportunities for the Iranians to prosper. At the same time, the attempted abductions of young Zoroastrian girls in the villages of Yazd by fanatical Moslems and their attempt to convert them to Islam was for the first time getting serious push back. Many of these attempts were getting interrupted. The families and Zoroastrian activists were able to rescue some of these girls. After rescuing them, the girls would typically be rushed to Sohrab Kianian's house. He had an underground safe room in his house that was used for temporary housing of the rescued girls until safe arrangement could be made for their safe transport to Tehran. It was well understood that once a girl was targeted and claims made as having converted to Islam, if they stayed in Yazd, they could be snatched at any time. Sohrab was also very effective with navigating the government bureaucracy. As soon as one of these kidnaping would be uncovered, he would appear at the Lieutenant Governor's and other officials' offices to demand action. Despite his small physical posture, once his car carrying him and his loyal assistant (Haji) would approach the officials' headquarters, everyone would recognize him and grant him access. There was a saying by the Zoroastrians of Yazd that "When Sohrab speaks, the royal palace in Tehran listens." Of course, justice afforded to Zoroastrian and other minorities was a uniquely Pahlavi Dynasty-era phenomena.

endowed schools in Yazd in 1896. Until that time, there was only one school for the Zoroastrians of Yazd. Khosravi School for Boys, which he founded, provided elementary and middle school level education to generations of youth in the community. The Jahanian School for Girls that he founded in later years was expanded and became the Markar School for Girls.[178]

Another notable act of Khosrow relates to his sponsoring the erection of the first mausoleum on the grave of the prominent poet Hafez of Shiraz. During a business trip to Brussels, Belgium, Khosrow met with a scholar familiar with the literary works of the Iranian poet Hafez. Based on that conversation, Khosrow got a greater appreciation for Hafez, the 14th-century poet born in Shiraz, Iran. Upon his return to Iran and during his trip to Shiraz for their family business, Khosrow searched for the site of Hafez's burial. Seeing it was unimpressive, he sponsored the building of a worthy mausoleum for Hafez. Unfortunately, years later, an influential Shiite ayatollah of Shiraz, on hearing that a non-Moslem had sponsored the building of Hafez's mausoleum, ordered its destruction. When the Pahlavis came to power, magnificent mausoleums for Hafez and Ferdowsi were constructed, which stand to this day.

Homayun grew up in a busy household and observed her parents' activism for the benefit of the Zoroastrian community. Much of the activities and comings and goings in their busy household were related to his father's community activities. Her father also conducted his trade business from his house, where his office was located.

Homayun attended the Markar School for Girls, which was among the first schools for girls established in Iran. She had vivid memories of her school years, her school friends, and growing up in her parents' busy household.

Every few years, Homayun and her entire family, along with her aunt, Firozeh, would travel to Kerman and stay with her uncle Kaykhosrow for several weeks. In other years, her uncle, Kaykhosrow, and his family would travel to Yazd to visit the rest of the family.[179] During their visits to Kerman, Sohrab and his family would also visit with their business partners in Kerman, the Soroushian brothers. It was during these visits to Kerman that Homayun came to know Jamshid, the son of Soroush and IranBanu Soroushian. Also, when Soroush and his son or other family members traveled from Kerman to Tehran, they would spend a night or two at Sohrab Kianian's house in Yazd en route to Tehran.

Homayun was about 20 years old when a proposal for marriage from Jamshid Soroushian was received. Homayun and her family accepted the marriage proposal. The marriage in Yazd at Sohrab Kianian's mansion happened a few nights after the marriage of Homayun's older sister, Azar, to her cousin, Mr. Shapour Kaykhosrow Kianian. The two wedding parties returned to

---

178 Markar School for girls is named after Peshotan Markar, a Parsi philanthropist who was focused on ameliorating the conditions of the Iranian Zoroastrians. Boarding facilities for young Zoroastrian girls from villages who had no family in the city of Yazd to stay with was added through the endowments from Peshotan Markar.

179 This annual family get-together continued through th e1930s. After that, Firozeh and her children gradually moved to Tehran, and with the onset of WWII and occupation of Iran by the British and Soviet forces, travel between the cities became less safe and less frequent.

Kerman. The two sisters lived for the rest of their lives in Kerman, where they both raised their families.[180]

Besides her sister Azar, her older brother, Khosrow, and his wife also lived in Kerman. Khosrow was married to his cousin, Simindokht, the daughter of Kaykhosrow Kianian.

Khosrow and his wife, as well as Azar and her husband, resided in stately homes on the north side of Zriesfe Avenue and were within walking distance of each other.[181]

Homayun was already used to extensive community activities conducted from their home in Yazd. Her husband's community advocacy in their new home in Kerman was very agreeable with her, and she was supportive of the same. She soon became accustomed to visits by scholars of Zoroastrian studies that her husband had invited. Visitors to her new home in Kerman who were coming to meet with her husband also included governmental dignitaries, cultural icons, ambassadors, and diplomats interested in learning about the Zoroastrian community.

Also, some of the Zoroastrians from Yazd and Tehran passing through Kerman would call on Jamshid and Homayun and be hosted during their stays in Kerman.

In time, Homayun came to provide marriage consulting and mediation to Zoroastrian couples who were experiencing marital issues. She also was active with the Zoroastrian Women Organization of Kerman. Homayun accompanied her husband on most of his foreign trips. At the same time, she was busy raising her five children and managing her household.

Homayun and Jamshid's first child and daughter, Mahavash, married and settled in Tehran. Their two sons, Soroosh and Mehrborzin, along with their twin daughters, Armity and Anahita, were sent to the US and England for studies. In view of the 1979 Islamic Revolution, all four of them settled in California. Mahvash and her husband Goodarz Goodarz sent their two daughters, Vesta and Mehrbanou, to the US for studies. Both daughters settled in the US after completion of their studies. Mahvash and her husband joined them and settled in Northern California. She spends some part of the year in Tehran, and Kerman attends to what remains of the family business.

Homayun survived her husband by seven years and moved between Iran and California to spend time with her children and grandchildren. In the final months of her life, she fell in her apartment in Tehran and was hospitalized. She never recovered and died after months of hospitalization. Her remains were moved to Kerman and buried in the Kerman Soroushian cemetery close to the grave of her husband. Her sister, Azar, passed away a few months later and

---

[180] The graves of both sisters are situated next to each of others at the Kerman's Soroushian Zoroastrian Aramgah, close to the burial site of Jamshid Soroush Soroushian.

[181] However, every time the other siblings from Yazd came to Kerman for visits or to attend to their agrobusiness, they would almost always stay as guests at Homayun and Jamshid Soroushian's home.

was buried next to Homayun's grave. On Homayun's gravestone is inscribed the following verse inspired by Zoroaster's Gathas: "Happiness to those through whom happiness comes to others."

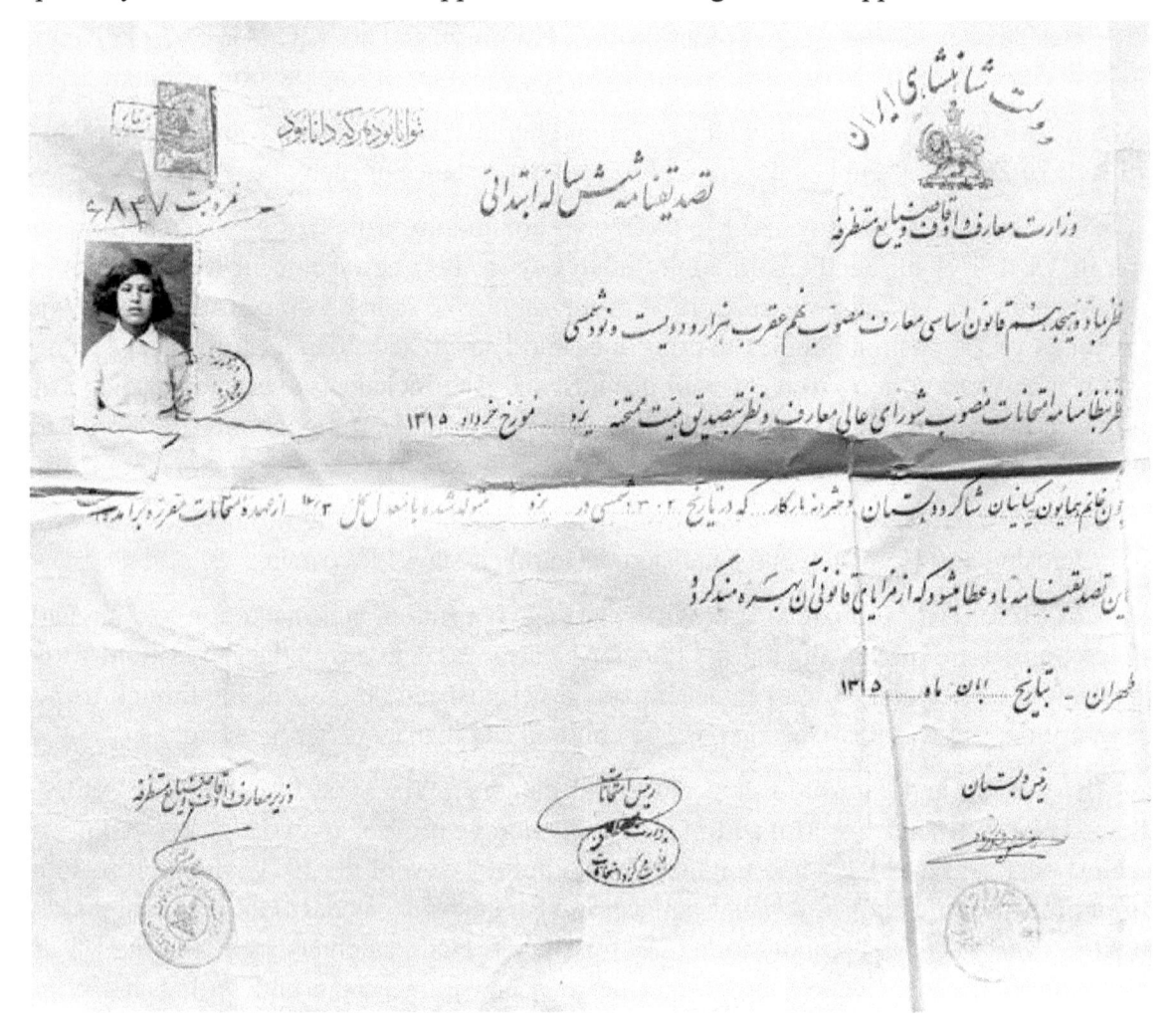

Figure 28: 1936, Yazd: Homayun Sohrab Kianian's Sixth Grade Graduation Certificate

Figure 29: 1934, Kerman: Jamshid Soroushian during his Mandatory Military Service

Figure 30: 1945, Kerman: Wedding photo taken in Kerman upon arrival of Homayun and Jamshid from Yazd. Jamshid's uncle, Faridu, and his wife, GoharBanu, are sitting on his left side. His mother and his sister, Katayun, are sitting on the right side of Homayun.

Figure 31: 1949, Kerman: Visit of Professor Pour-Davoud (3rd from right in the front row) to Kerman as a guest of Jamshid Soroushian

Figure 32: 1957, Kerman Airport: Jamshid Soroushian (first from right) welcoming Mohamed Reza Shah Pahlavi to Kerman for a Royal Visit. Standing next to Jamshid is Mr. Shahpur Kaikhosrow Kianian

Figure 33: 1963, Kerman: A family photo of Jamshid and Homayun Soroushian with their five offspring and Homayun's older sister, KhorshidBanu.

Figure 34: 1964, Kerman: Novruz community-wide celebration hosted by the Zoroastrian Association. Jamshid (second from right in the second row) was the president of the Anjuman.

Figure 35: 1965, Kerman: Jamshid Soroushian in the audience with Mohamed Reza Shah Pahlavi during a royal visit to Kerman

Figure 36: Decorative Wall Carpet commissioned by Jamshid Soroushian depicting the artist's impression of the burning of Persepolis by Alexander of Macedonia in 330 BCE

2.9 Mehrborzin Jamshid Soroushian and Mehrbanou Mehraban Zartoshty

2.9.1 Mehrborzin Jamshid Soroush Soroushian
1952, Kerman

The narrative of the Soroushian family extends to the generation born subsequent to Mohamed Reza Shah Pahlavi's accession to the throne of Iran in 1941. They came of age during an unprecedented era in Iran's history compared to the prior 14 centuries, a period characterized by peace, prosperity, and remarkable advancements across various aspects of national life. Growing up in Kerman, many of us were deeply entrenched in the notion of residing within the Zoroastrian Mahalleh for security and sanctuary.[182] However, as years went by, we gradually became open to the prospect of dwelling beyond its confines.

I was born in Kerman in the winter of 1952, the third child of Homayun and Jamshid Soroushian. Alongside my four siblings, we were raised in Kerman, surrounded by relatives, cousins, and the tight-knit Zoroastrian community of the city. Our formative years were spent in the historic schools established by preceding generations of Zoroastrians. Enrollment was inclusive, welcoming Iranians from all religious backgrounds.

The house where we spent our formative years, situated on the north side of Zriesfe Avenue,[183] marked a notable boundary of the expanding Zoroastrian quarters in Kerman. By the 1960s and early 1970s, the majority of Kerman's Zoroastrian community resided within these quarters. Interestingly, alongside Zoroastrians, there were also non-Zoroastrians, including a handful of foreign nationals primarily from Eastern and Southern Europe, living within the confines of the Zoroastrian quarters.[184]

Despite being occupied with managing the farms inherited from his father, my father remained deeply engaged in community affairs, with a particular zeal for Zoroastrian studies. As a farm owner, he fostered connections with high-ranking government officials, including governors and heads of various governmental agencies. On occasion, some of these officials were invited to our home when my parent hosted receptions for visiting dignitaries, including esteemed Zoroastrian priests from India.

During meals, my father often led discussions on significant issues affecting both the Zoroastrian community and Kerman at large. He also lauded the achievements of young Zoroastrians and Iranians who had excelled in fields such as medicine, sciences, and beyond.

---

[182] For those born in Tehran, the concept of residing in integrated neighborhoods was simply an accepted reality.

[183] In a post made in February 2023, a former Muslim student from Kerman who had attended Zoroastrian schools in the city referred to the Zriesfe Quarter of Kerman as the "Kindness Quarter"

[184] In contrast, in Yazd, occupancy within the Zoroastrian quarters was by members of the Zoroastrian community..

Mehrborzin Jamshid Soroushian

There was a strong emphasis on academic excellence,[185] particularly in the sciences and medicine.

During the summer months, our family typically retreated to a village nestled at the foot of the Hezar Mountain range[186] in the Western part of Kerman.[187] As the sun sets, casting a warm glow over the landscape, we gather under the vast, clear sky adorned with distant stars and celestial wonders. It's a nightly ritual, eagerly anticipated.

My father, a man of profound dedication and scholarly passion, always brought with him a cherished volume of Ferdowsi's Shahnameh. With eloquence and fervor, he regaled us with the timeless tales woven within its pages. His recitations were not mere readings; they were performances, each word resonating with the essence of the ancient narrative. Remarkably, he effortlessly recited extensive passages from memory; his voice imbued with the spirit of the epic.

Through these stories, my father imparted more than mere entertainment; he shared invaluable lessons about morality and life. Each poem he recited carried within it a profound insight, a guiding principle that resonated with us long after the echoes of his voice had faded into the night.

There was a stream of scholars of Zoroastrian studies who came to visit and stay with us in Kerman for the duration of their stay. Professor Mary Boyce of London University took a sabbatical leave in 1963 and came to Kerman. Her stay at our house for several months presented a good opportunity for me. I was learning English at Iranshahr High School and could practice it with her when I got back home in the late afternoon, and would, even at times, translate for

---

185 The admiration shown towards high-achieving individuals in academia served as a powerful form of role modeling for my generation, reinforcing the importance of academic excellence.

186 The Hezar Mountain range stands as the loftiest in the Kerman province when measured from sea level. The village, known by the Arabic appellation Qaryat-ul-Arab (village of the Arabs), traces its origin to the reign of King Khosrow Anushiravan (Khosrow I, 540 A.C.) of the illustrious Sasanian dynasty. Legend has it that Khosrow orchestrated the relocation of a tribe of warring Arabs from the southwestern frontier to this locale in Kerman. The intent was to acquaint them with agricultural and farming practices, with the expectation that they would eventually return to their ancestral lands to cultivate the soil. However, contrary to expectations, the Arab settlers chose to remain, leading to the village being christened in their honor.

In the more recent annals of history, during the 19th century, this village formed a part of the Royal Qajar holdings. Subsequently, in the early 20th century, under the auspices of the Pahlavi regime, the Qajar estates were divested by their proprietors. Jamshid's father, in conjunction with his brother and the Kianian and Aamari brothers, acquired this agricultural expanse. Within one of the fruit orchards flanking the village's main thoroughfare, Soroush Shahriar Soroushian undertook the construction of a residential enclave utilizing state-of-the-art building materials of the era. Adjacent to this residential quarter, a brick production facility was erected within the confines of the same orchard to cater to the demand for bricks required for the construction not only of residential quarters within the garden premises but also for a residential dwelling in another village situated further southwest, which he had procured. Upon the completion of the constructions, the brick production facility was disassembled, and the land was replete with the verdant foliage of newly planted trees.

187 The half-day journey from Kerman to the countryside village provided my father with an excellent opportunity to mentor my brother and me in driving the family automobile. In 2023, one of Jamshid Soroushian's granddaughters, Mehrbanou Goodarz, reminisced about her childhood visits to Kerman to see her grandparents. She fondly recalled how her grandfather would allow her to take the wheel of his car during their countryside outings, where minimal traffic was encountered.

her.[188] There were also a number of young Americans, part of the Peace Corps, who had been assigned to Kerman for a few years. They would typically teach English at various schools in Kerman, including the Zoroastrian boy schools.[189]

Another young American couple was also involved in several development projects in Kerman. They resided in a rented house on the opposite side of Zriesfe Avenue. Our association with them provided me with an opportunity to practice my English.

Reflecting on our upbringing, it was a time of great joy. Looking back years later, I contemplated the environment in which we were raised, especially in comparison to prior generations of Zoroastrians during the Qajar era. I realized how fortunate my generation had been.

Through our study of Iran's history over the centuries, it became evident that we grew up during an extraordinary period of peace and stability throughout Iran and its neighboring regions. From the 1950s to the 1970s, Iran's economy flourished and remained stable. The White Revolution was initiated through a national referendum in the early 1960s, which granted Iranian women the right to vote and participate in elections. We also learned about the disturbances incited by some mullahs and their followers who opposed the reforms of the White Revolution. Fortunately, peace was swiftly restored in Qum and Southern Tehran.

In 1965, the assassination of Prime Minister Hassan Ali Mansur in Tehran by an Islamic fanatic caused unease among my parents. My father closely followed the news broadcasts from Tehran, staying abreast of unfolding events.

The birth of the crown prince, the coronation of the Shah and Queen, and, later, the celebration of the 2500th anniversary of the Persian Empire[190] were all joyous occasions that instilled a deep sense of pride in our country and its significant role in world history.

During these moments, there prevailed an overarching sense of optimism, accompanied by the belief that ample opportunities awaited all Iranians. It was incumbent upon each of us to strive toward realizing our fullest potential.

---

[188] My contact with Professor Mary Boyce resumed once I arrived in the UK in 1968 to pursue my education and undergraduate studies at London University. At times, she would send me list of questions, that I would translate into Farsi and send to my father to get the answers. Once I received the answers, I would translate them into English and send them to Professor Boyce. Even after I departed for the US for my graduate studies, I would exchange a new year greeting card with her. She had come to expect the card exchange, as one year when I failed to send her a card, she made me aware of it.

[189] We invited a few of them to our homes. One of them, Mr. Tom Sisul was in Kerman in 1963-1964 and thought at the Zoroastrian schools. Tom was originally from Washington State. In 2022 in San Diego, going through the family photos I had brought from Kerman, I found a picture I had taken with him and two other Peace Corps volunteers in Kerman. I was able to trace Tom on the internet. He lived in Alaska, and could recall coming to our house in Kerman.

[190] While the Western media heavily criticized the 2500th anniversary celebration of the founding of the Persian Empire, it notably omitted acknowledgment of the significant investment made in attracting international tourists and developing the national infrastructure to support a flourishing hospitality sector in the aftermath of this event.

In both school and social circles, approximately half of our friends and acquaintances belonged to the close-knit Zoroastrian community, while the other half were Muslims. Additionally, there were Jewish, Bahai, and Armenian students attending Zoroastrian schools.

One notable observation I made was that the Zoroastrians, as a whole, were remarkably open to new ideas and technological advancements, particularly those originating from the West. They embraced such innovations to the extent that they could enhance their lives.[191] In contrast, Muslims tended to adhere closely to the directives prescribed by their older and more conservative mullahs, who dictated a more traditional worldview.

The clash between these contrasting dynamics became apparent in the aftermath of the 1979 Islamic Revolution. Many devout Muslims ascended to positions of influence following the Revolution, disrupting the societal norms established during the Pahlavi era. Some of these individuals, who had previously benefited from their interactions with the Zoroastrian community – whether through attendance at Zoroastrian schools or through close business ties – found themselves torn between recognizing the progress and achievements of the Zoroastrians and adhering to the religious beliefs ingrained in them, which asserted that only Muslims were deserving of Allah's blessings,[192] while non-Muslims should be deprived of such blessings.[193]

Upon assuming positions of power in the post-1979 era, some of these individuals chose to erase any traces of their past associations with the Zoroastrians – whether in schools or elsewhere – and appropriated them for the benefit of Muslims. This approach seemed to represent their attempt to reconcile the perceived conflict between their moral considerations.

When I was eleven years old, my parents organized a celebration at our home to mark the initiation of both my older brother and sister, as well as myself, into the Zoroastrian religion.[194] Our maternal grandmother, uncles, and aunt from Yazd traveled to join us for this special occasion. The event was truly memorable, filled with the presence of family, friends, and even some dignitaries.

---

191 In the early 20th century, with the introduction of electricity and distribution lines in Kerman, Zoroastrian neighborhoods were among the first to adopt this technology, allowing for the extension of aerial copper wires to their homes. In contrast, due to numerous Fatwas issued by Islamic religious authorities against the adoption of electricity, Muslims exhibited resistance. A similar pattern emerged during the initial deployment of telephone lines.

192 Reference to God according to the Quran - the Almighty, who governs all aspects of the material world and the afterlife.

193 The best example of this mindset is reflected in a poem from the famed poet Saadi of Shiraz who lived in the 13th century. "O' God who from your invisible sources keep feeding the Gabres (derogatory term for Zoroastrians) and the Tarsas (derogatory term for Christians), why deny your own lot (implying Moslems), and keep the enemies in your good graces."

194 The Sedreh-Pushi, also known as Novjote, marks the initiation celebration for young Zoroastrians into the faith, tracing its origins to the inception of the religion. However, historical records indicate that in Iran, following the country's conquest by Muslims, this tradition faced intermittent observance due to the challenging and uncertain circumstances endured by Zoroastrians. Yet, the 20th century witnessed a resurgence of interest in reviving this ancient rite. Conversely, among Zoroastrians who sought refuge in India, the Novjote ceremony has persisted without interruption since their settlement in the region.

Echoes of Survival

As our cousins and others embarked on their journeys abroad for university education, my siblings and I found ourselves drawn to the prospect of pursuing advanced studies overseas as well. Fortunately, our parents embraced this aspiration and generously offered their financial support. Inspired by the example set by my aunt, Katayun, and her husband, Mr. Jamshid Faravahar, who had sent all five of their daughters to the UK, with three of them securing admission to medical Schools, my older sister too, harbored a desire to study in the UK.

However, shortly after her high school graduation, she received a marriage proposal from a distant relative, Mr. Goodarz Goodarz, residing in Tehran. The groom's family visited Kerman, and we hosted a memorable formal engagement party for them in the spring of 1965. Subsequently, in early autumn, we traveled to Tehran and stayed at the groom's parents' residence for the wedding ceremony.

Meanwhile, the following year, my brother Soroush graduated from Kerman's Iranshahr High School and successfully gained acceptance to California Polytechnic at San Luis Obispo. Without delay, he departed for the United States to pursue his studies.

In 1969, I was 17 years old and had completed my 11th grade in high school. I realized that if I had waited for another year to graduate from high school, I might have been barred from leaving the country until I had completed my two years of compulsory military service. Therefore, I decided to try to get a student visa to leave. My father applied for my Iranian passport from Kerman that summer while I was in Tehran, staying at my sister's apartment and trying to secure a visa. My passport was issued along with an exit permit that was for a short duration. I realized I had a short timeframe to secure a visa and make my trip arrangements.[195] Since I had no formal student acceptance from a US-accredited educational institution, I did not try to seek a US visa. My attempt at getting a Canadian visa was not successful. After leaving the Canadian consulate in Tehran, I headed to the British Embassy, consular section and made an application for a visa. The consular office advised me that he could issue me a visa that is short-duration and lasts for several months. He further advised that once I was in the UK and enrolled in a school, I could take an enrollment confirmation letter from the school along with my bank statement to the Home Office to get a student stay extension.

With my passport and visa both secured, I made a quick trip back to Kerman to say goodbye to family and friends and to return to Tehran to launch the next phase of my life, which involved separation from my family, living by myself outside Iran for a prolonged period, and studying in a second language. Within a week, we drove in our family car towards Tehran, stopping in Yazd for two days. I had a chance to say goodbye to my maternal grandmother, my maternal aunt, and my uncles and cousins who lived in Yazd. Then, we were on our way to Tehran. We stayed another night in Isfahan, and the day after, we were heading to Tehran, and

---

195 Thanks to the wise and peaceful policies of the Iranian government, most Western and Southern European countries had waived visa requirements for Iranian passport holders. The exception at the time were Austria, England, Portugal and Switzerland. A few years later, England and Iran agreed to drop visa requirements for passport holders from each other's country. After the Revolution, almost all those countries imposed stiff visa requirements on Islamic Republic passports.

we arrived at my sister's place the same night. The next day, my father and I went looking for an airline ticket for the flight to London. Iran Air[196] had started daily flights to London. All the flights made a stop (Istanbul, Rome, Geneva, Frankfurt, Paris). One of the weekly flights transited through Moscow. We were told flights through all other cities were fully booked for several weeks in advance. The only flight that had vacancies was the flight through Moscow. I got excited about catching aerial views of Moscow on the way to London. At the same time, arrangements had to be made for someone to help on my arrival in London. Having a few cousins living in London was reassuring. I also had an Armenian school friend by the name of Henry Haghlatian, who had been sent to London by his parents to study. He was staying with his sister and brother-in-law, who was studying in London. We wrote to Henry and advised him of my arrival a week later, and asked if he could meet me at the airport on my arrival. The letter was mailed to London.

Five weeks after receiving my passport, my family and I drove to Tehran's Mehrabad International Airport. I was excited to start this adventurous trip that I expected to last for several years. My expectation was that after completing my studies, I would return to Iran and start contributing. Little did I know that trip would turn out to be a one-way departure. The next five years of stay in England, which included three years of studying at University College London, where I got my bachelor's degree in Physics, was followed by a month's stay in Paris. Following that was five years of Ph.D. studies at the University of California Los Angeles. I returned to Iran twice to visit with family and friends, and my parents came to visit me and my siblings twice.

I left Iran with wonderful memories of the place and the people and the sense of possibilities it conveyed. While pursuing my studies in Europe and later in the US, I came across a growing number of Iranian students. In the earlier part of my stay in Europe (early part of the 1970s), most of the Iranian students I came across had been sent overseas by their families who could afford to do so. From 1975 onward, when I came to the US for graduate studies, the number of Iranian students who were receiving financial support from the Iranian government was on the ascent. Besides, many of them enrolled in the Ph.D. programs in Engineering and Science were also getting financial assistance from the universities they were attending. Amongst these groups, some were politically active on university campuses,[197] especially in the US. I kept my distance from them, as I could not find anything appealing in their political narratives or any of their expressed desires for the future of Iran. Many of them came across as being very religious and conservative. I was amazed at those students harboring such dislike of the Shah and the government that had given them full scholarships and financial support for their studies overseas. One question that always came to me was, "Who was financing these

---

196 Iran Air offered a discounted fare to Iranian students who studied abroad.

197 They would usually hoist banners around the Student Union and dining facilities. The message conveyed by the banners were very anti-Shah and anti-Iranian government. They would also hand out fliers filled with anti-Shah propaganda.

activities?" Some of these so-called students seemed to be dedicating a lot of their time and energy to organizing anti-Shah protests.

Within a year of my arrival in the US to undertake my graduate studies at UCLA in Nuclear Physics, my brother Soroosh, who was also working towards a Ph.D. in Mechanical Engineering at UCLA, made a trip back to Iran and got married and returned with his wife, Shirin Zomorrodi.[198] My twin sisters, Armity and Anahita, were sent to the US by my parents to complete high school and pursue higher education. They flew to London in 1972 and visited with me for two weeks before flying off to Los Angeles, where my brother Soroosh was located. In 1976, Armity was courted by a medical doctor, Dariush Shahriari, who studied medicine in Germany and practiced there. She agreed to marry him and moved to West Germany. My youngest sister, Anahita, went to Iran in the summer of 1976 and met her future husband, Mr. Feridon Sioshansi, who was pursuing his Ph.D. studies in Economics at Purdue University in Lafayette, Indiana. They were married, and soon after her return from Iran, she packed up and left for Indiana to join her husband. By 1977, my brother and two younger sisters were gone from Los Angeles. Two of my maternal cousins were in Los Angeles studying engineering, one at UCLA and the other at the University of Southern California. Later on, another cousin was admitted to the engineering Ph.D. program at UCLA and arrived in Los Angeles.

I was working towards my Ph.D. and had plans to return to Iran upon getting my doctorate degree, and, as such, I was not making any career plans in the US post-graduation. Neither was I thinking of buying a residential unit for myself. As I was working on the completion of my Ph.D. thesis in 1978, worrying news from Iran kept coming. Riots were escalating in Tehran. On the campus of UCLA, the revolutionary Iranian students were overly busy staging demonstrations against the Shah and attempting to swing public opinion in favor of the Islamic Revolution. I had no illusion that the event that was about to unfold would have existential consequences for my motherland and for the Zoroastrian community[199] and other minority groups in Iran. Worried about the course of events, I found myself glued to the TV news and reading newspaper coverage of the events in Iran in the print media a lot of the time. I recall at one point reflecting back on my ten years of being away from Iran and the news coverage of Iran I had read in the UK press as well as the US media. I realized almost all the media coverage in the UK was very critical of the Shah and the government of Iran. I had, at times, wondered how the reporters could have missed all the progress being made. At the same

---

[198] She was also admitted to UCLA to pursue her Bachelor Degree in Chemical Engineering. Two years later, Soroosh earned his Ph.D. and, with his wife, moved to Cleveland, Ohio. He had accepted an academic position in engineering at Case Western Reserve.

[199] The years before the revolution, taped messages from an exiled cleric in Iraq by the name of Ayatullah Rouh-ulla Khomeini were being passed amongst the revolutionary Iranian students. An Iranian student with who I shared an office with at UCLA at one point had got hold of one such tapes. He had brought the tape and tape recorder to the office one day, and was playing the message. That was the first time I heard the voice of Khomeini, and one of the first things he said to attack the Shah was that the Shah, while in Bombay, had embraced the fire-worshippers. That was one of his crimes. The reference to fire-worshippers was the Parsis or the Zoroastrians of India. I noticed the impression on the Iranian student's face who was in possession of the tape and who knew I was Zoroastrian was one of shamefulness.

time, there was very little negative coverage of Middle Eastern Arab countries that had questionable human rights records compared to Iran. It appeared to me, and I concluded there was no objectivity in the Western press coverage of the Pahlavi era. Another puzzling point for me was that during the early presidency of Jimmy Carter in the US, on many occasions, when the press asked him about the Shah and the events unfolding in Iran, he would always raise the issue of human rights in Iran. Oddly enough, as soon as the Islamists took over in Iran in 1979 and started executing former officials and disenfranchising the women of Iran and the Bahai minority community, President Carter and his administration made no mention of human rights.[200] Likewise, the Western reporters who had produced overly sensational accounts of the events in Iran, always blaming the Shah's regime and projecting the Moslem mobs as victims, were nowhere to be found once the Islamic regime formed and started their mass killings and depriving the women of Iran of their basic rights. There was never a word of reckoning as to how baseless their prior analysis had been.

I was in regular communication with my parents in Kerman and my sister in Tehran, and I watched with great sadness as my motherland fell from grace and reversed back on its social progress to the Middle Ages.

With the reality of the Islamic regime sinking in and all the societal norms upended, my parents were no longer insistent that we should return to Iran. Although, with their advancing age, the need for family business continuity was ever so evident. My parents had expected that my brother and I would return to Kerman after the completion of our studies, help them run the family business, and relieve them of that heavy burden. Unfortunately, with the onset of the Islamic Revolution, that plan was no longer appealing.

With my Ph.D. studies coming to an end in 1979, within a few months of the establishment of the Islamic Republic, I realized I needed to think of establishing a career in North America. My plan had always been to return to Iran upon the completion of my doctorate studies. But now, with the reality of the Islamic Revolution, that urge was no longer there. I applied for and received an offer of a post-doctoral position at Simon Fraser University in British Columbia, Canada.

For the next three years, I lived in Greater Vancouver, British Columbia. During that period, I married Mehrabnou Zartoshty, who, with her parents and sister, lived in London, England. They had left Iran in view of the Islamic Revolution. Our marriage took place at the Zoroastrian House in London, and a few days later, Mehrbanou and I flew back to Vancouver. Her parents also moved to Vancouver within a year of her move. Our first son, Vishtasp Mehr, was born in Vancouver in December of 1981.

---

[200] Soon after the take-over by the Islamists in Iran, the US embassy was overrun by a revolutionary mob who took 52 US diplomats as hostages for 444 days.

Echoes of Survival

In 1983, we decided to move to the United States[201] for permanent settlement.[202] My career path, starting in academia and ending in the telecommunication sector, involved several relocations for the next thirteen years to Jackson, Mississippi; Ithaca,[203] New York; and Howell, New Jersey. Our second son, Viraf Mehr, was born while we lived in Jackson.[204]

Living in the Greater New York City area put us close to a sizeable Zoroastrian and Iranian diaspora settled in the tri-state areas of New York, Connecticut, and New Jersey. With my sons going through elementary and middle school, we would drive to New Rochelle, New York, the site of the Zoroastrian center of NY, once a month. The purpose was for my sons to attend the religious classes taught by a group of volunteers, mostly Parsis from India.

During my nine years living in New Jersey, we attended three North American Zoroastrian congresses held in Toronto (1988), Vancouver (1992), and Philadelphia (1996).

Finally, in 1996, we made a final move to San Diego, where we settled down.

Southern California at the time had the largest Iranian diaspora outside Iran that has come about as a direct result of the 1979 Islamic Revolution. The largest Iranian Zoroastrian diaspora is also in Southern California. Moving to San Diego brought us physically closer to some of our relatives.[205]

My two sons and seven of their cousins who grew up in North America[206] have all completed their undergraduate studies. Two-thirds of them have completed graduate studies and are professionally active as of the year 2023. Most of them are married and raising families.[207]

In closing this chapter of the family story spanning from the early 18th century down to the 21st century, different thoughts and feelings come to me. This journey of a family through nine generations, starting in Khorasan and ending in the US with a sustained stay in Kerman for much of the 19th and 20th centuries, has been a tale of survival and endurance. It also highlighted the sustained will of each generation to do its best to safeguard its heritage and pass it on to the

---

[201] Having lived in a number of countries, I felt that if the conditions were not right for my family to return to Iran, the preferred place to settle would be the US.

[202] Since my wife's sisters were born in the US and had US citizenship, they were able to sponsor my wife for permanent residency. Her application was approved and the approval was extended to me and our son, Vishtasp Mehr.

[203] During the year I was a visiting assistant professor at Cornell University, I also managed to earn a Master of Engineering in Electrical Engineering. After that, I accepted a position at Bell Laboratories in Central New Jersey.

[204] Viraf was born in San Diego where Mehrbanou's parents lived at the time. We were visiting San Diego from Jackson.

[205] As far as my own siblings are concerned, my older brother and his wife also moved to Southern California from Tucson. He was appointed as the director of the Hydrometeorology program at the University of California, Irvine. My three sisters reside in the San Francisco Bay area.

[206] They have two cousins who live in Germany and Switzerland. Those cousins completed their high school studies in California. One studied medicine in Northern Ireland and is now practicing in Germany. The other did not attend college.

[207] During the COVID-19 pandemic years of 2020-2021, we held several remote video calls with descendants of Soroush Shahriar and Faridun Shahriar Soroushian who are now outside Iran. The attendees were born in Iran during and after WWII and have settled outside Iran mostly due to the 1979 Islamic takeover. Members of the next generations born in the decade of 1970s and beyond were also included. The majority have settled on the west coast of the US. Smaller numbers have settled in the UK and in other regions of the US and Europe.

next generation, make the best of the situation, and prevail. They did not let the limitations imposed on them by external forces define them. At the same time, these stories reveal the struggle for the survival of the remaining Zoroastrians of Iran and what it took to make it through the dark days of prejudice and intolerance imposed on them.

2.9.2 Mehrbanou Mehraban Jamshid Zartoshty
Tehran, 1952

Mehrbanou, the youngest of the three daughters of Paridokht Rostam Mavandad and Mehraban Jamshid Zartoshty, was born in Tehran in 1952.

Her father, Mehraban Jamshid-Kaykhosrow-Khodadad-Bahmard-Hoshang,[208] was born in Yazd city in a priestly Zoroastrian family in the early part of the 20th century[209]. Mehraban was raised mostly by his mother, Farangis[210]. Mehraban's father, Jamshid, had gone to Bombay during the later era of the Qajar dynasty and established an import-export business in Bombay. Jamshid also provided money transfer services to Zoroastrian expatriates working in India who were in need of money to send to their families, mostly in Yazd and Kerman. Jamshid's older son, Faridun, and later his youngest son, Mehraban, took the onerous trip to Bombay to first receive higher education and then join the business he had started. The two brothers succeeded in expanding their father's business considerably.[211]

Mehrbanou's mother, Paridokht, was from a priestly family. Her paternal ancestry goes back nine generations and traces to Mobed Bahram Shah Baghi, who was among the few Zoroastrians who managed to escape from Isfahan in the early 18th century when the last Safavid Ruler, Sultan Hussain ordered the massacre of Zoroastrians in Isfahan.[212] He ran away eastwards and took refuge in the village of TurkAbad close to Yazd.[213]

---

[208] Forenames of Five generations of Mobed Mehraban Zartoshty is appended to his name. They were all practicing Zoroastrian priests.

[209] Excerpts from the "Life Story of Mobed Mehraban-Mobed Jamshid Zartoshty", published in 2004 in Farsi. The book was written by Mr. Jamshid Pishdadi and Printed by Speedy Press Services, Inc. in Simi Valley, California. The source for the book's content was mostly from recollections of Mobed Mehraban Zartoshty.

[210] Well regarded for her wisdom and leadership qualities by her Zoroastrian neighbors and acquaintances, she was affectionately referred to by the title of Usta Farangis. Usta meaning a person who has mastery of her practices. With her husband away for prolonged periods to make a living, she had to raise her three offsprings by herself.

[211] Their reputation for dependability and honesty had resulted in a number of major importers of grains and tea in the Tehran bazar to open standing letters of credit in large amounts for the Zartoshty brothers to source and forward their product needs without delay and as soon as such products became available. During the famine years and WWII years in early 1940s, the demand for grains in Iran was exceedingly high. The brothers were able to meet the need to the extent possible.

[212] The family biographical information for the Mavandad priestly family of Yazd was featured in the Memoires of the Late Mobed Hormuzdyar-Ardeshir Khorshidian produced during his life in the first half of the 20th century.

[213] His grand-daughter named Delbar who was born in TurkAbad married a Zoroastrian priest who had escaped from Khorasan and had fled to TurkAbad. Their grandson, Mobed Mavandad was the one who made the move to Yazd city in the early parts of the 19th century.

Echoes of Survival

His descendants, some five generations later, made the move to Yazd city and took residence within the Zoroastrian priestly section of Yazd Gaber-Mahalla. Paridokht grew up in Yazd and attended the Zoroastrian Markar school for girls, which was amongst the first girls' schools established in Iran in the later years of the Qajar dynasty and provided for secular education.[214]

One year after the end of WWII, Mehraban traveled back to Yazd and married Paridokht. Soon after, they left for Bombay. In 1947, one year after India's independence, the business climate in India had deteriorated. Mehrban and his wife decided to leave India and move to New York City, where he was engaged in export business with Iran and India from the US. The business climate was very promising in the US, and their first two daughters were born in the US. Encouraged by his brother, Mehraban and his family relocated to Iran in 1951 after three years of stay in the US. The family settled in Tehran, the fast-growing capital city of Iran, under the Pahlavis. Tehran was becoming a major metropolitan city in the Middle East and a magnet for Iranians from the provinces. Their third daughter was born in Tehran within a year of their arrival and was named Mehrbanou in honor of her maternal grandmother.

The decades of 1950 through 1970s were exciting times in Iran. Amongst the Zoroastrians and other Iranians, there was a tacit desire for their youth to be sent to Western countries for higher education. Mehrbanou grew up in Tehran surrounded by her cousins, uncles, and aunts' families who had moved to Tehran from Yazd. In her early years, she was also around her paternal grandmother, Usta Farangis, and her maternal grandfather, Rostam Mavandad, both of whom had relocated from Yazd to Tehran to be close to their children who had moved to Tehran. Mehrbanou and her family also made a short visit to Yazd, mostly because of her father's attachment to Yazd. Besides that, the environment in which she was growing up in Tehran was conducive to the embracement of the good tidings of life and the modernity that Pahlavi Iran provided.[215] Along with her sisters and cousins, Mehrbanou attended Tehran's Zoroastrian schools for girls, the Guive Elementary and Anoushiravan Dadgar High School. After completing her high school studies, Mehrbanou took the test for the students planning to go overseas to study and passed the tests.[216] She was eager to come to the United States to attend

---

[214] Secular education for girls as well as for boys was forbidden in Iran due to the influence of the Islamic priests. Maneckji Hataria who had arrived in Iran in the second half of the 19th century engaged in intense lobbying with king, Nasser-ul-Dinshah Qajar on behalf of the Zoroastrians of Iran. He was able to get royal permission from the king for the establishment of a number of schools in Kerman, Yazd cities and villages. Those schools had limited size and scoop. It was towards the end of the Qajar period and during the reign of the Pahlavis that schools providing secular education were established throughout Iran by the central government. The Zoroastrian schools were funded by Zoroastrian benefactors from India as well as well off Zoroastrian merchants in Iran. The funding for the establishment of the Markar school came from the famed Parsi Philanthropist, Peshotan Markar.

[215] For most Iranians growing up in Tehran in 1950-1960s felt like a new beginning, without constant reminders of the past limitations that growing up in the ancestral cities would have imposed on them.

[216] The decades of 1960 and 1970 under the progressive rule of the Pahlavis witnessed a noteable number of Iranian students attending universities in the US and Europe, studying in various fields of engineering, science and humanities.

college and was admitted to Ohio State University, where she completed her undergraduate studies.

In the mid-1970s, Mehrbanou, having completed her university studies, returned to Iran along with her older sister, Homa, to the delight of their parents and family. In view of the booming Iranian economy and the opening of opportunities in civil construction and design, Mehrbanou was able to find jobs in Tehran that were in line with her college training. For the second half of the 1970s, she was actively working in Iran. She was also active in Zoroastrian Women's Organizations in Tehran. As the year 1979 approached and the Islamic Revolution started to gain steam, she decided to leave Iran for London, where her sister, Vida, and her family had moved. Her older sister had also left for the US. Soon after the takeover by the Islamists in Iran and the security conditions in Tehran and the rest of the country deteriorating, Mehrbanou's parents managed to leave Iran[217] for the last time and joined their two daughters in London.

It was within a year of departing from Iran that Mehrbanou met Mehrborzin Soroushian in London. They had family acquaintances from earlier times in Iran. The two decided to get married. At the time, her future husband resided in Vancouver, Canada. In August of 1980, they were married at the Zoroastrian House in London and moved to Canada. Her parents followed her to Vancouver within a year. In December of 1981, Mehrbanou gave birth to their first son, Vishtasp Mehr. Two years later, the young family moved to the United States. Their second son, Viraf Mehr, was born in August of 1984 in San Diego. After several relocations in the US, including a nine-year stay in New Jersey, the family relocated to San Diego, California, in 1996 to be close to the rest of the family who had relocated to Southern California. Mehrbanou's parents also moved to San Diego from Vancouver to live out the remaining years of their lives. At this time, Mehrbanou and her husband, Mehrborzin, have lived in San Diego for more years than in any other location. She has maintained a busy professional life in tax accounting. Their two sons have completed graduate studies and established their own lives.

---

[217] Under Mohamed Reza Pahlavi, visa restrictions for Iranian citizen to most countries in Europe and elsewhere had been lifted. Iranians could enter countries such as the UK without a visa. Visa restriction was imposed on Islamic Iranian passport holders within a short period after establishment of the Islamic Republic. At this time, the Islamic Iranian passport bearers require to obtain visa for most countries.

Figure 37: 1956, Kerman: Mehrborzin (1st from right) standing next to his father at a reception for a group of Parsis visiting from India.

Figure 38: 1956, Tehran: Mehrbanou standing in front of her mother with the rest of her family posing for a family portrait.

Figure 39: 1963, Kerman: Iranshahr School Boy Scout Troops at the Main Kerman Stadium

Figure 40: February 1964, Kerman: Birth Day celebration for Mehrborzin and his sisters, Armity and Anahita, at home with Cousins, Aunts, Uncles, and friends

Figure 41: 1980, London, UK: Wedding Ceremony of Mehrbanou and Mehrborzin at the Zoroastrian House in London

Figure 42: September 1992, Vancouver, Canada: NovJote[218] Ceremony of Vishtasp (left) and Viraf (right) sited with their parents Mehrborzin and Mehrbanou

---

[218] Initiation ceremony for the Zoroastrian youth, once they reach the age of maturity

Chapter 3
Other Descendancies of Khodabux Shahriar Jamshid

In the late 19th century and throughout the 20th century, conditions for Zoroastrians in Iran, along with other Iranians, witnessed significant improvements due to various factors.[219] These enhancements became notably tangible with the emergence of the Pahlavi Dynasty in the 1920s, creating an environment ripe for individuals and families to realize their full potential and contribute to the development of a modern nation.

In the preceding chapter, the lineage through the eldest son of Khodabux Shahriar was traced. In this chapter, we delve into the life stories of several other offspring of Khodabux Shahriar-Jamshid:

The narrative begins with the descent of Esfandiyar Khodabux, the second child of Khodabux Shahriar.

1. Following that, we explore the story of a descendant of Daulat Khodabux (Shahriari) and his spouse, a descendant of Shahriar Khodabux. Their pioneering life journeys, particularly in pursuing education overseas in the 20th century, are highlighted.

2. Subsequently, we recount the achievements of a descendant of Khodamorad Khodabux, emphasizing their professional accomplishments.

3. The tale of a descendant of Sultan Khodabux and his spouse, a descendant of Shahriar Khodabux, is presented next, focusing on the pioneering aspects of their life journeys.

4. Lastly, we delve into the life stories of two sons of Kaykhosrow Khodabux, who migrated to the United States in the early 20th century.

Most of these narratives have been generously provided by descendants of the individuals in question.

3.1 Esfandiyar Khodabux Shahriar and Sultan Khosrow Hormuzdyar
3.1.1 Esfandiyar Khodabux Shahriar Jamshid
1858-1910, Kerman

Esfandiyar, born a year after his eldest brother Shahriar, was the second child of Khodabux and Katayun. Tragically, he lost his father while still in his teenage years, leaving him, along with his siblings and mother, to shoulder the responsibility of earning a livelihood from a tender age.

While his elder brother managed the business dealings between Kerman City and the surrounding villages, procuring produce for sale in Kerman's markets, Esfandiyar assisted with

---

[219] Establishment of rule of law, increased security, improved health care, establishment of schools and universities focused on secular education, and embrace of modernity.

the urban operations. He often accompanied Shahriar on trips to the countryside, and when at home, he contributed to caring for his six younger siblings and toiled on the farms outside the city to supplement the family income.

Esfandiyar's dedication, competence, and integrity caught the attention of the governor of Kerman, Farmanfarmayan, who entrusted him with the management of the Qajar farm holdings near the village of Qanat Qasan. Over time, Esfandiyar acquired ownership stakes in some of these properties, partly through payments and partly as compensation for his services. These landholdings formed a significant part of Esfandiyar's legacy, passed down to his surviving children.

Esfandiyar and his wife, Sultan, were blessed with six sons and two daughters: Mehraban, Darab, Iranbanu, Khosrow, Sohrab, Khodabux, Daulat, and Rustom. Tragically, their two eldest sons, Mehraban and Darab, succumbed to epidemics at a young age. Darab, engaged in trade with Bombay from the port of Bandar Abbas, lost his life in the course of his business dealings. Meanwhile, Sohrab and Khosrow were involved in commerce in Kerman and Tehran, respectively. Khodabux ventured to Bombay in pursuit of business opportunities but later returned to Kerman when his endeavors there proved unfruitful. Their youngest son, Rustom, fell victim to a kidnapping at the age of six. Remarkably, four decades later, he was reunited briefly with his family in Kerman and Tehran.

The two daughters, Iranbanu and Daulat, married and raised families of their own.

3.1.2 Sultan Khosrow Hormuzdyar
1865 – 1929, Kerman

Sultan Khosrow's parents were Zoroastrian farmers residing on the outskirts of Kerman city. Esfandiyar's father, Khodabux, had initially met them during his business ventures in their village, and their families maintained a connection over time. Esfandiyar and Sultan crossed paths during their youth, and when the time came for Esfandiyar to wed, Sultan became his chosen partner. Sultan was a steadfast, hardworking wife devoted to nurturing her children. Her upbringing instilled strong Zoroastrian traditions in her, which she imparted to her offspring. With her husband frequently absent due to business, Sultan bore the responsibility of caring for their expanding family.

The kidnapping of her youngest son, Rustom, at the age of six in 1911 dealt a devastating blow to the Sultan. Additionally, she endured the loss of her husband and eldest son, Mehraban (Hormuzdyar), to poisoning and her son Darab's passing from malaria in Bandar Abbas. Her eldest daughter, Iranbanu, stepped in to assist in caring for her younger siblings while the extended family rallied around them following Esfandiyar's passing.

Years later, Rustom, who had been kidnapped, miraculously reconnected with the family. Despite being only six years old at the time of his abduction, he retained memories of his Kermani origins and his mother's name. Much had changed in Iran during his absence. In 1924, Reza Shah Pahlavi ascended to the throne, reasserting central control over the Southwestern Province of Khuzestan and abolishing slavery in the region. As part of a broader initiative, Iranians were required to adopt surnames and obtain birth certificates for the first time. While the family in Kerman had adopted the surname Soroushian (Sorooshian), Rustom, unaware of his familial ties, chose the surname Sultani during his time in Khuzestan.

Esfandiyar Khodabux Shahriar Jamshid *Sultan Khosrow Hormuzdyar*

1856– 1910 (Kerman)   1865 – 1959 (Kerman)

Mehraban[220]
1884-1910
(Kerman –
Bandar Abbas)

Darab[221]
1888-1915
(Kerman –
Bandar Abbas)

IranBanu
1892-1981
Kerman

Khosrow
1893-1972
(Kerman-
Tehran)

Sohrab
1895-1955
Kerman

Khodabux
1901-1942
Kerman

Daulat
1903-1979
Kerman-Tehran

Rustom
1905-1954
Kerman-Tehran

Photo 44: 1907, Kerman: First and the second from Right are Sohrab Esfandiyar, and Darab Esfandiyar

---

[220] The other name associated with him is Hormuzdyar. Mehraban was three years old when his paternal uncle, Hormuzdyar suffered a premature death. To keep his name alive, Esfandiyar changed his son's first name to Hormuzdyar to keep his brother's memory alive. Changing first name in views of events such as this one was fairly common until 1925 when births had to registered with the central government and birth certificates were issued.

[221] Darab died in Bandar Abbas, a victim of Malaria

Figure 43: 1935, Kerman: Arastu (standing behind his parents). Hamayun & Khosrow Soroushian (holding their second daughter, PouranDokht Sitting in the Front row: Parvin and her brother Aflatoon.

Figure 44: 1941, Tehran: From left: Khosrow Esfandiyar and Rustom Esfandiyar

Mehrborzin Jamshid Soroushian

3.2 Mahindokht Soroush Soroushian and Manutchehr Dinyar Shahriari [222]
3.2.1 Mahindokht Soroush-Shahriar Soroushian
1927 – 1983 (Kerman, Vancouver-Canada)

Mahindokht, the youngest among six siblings born to Soroush Shahriar Soroushian and IranBanu Esfandiar Soroushian, grew up in a tightly knit family environment, surrounded by her parents, four brothers, elder sister Katayun, cousins, and other relatives. At the age of 13, the loss of her father was a profound shock. She also witnessed the harsh conditions endured by the citizens of Kerman during World War II, exacerbated by famine and epidemics resulting from the Allied forces' occupation of Iran and the influx of refugees to Kerman. Her older brother, Jamshid, nearly succumbed to the imported diseases.

Mahindokht received her primary education at Kerman's Zoroastrian school for girls.[223] The conclusion of World War II heralded a wave of optimism. At the age of 22, Mahindokht expressed a keen interest in pursuing further studies in Europe. Encouraged by her family, she embarked on a significant journey to London to pursue studies in home economics and nursing—a milestone as it marked her first venture beyond Iran's borders. To facilitate her transition, the family sought the assistance of Mr. Khodadad Mehrabi,[224] a prominent Zoroastrian figure from Kerman who had established himself in London, where he ran a successful retail rug business for many years. Mahindokht's solo journey abroad made her the first female member of her family to undertake such a venture.

Her voyage to England commenced from the Persian Gulf port of Bandar Shahpur aboard a commercial ship, following the acquisition of her visa from the British Consulate in Kerman, accompanied by her brother Esfandiyar and a British nun returning to England. Mahindokht exhibited determination in overcoming obstacles and establishing herself in her new surroundings. Over time, she aided her young nieces from Kerman in settling in London, facilitating their transition, along with other Zoroastrian female acquaintances.[225]

During her stay in London, Mahindokht witnessed the great smog of London, became sick, and was admitted to a hospital. Back in Kerman, her family was worried about her condition. Her brother Parviz was to go to London to check on her sister. While in Tehran making trip arrangements, Parviz received word that she was in recovery.

---

[222] This narrative was produced by Mahdokht Shahriari, the sole daughter of Mahindokht and Manutchehr.

[223] The Shahriari school stands as the oldest educational institution for girls established in Kerman. Situated in the heart of the Zoroastrian quarter, which emerged as the primary residential area for Zoroastrians by the late 19th century, its campus holds historical significance. The construction of the school building was made possible through the generous donations of the late Shahriar Khodabux Tafti's two sons in the latter part of the 19th century. In homage to their father, the school was aptly named Shahriari.

[224] Mr. Mehrabi hailed from the esteemed Farvahar family of Kerman and had served in the Southern Persian Rifles force stationed in southern Iran in the aftermath of World War I.

[225] Miss Kiandokht Kaikhsrow Kianian, a neighbor of Mahindokht in Kerman, later relocated to London a few years after Mahindokht and received assistance there.

It was in Europe that she met her future husband, Manutchehr Shahriari, who also hailed from the Zoroastrian community of Kerman and was studying medicine in West Germany at the time. Within a few years, they were married, and Mahindokht moved to Gottingen, Germany, where their daughter, Mahdokht, was born in 1959. A few years later, Mahindokht and her young daughter returned to Kerman.

In Kerman, Mahindokht engaged in active management of the agricultural lands she had inherited from her parents. She proved to be very efficacious and gained recognition for being as effective as her male peers.

She also got involved with the Women's Organization in Kerman and represented the Kermani chapter at a national meet in Tehran. Following her, a few other women of the family got involved with the national organization to represent the women of Kerman.

Once her daughter had completed high school, she was sent to Switzerland and the US for undergraduate studies.

Following the 1979 Islamic Revolution in Iran, Mahindokht and her husband moved to the US and finally settled in Vancouver, Canada.

While living in North America, Mahindokht made several trips to Iran. On her last trip, happening in the wake of her mother's passage in Kerman, Mahindokht asked her daughter, Mahdokht, what memorabilia she desired from her grandmother. Mahdokht asked for her grandmother's prayer book, which she would recite every evening, and she received it.

Mahindokht was diagnosed with fast-advancing cancer and finally succumbed to it in 1983. Her remains were buried in the Zoroastrian cemetery of British Columbia. Mahindokht loved the Iris flower. For a number of years, every spring, when her daughter goes to her mother's grave, a wild Iris blooms next to her stone. It is the only wild Iris in that section of the cemetery.

3.2.2 Manutchehr Dinyar-Bahram Shahriari
1929-2022 (Kerman, Vancouver-Canada)

Manutchehr was the oldest of 6 children born to Dinyar Bahram and Tabandeh Darab. He was born in Kerman in 1929.

Manuchehr's paternal great-grandfather, Shahriar, arrived in Kerman from Yazd in the 19th century and settled in Kerman. Very likely, he was descended from the Zoroastrians of Khorasan who had to flee and take refuge in Yazd during the 18th century. As with most of the Khorsani Zoroastrians of the 18th century, they possessed wealth. In Kerman, he married a Zoroastrian girl, Daulat Khodabux, and sired three sons, the oldest of whom was named Bahram (1878-1907).

At age 14, despite his father's desire for him to help with his farmland, Bahram was intent on going to Shiraz to study literature and history. That move was very uncommon for a person of his age, and considering all the risks he was exposed to due to his minority status as a Zoroastrian. He managed to hide his identity and, undertook the journey and returned safely to Kerman 4 years later.

The conditions were still difficult for religious minorities in Kerman, and upon returning, he found that his family was in a dispute over their farmland. The young Bahram decided to take the matter into his own hands, wrote a letter of grievance to the governor Farmanfarma, and tried to deliver it himself. Bahram was denied admission to the governor's mansion but was reassured his letter would be delivered.

When the governor read the letter, he was impressed with the literary composition of the complaint and summoned Bahram. He tested Bahram's knowledge and concluded the letter was indeed written by Bahram. The governor bestowed the title of Mirza[226] on Bahram and ruled in his favor. He was the first Zoroastrian to be given that title by that governor. The fact the governor was siding with a Zoroastrian in dispute with Moslems was also a novel phenomenon.

Mirza Bahram also managed to get a store and storage space in the Kerman Bazar to conduct business.

Mirza Bahram was a humanitarian. Through the end of his short life, he delivered flour and other food items to needy Kermani families. He carried out his care package deliveries at night and conspicuously. It was only after his death that his benefactors came to know his identity. Mirza Bahram died prematurely at the age of 29 and left behind his wife and three young sons, Shahriar, aged 7, Dinyar, aged four, and Soroush, aged 2. The three brothers grew up in the care of the larger family.

In the decade of 1920s, when Reza Shah ascended to the throne and mandated that all Iranians must adopt a last name and obtain government-issued birth certificates (all for the first time), the older son, Shahriar (1898-1950), adopted the last name of Shahriari. The rest of the family followed suit. Even some of the non-Zoroastrians who worked for the family adopted the last name of Shahriari-Panah. Shahriar married Gohar Faridun-Khodamorad-Khodabux. They sired four children: their first son, Siross, followed by their first daughter, Irandokht; their second daughter, Tooran; and their youngest son, Shahrokh.

Dinyar (1903-1980), like his father, Mirza Bahram, was interested in Persian literature and comparative religious studies. He was a dedicated Zoroastrian and felt it was our moral calling to keep our religion alive. Dinyar had studied the Avesta and knew the Shahnameh by heart. He had analyzed the poetry of the Shahnameh, Rumi, Hafiz, and Sadie. Dinyar was also fluent in Arabic and had a good understanding of the Quran. His knowledge of the Quran was so thorough that even the Imam Jumeh of Kerman (Moslem prayer leader) would often call on him to ask Quarn-related questions. He also had knowledge of the bible.

Dinyar received his basic education at the Zoroastrian School for Boys in Kerman and then attended the British Missionary school in Kerman, where he learned English. The school officials saw much potential in him and encouraged him to go to England for higher education. Dinyar decided to stay and married Tabandeh Darab Shahriari.

Dinyar became active in agriculture, and from his inheritance, he bought a big parcel of fertile land in the North Western suburb of Kerman City. An underground irrigation system (Qanat) was dug to bring in water from a mountainous basin to the village that he named Ferdows[227]. Once irrigation water was secured, the land was cultivated. Fruit orchards and

---

[226] Literally meaning a scholar.

[227] The name was chosen in honor of the national poet of Iran, Ferdowsi

pistachio gardens were developed, and other crops, such as saffron, were grown. In a few years, Ferdows became a productive agricultural village.

Besides managing his farms and attending to his family, Dinyar spent time reading literary books. He understood the importance of education and paid for the medical school expenses of a relative at Tehran University and in Germany. Besides, he sent his son, Manutchehr, and his youngest daughter, Iranbanoo, to study in Germany, something the progressive Pahlavi dynasty of Iran facilitated. Dinyar died in Kerman around the time of the Islamic Revolution.

Dinyar and Tabandeh had six children, the oldest of whom was Manutchehr (1929 -2022), followed by four sisters and a young son, Bahram, who died of sickness at a young age and was buried at the Tehran Zoroastrian cemetery of Qasar-Firozeh.

Dinyar's son Manutchehr grew up in Kerman and attended the Zoroastrian schools for boys.

Manutchehr had a happy childhood. He attended the Zoroastrian schools in Kerman and pursued his passion for music by learning to play the Tar[228] professionally.

By that time, conditions were improving for the Zoroastrians of Kerman and Iran. Manutchehr was active in sports and mountain climbing.

As he was reaching the age of 18, his father started mentoring him on attending to the farms and bought him a motorcycle for him to travel to Ferdows.

After high school graduation, his father encouraged him to go to America and study medicine. Dinyar told Manutchehr that America is a new land with unlimited opportunities. Manutchehr, though, decided to go to Germany as few of his friends had already gone there to study. In the year that he was waiting for his travel documents to be completed, he attended English language classes associated with Tehran University.

As soon as his visa was ready, he took a flight to Germany in late 1951. WWII had ended. He arrived late at night, did not speak a word of German, and did not know where to go. He remembers as he walked away from the airport, a US tank stopped in front of him, and an American soldier emerged and asked him if he needed help. At that point, Manutchehr was so happy to have learned English in Tehran. He explained his situation to the American soldier, who helped him find a place to stay for the night.

From there, he contacted his friends, enrolled in a German language school, and, after a while, started his studies at the prestigious medical school in Gottingen.

His first Anatomy lab session brought back the memories of Kerman when he helped skin dead sheep. He had done that many times in Kerman. So when the professor in the anatomy lab asked the students to carve a human corpse and remove the skin, Manutchehr just got to it while the other students were struggling.

The professor looked at him in disbelief. That was enough for Manutchehr to decide medical school was the right choice for him.

---

[228] A popular string musical instrument of Iran

Mehrborzin Jamshid Soroushian

While still in medical school, he met and married Mahindokht Soroushian, and their only daughter, Mahdokht, was born in 1959 in Gottingen. In fact, after their daughter was born, Manutcher changed his specialty from internal medicine to pediatrics.

He continued in medical school and finished at the top rank of his medical class, only second to a German who was one of his best friends. No other foreign students in that university had ever achieved that level of accomplishment.

The word of his accomplishment had been sent to the Iranian embassy in Cologne, West Germany. The ambassador extended an invitation to Manutcher and Mahindokht as guests of honor and offered him a monetary prize for this achievement. His name appeared in some Iranian newspapers.

After finishing his studies, Manutcher worked as a pediatrician in a hospital in Hanover, Germany, and ran a practice with another doctor. He was given an honorary residency in Germany to enable him to stay and work in Germany.

His father, Dinyar, was getting old and asked him to go back to Iran. Manutcher agreed, and in 1966, after fourteen years of living and working in Germany, he went back to Iran. The opportunities for all Iranians based on merits had blossomed under the Pahlavis.

In Tehran, he was offered the position of head of pediatrics at the Air Force Hospital, which he accepted, though he had never enlisted in the military. He also started his own practice.

Two years later, his father had a stroke, and Manutcher and his family moved to Kerman. In Kerman, he became the head of pediatrics at the biggest hospital in Kerman and started his own busy practice as well. He also started looking after his father's pistachio farms.

He was a dedicated doctor with a deep sense of devotion to his patients. The sickest of children were brought to his practice from all parts of Kerman and Yazd. He spent countless hours attending to his patients and helping those who could not afford their medical care. He would not charge them and, in some cases, would call the Pharmacy ahead of time and ask them to charge him for the medications and not the patient.

He was the chosen pediatrician to the dignitaries in Kerman, as well as the less privileged. He did his best for all. To date, there are people who still remember how he saved the life of a brother, sister, or child.

His daughter says that Manutcher's loyalty and dedication towards family, friends, and patients were among his highest attributes. He was there when people needed him.

Manutcher and Mahindokht eventually moved to the US, where their daughter was attending university. They later moved to Canada as a family. Mahindokht and Manutchehr traveled back and forth between Canada and Iran. Eventually, Manutcher moved to Vancouver permanently, where his daughter and her family lived.

After the death of his first wife Mahindokht, Manutcher married Mehrnaz Khosravi-Kermani in 1990. Mehrnaz joined him in Vancouver. She passed away in North Vancouver in December 2014. Manutcher passed away in North Vancouver at the age of 92. He is buried at the Zoroastrian cemetery of British Columbia, where both of his wives are buried as well.

Figure 45: 1938, Kerman: Standing from Left, Hormuzd, Mahindokht, Katayun Seated in the front is their grandmother, Banu Gushtasp Dinyar, and Katayun's firstborn daughter, IranBanu

Figure 46: 1945, Kerman: Manuchehr Dinyar Shahriari

Figure 47: 1951, London: Front row (L to R) Mrs. Mehrabi, Kiandokht Kianian, Mahindokht Soroushian. Back row (L-R) Mr. Khodadad Mehrabi, IranBanu Jamshid Fravahar

Figure 48: 1957, Germany: Mahindokht and Manutcher

3.3 Tooran Shahriar Shahriari and Bahram Bahman Bahrami [229]
3.3.1 Tooran Shahriar Bahman Shahriari
1931-2024 (Kerman, Tehran)

Tooran Shahriari was born in Kerman in 1931 into a well-known and respected Zoroastrian family. Her grandfather, Mirza Bahram, was a big landowner, an anomaly for his time. Not only the extent of his land ownership was uncommon for religious minorities, but more importantly, the respect paid him by Muslims and Zoroastrians alike was highly unusual. He was well known for his benevolence, which extended to both groups.

Tooran's father, Shahriar, was a landowner like his father, while her mother, Gohar, was a homemaker. Tooran had two older siblings, Siroos (the Persian pronunciation of Cyrus) and Iran, and a younger brother, Shahrokh.

Within the family, there was always respect for books, history, and literature. Her father, Shahriar, enjoyed reading books and was known for his amazing memory, whereby he could recite long poems by heart and also talk about historical events with fluency and ease. Her mother, Gohar, was fascinated by world and national events and would follow up on national news on the radio. Like her father, Tooran was an avid book reader, and like her mother, she followed the news with passion.

The 1940s and the 1950s were tumultuous years in Iran, both politically and socially. Nationalism and women's rights were on the rise, notions that appealed to Tooran.

Belonging to a landowning class, her family - unlike many others who migrated to Tehran and took advantage of the newfound opportunities offered by the social changes taking place - remained in Kerman.

However, Tooran wanted to be a part of the change. She was determined to make her mark and to be her own person.

At her insistence and against her father's misgivings, but with the support of her mother, she moved to Tehran, where she boarded at a well-known girls' boarding school run by the Bahadin sisters.

Passionate about social justice, she applied and was accepted to study Law at the University of Tehran.

Out of the total 120 law students in her year, the percentage of female students was 10% or 12 in total number. Tooran was one of the 12.

In the midst of her undergraduate studies, she met her husband, Bahram Bahrami, and married him in December 1953. Together, they had three daughters, Homa, Mitra, and Vida.

---

[229] This life journey of Tooran and Bahram Bahrami narrative was produced by their youngest daughter, Vida Bahrami Keyani

Tooran graduated from law school in 1955, passed the bar exam in 1963, and obtained her Masters in Criminal Law in 1968.

While completing her studies, she also worked at the Ministry of Labor, first as a legal advisor on issues related to working women and children (1955-57), then headed that same bureau from 1957 to 1970, and later became a chief labor specialist and arbitrator in that same ministry from 1970 to 1982.

She was also an active member of many organizations, namely the International Literary Association or "Anjoman-e-Ghalam," the Zoroastrian Women's Association of Tehran, the Zoroastrian Association of Tehran, and the Iranian Lawyers' Association.

Blessed with a poetic frame of mind, she has also published four books of poetry, covering such varied themes as social justice, Zoroastrianism, and nationalism, amongst others.

Her books of poetry are entitled Gohar, Negar-e-Zan, Divan-e-Tooran, and Mehr-e-Iran, respectively, published in 1966, 1973, 2000, and 2012.

Also, for many years, she was a sought-after and well-respected speaker within the Zoroastrian community as well as the larger Iranian community.

Today, many women are to be found in the highest and most accomplished of positions, and we owe a debt of gratitude to those brave women who paved the way.

Tooran was one such pioneer and trailblazer. She was the first Zoroastrian woman to attend law school in Iran, the first to pass her bar exam in Iran, and the first Non-Muslim to become an elected board member of Iran's Central Bar Association. She was also the fifth Iranian woman to pass her bar exam in Iran.

The social changes that impacted Iranian society during the Pahlavi era certainly allowed Tooran to achieve all that she did. However, had those changes not happened, it's still possible that Tooran would have written her poems and possibly even published them in book form. In that case, and without the Pahlavi era social changes, she might still have become a known poet, maybe even the Zoroastrian's very own Emily Elizabeth Dickinson.

3.3.2 ShahBahram Bahman Bahrami
1921-2013 (Kerman, Tehran)

Bahram Bahrami (Bahram-Bahman-Bahram-Behruz-Eskandar-Goshtasp-Bahman) was born in Kerman in 1921, the oldest child of the family. He had four younger sisters, Faranguiss, Nahid, Parvin, and Berdjis.

His mother, Sarvar, like most women of her time, was a homemaker, and his father, Bahman, was an accountant but came from a long line of well-known astrologers.

According to legend, one of Bahram's astrologer ancestors, most likely Goshtasp-e-Bahman, correctly foretold the victory of Mohamad Khan Qajar over Lotf-Ali-Khan of the Zand dynasty in 1794, and for that correct prediction, the Zoroastrian men were spared the brutal revenge of eye gouging by the Qajar forces, a lot that befell most other Kermani men, for the crime of having sided and given refuge to Lotf-Ali Khan.

Echoes of Survival

Bahman, Bahram's father, was a hardworking and honest individual. His city of birth, Kerman, was well known for its handmade rugs and attracted many non-local merchants and traders. One such individual was a merchant from the city of Tabriz, Mehdi Dilmaghani, who came to Kerman in the 1920s and established his own carpet production and sourcing company there. Looking for an experienced and trustworthy accountant/second in command and learning of Bahman's good character, capabilities, and honesty, he soon offered Bahman the job. As a result of his new post, Bahman met many visiting notables, as well as domestic and foreign merchants, some of whom engaged in sourcing carpets for export to Europe and the US.

It was through such contacts that Bahman began to better appreciate the social changes that were taking place within the larger Iranian society, amongst them the emerging importance of higher education. For that, amongst other reasons, the Bahrami family moved to Tehran, where the best educational institutions and the only national university, namely the University of Tehran, could be found.

Bahram moved to Tehran around the age of 16 and attended the Dar-ul-Funun school, the oldest Western-style institute of higher education, established in 1851 by the royal vizier Amir Kabir. Upon completing his high school education, he was admitted into the Pharmacy department at the University of Tehran, but not feeling excited by the job prospects that such an education would offer, he left the university during his second year and embarked upon his burgeoning business interests.

During his 20s, he tried his hand at various jobs, amongst them becoming a distributor of sugar and sugar cubes in Tehran. Of such importance were these two items for the Iranian economy during the 1920s well into the 1940s that the tax money accrued from their sale (as well as the sale of tea) provided most of the funding for the construction of the North-South Trans-Iranian railway, which was started in 1927 and was completed in 1938. This construction was a major feat by Reza Shah Pahlavi, for unlike other regional national railroads, the Iranian railway system was fully funded by indigenous capital.

After that, encouraged by Mr. Dilmaghani, Bahram opened his own carpet stall in the capital city's main bazaar. That experience lasted a few years until he found his true passion, namely construction and architecture.

Bahram took some classes in architectural drawing and design. The first project that he worked on was a beautiful combination of two sets of buildings, with the two sides separated from each other by a pool, flower gardens, shrubs, and fruit trees.

Upon the completion of that first construction, friends and family members, realizing Bahram's architectural talent, attention to detail, amazing work ethic, honesty, and kind, approachable, and generous personality, started trusting him with their own housing needs, and it was thus that Bahram's flourishing construction business started.

He married his wife of almost 60 years, Tooran Shahriari in 1953, and the result of that marriage was three daughters, Homa, Mitra, and Vida. All three were sent to England around the age of 15 in order to pursue their education. All three finished their university studies in England, after which they all moved to California.

Bahram's story is not unique, for many such successes and stories may be encountered as a result of the social and economic changes that the Iranian society was going through at the time. Reza Shah, the founder of the Pahlavi dynasty, through his many social, economic, and political reforms, helped lay the foundation of the modern Iranian state. Religious minorities, who until then had limited prospects for growth and felt more secure living amongst their own, mainly in the provincial towns of Kerman and Yazd, were quick to take advantage of the changes and, with a newfound sense of hope and liberation, began migrating to Tehran.

The genie was truly out of the box, and those with ingenuity and a willingness to work hard now found ample opportunities to prove themselves and create a good life for themselves and their families.

Thus, when Bahram arrived in Tehran, the capital city seemed like a most welcoming place. From the 1880s to the 1940s, the country experienced many changes, namely an end to the Jizya tax - a poll tax levied on religious minorities, and the establishment of a national parliament in 1906, where religious minorities were also granted the right of representation.

By 1940, the Zoroastrians had their own schools, their own temple, and their own Zoroastrian association, "Anjoman-e Zartoshtian-e Tehran," which was in charge of taking care of the needs of the burgeoning Zoroastrian community residing in Tehran. That sense of communal support must have made Bahram and Bahram's generation's move to Tehran not only easier but also more productive.

Though Bahram's story might not be unique for his time, it is still worth mentioning that his success proved a valuable lesson to others within the family and also amongst friends who were encouraged by his achievements and decided to migrate to Tehran.

It was on the basis of this most important of migrations, its lessons in communal organization, and the individual successes it produced that a subsequent and younger generation was ready, willing, and better prepared to take the process one step further and repeat it in countries other than their own, in the hope of a better life for themselves and their children.

Figure 49: 1934, Kerman: Tooran seated in the front (right side) for a family photo

Figure 50:1957, Tehran: Tooran (seated first from left) with her first daughter, Homa, husband, Bahram mother, Gohar, and her two brothers, Siross and Shahrokh.

Figure 51: 1961 Tehran, Family photo taken in their home garden in Tehran, Bahram (holding Vida), Tooran (holding Mitra) and Homa are standing.

3.4 Banu Faridun-Shahriar Soroushian and Mehraban Kaykhosrow Rustom Hormozdi[230]

3.4.1 Banu Faridun-Shahriar Soroushian
1919 – 1998 (Kerman – Tehran)

Banu, the second child of Faridun Shahriar Khodabux and GoharBanou Dinyar Klantar was born in Kerman in the year 1919. Along with her four brothers, a younger sister and their parents, she grew up in a closely knit household surrounded by her cousins and other family.

Banu attended the Zoroastrian girl school of Kerman. At the age of 13, her parents sent her to the American Boarding School for Girls in Tehran, a pioneering institution permitted to operate in Iran. Named Iran-Beatel, the school, with its secular education program modeled on the American system, catered to girls from diverse religious backgrounds.[231] The progressive Pahlavi dynasty made it possible for institutions dedicated to the education of Iranian girls of all persuasions to operate in Iran. The school's secular education program was modeled on the American educational system. While originally intended for Christian and diplomatic families, it also attracted upper-class Iranians and members of the Qajar clan, providing Banu with an opportunity to forge friendships with daughters of prominent Iranian families. Attendance at this school was a new experience for Banu, and it offered her an opportunity to make friends with daughters from other prominent Iranian families.

Upon completing her studies and before returning to Kerman in 1940. Banu met Dr. Mehraban Hormozdi at a mutual acquaintance's house. Dr. Hormozdi, having recently returned to Iran from England, where he obtained a Ph.D. in Engineering, formed a close bond with Banu, leading to their marriage.[232] The couple enjoyed a long-lasting union and were blessed with four daughters: Homa, Mahshid, Mitra, and Mina.

With her husband working at the National Iranian Oil Company (NIOC), the family lived in the Western Province of Kermanshah for eight years, and that is where some of her children were born. Finally, her husband's job was transferred to the headquarters in the capital, and the whole family moved to Tehran.

Both Banu and her husband, Dr. Hormozdi, passed away in Tehran and were buried at the Zoroastrian cemetery of Tehran. Of their four daughters, two have moved to the US. The youngest one lives in Vienna, Austria, with her husband and children. Their second daughter,

---

[230] The story of the life journey of the Hormozdi family was narrated by their youngest daughter, Mina Hormozi-Amighi, of Vienna, Austria.

[231] The school was led by a Ms. Doolittle.

[232] The family elders had tried to follow Memas Banu's lead on selecting spouses for the eldest sons of Faridun Shahriar and Soroush Shahriar from birth. The plan was that once of marriage age they would marry their girl cousins who were younger than them. However, this arrangement was rejected by all the cousins when it came time for marriage.

Mahshid, continues to practice medicine in Tehran, but both her sons have relocated to the US in the wake of the Islamic Revolution.

3.4.2 Mehraban Kaykhosrow-Rustom Hormozdi
1909 – 1977 (Kerman – Tehran)

The Hormozdi family traces its lineage back to a priestly lineage in Kerman dating to the 18th century. For generations, they held prominent positions as Zoroastrian priests in Kerman, with their roots extending to the Khorasan province of Iran. Dastur Rustom Jahangir-Rustom (Hormozdi) (1853-1898), bearing the title of Mobed-e-Mobedan[233] of Kerman, also served as the third president of the Nasseri Zoroastrian Anjuman of Kerman.[234]

Dastur Rustom Jahangir-Rustom and his wife, Sultan Khodabux Shahriar (1867-1929), were blessed with a son named Kaykhosrow (1881-1913) and a daughter named Firuzeh Mulla[235] (1886-1946).

Kaykhosrow followed in his father's footsteps as the high Zoroastrian priest of Kerman. Kaykhosrow and his wife, Makhmal Behruz, had four children: a son by the name of Khodadad, followed by a daughter named Sultan, followed by second and third sons Khodayar and Mehraban.

Dastur Kaykhosrow died prematurely, a victim of a plague that had spread in Kerman. Upon his passage, the Zoroastrian Anjuman of Kerman agreed to pay Dastur Kaykhosrow's full salary to his wife, subject to one condition. His eldest son, Khodadad (1901-1939] was 12 years old at the time and was attending school. The Anjuman requested that Khodadad continue his education while also tutoring younger students.

Though the financial support was modest, it sustained the family. Khodadad finished high school but did not get a chance to attend University. However, Khodadad had intellectual and literary tendencies and a progressive outlook. He published a monthly newsletter under the title of…Homay. In this newsletter, he presented new ideas and covered modern thinking on motherhood and the vulnerability of pregnant women at the time of delivery.

---

[233] Title reserved for the high Zoroastrian priest.

[234] Charter for the establishment of Zoroastrian associations in Kerman and Yazd was issued by Nasser-ul-Dinshah Qajar (1831-1896) thanks to the ceaseless lobbying efforts of Maneckji Limji Hataria (1813–1890). The association of the name of Nasseri with that of the Anjuman is in recognition of Nasser-ul-Dinshah granting the official charter for the establishment of these two associations, which meant the local governors had to recognize these bodies and be responsive to them. Although, Maneckji and his successor Ardeshir Reporter did not get to spend time in the organization and management of the Anjuman in honor of their contribution, Maneckji is recognized at the first and founding father of the Kerman Anjuman, and Ardeshir Reporter is considered as the second president. The fourth president of the Anjuman was Gushtasp Dinyar-Bahram. Shahiar Khodabux served as the 5th president and was followed by his sons Soroush and Faridun as the 6th and the 7th presidents.

[235] She was bestowed with the title of "Mulla" by her contemporaries, acknowledging her exceptional wisdom and leadership skills

Echoes of Survival

Khodadad married Homayoon Rostam-Khosrow-Jamshid, and they raised four children: their first daughter, Irandokht, followed by two sons, Kaykhosrow, Fraydoon and their youngest daughter, Parvin.

The family arranged for their second son, Khodayar, to receive religious training in India. However, Khodayar pursued literature and poetry upon his return to Iran. He settled in Tehran, married Homayoun Esfandiyar Ravary, and had three children: Manijeh, Manouchehr, and Mehran.

Mehrabon, the youngest son, completed his high school education in Tehran and prepared for higher education abroad. Despite facing challenges, including studying under streetlights at night, he was selected to study in the UK at the University of Birmingham. He earned his Ph.D., becoming the second Iranian student to achieve this feat at the university.

The youngest son, Mehraban, pursued his high school education at Tehran's Sherafat High School. There, he diligently prepared for the qualifying exam, often burning the midnight oil under the illumination of street lights. At the age of 19, along with several other promising young Iranians, he was selected to study abroad in the UK for higher education[236]. In the UK, he secured admission to the Mechanical Engineering program at the University of Birmingham. He successfully completed his Ph.D., earning the distinction of being the second Iranian student to achieve this feat at the university.

During his time in Europe, Mehrabon attended the Berlin Olympic Games in 1936 and witnessed the rise of the National Socialists in Germany. After completing his studies, he returned to Iran, reuniting with his family after an eleven-year absence.

During his time in Europe, Mehraban attended the Berlin Olympic Games of 1936, resided in Germany for a period, and bore witness to the ascension of the National Socialists to power. Apart from fluency in Farsi and English, he also possessed proficiency in French and a rudimentary grasp of German.

Upon completing his educational pursuits in 1940, Dr. Hormozdi embarked on an ocean voyage from the British port of Southampton bound for Bombay, India, traversing the Suez Canal. Fortunately, his vessel navigated the treacherous North Sea unscathed, unlike two commercial ships departing from Southampton earlier that day, which fell victim to a German U-boat lurking beneath the waves.

Upon reaching Bombay safely and after a brief stay, Dr. Hormozdi continued his journey from Bombay to the Persian Gulf port of Bushehr, proceeding overland to the capital city of Tehran. After an absence of eleven years, he rejoined his family upon returning to his homeland.

Amidst Iran's ongoing modernization initiatives spearheaded by Reza Shah, doors opened for highly educated Iranians. Dr. Hormozdi seized his initial employment opportunity as

---

[236] To cultivate expertise in engineering, medicine, and other core subjects among young Iranians, the government of Reza Shah sponsored meritorious Iranian students to pursue overseas studies.

the director of Tehran Silos under the purview of the Agriculture Ministry. Subsequently, he transitioned to the Treasury Department. During the Allied occupation of Iran, he collaborated closely with the American advisor Arthur Millspaugh,[237] who played a pivotal role within the Ministry.

He later joined the National Iranian Oil Company (NIOC) and held the position of vice-director at the Kermanshah Oil Refinery for eight years.[238] Subsequently, he relocated to the NIOC headquarters in Tehran, where he remained for the next 25 years. During his tenure at the Tehran headquarters, he was elected as the president of the Engineers' Union.

The family generously donated a multi-level, multi-unit house they owned in Tehran for the benefit of the Zoroastrian community.

Mehraban Hormozdi passed away in 1977 due to a stroke two years prior to the Islamic Revolution.
After his passing, his wife and daughters donated an extensive library of books that he had collected to the library of the Zoroastrian Anjuman of Kerman.

---

[237] Arthur Chester Millspaugh was an American economist who was hired by Reza Shah's administration to help put Iran's financial house in order. He had recommended new taxes to be imposed, and the delinquent tax payers to be identified and subjected to legal action. He had a break with Reza Shah, after he tried to dissuade Reza Shah from increasing his defense budget and left Iran. Due to his familiarity with Iranian financial issues, the allied forces asked him to return to Iran and recommend measures to heal Iran's financial woes. In total, he spent eight years in Iran and named his son born in Iran, Tehran.

[238] During the progressive Pahlavi dynasty, opportunities were indeed accessible to Iranians regardless of their religious beliefs. However, remnants of the 1907 constitution imposed certain limitations. According to its provisions, key positions such as heads of government agencies, ministers, governors, and judges were reserved exclusively for Shia Muslims.

Figure 52: 1944, Kerman: Banu standing between her brother Shahriar and father Faridun behind her grandmother (seated).

Figure 53: 1945, Kerman: Wedding of Banu Soroushian and Mehraban Hormuzdi surrounded by family members

Figure 54: 1953 Tehran's Shah Reza Boulevard. Photograph captured by Dr. Hormuzdi depicting the return of Shah Mohamed Reza Pahlavi and Queen Sorraya from Italy amidst the constitutional crisis involving Prime Minister Mosadeq.

Figure 55: 1958, Kermanshah: Banu and Mehraban Hormuzdi with their four daughters

Echoes of Survival

گزارش ۱۲

گشایش خانهٔ دکتر مهربان هورمزدی

سازمان زنان زرتشتی

برحسب دعوت قبلی درگشایش خانه روانشاد دکتر مهربان هورمزدی حضور بهم رساندم و شاهد رویدادی دیگر و فشنگ در تهران بودم. در این آیین نخست سه دختر وسیله موبدان و ارستهٔ سدره پوش شده و بیا به دینداری رسیدند سپس ریاست سازمان زنان زرتشتی بروا گذاری خانهٔ آنروانشاد وسیلهٔ بازماندگان محترم به سازمان زنان سخنی کوتاه بیان داشت. آنگاه دکتر جهانگیر اشیدری و خانم توران بهرامی ازد هنر خانواده هورمزدی و خواهرش روانشاد سلطان خانم به نیکویی یاد کردند و تاریخچه ای از برادران هورمزدی و خواهرش سلطان خانم ایراد نمودند. در پایان خانم دکتر مهشید هورمزدی (ورزا) ازمدعوین تشکر کرد و مجلس با پذیرایی گرمی پایان یافت.

روانشاد دکتر هورمزدی و خواهرش روانشاد سلطان خانم در یک خانوادهٔ روحانی درکرمان زائیده شده اند که از بدر در بدر و ا زبدر بزرگ از ستور و عالم بوده اند. نسب آنها بد ستور کیخسرو ستور رستم د ستور جهانگیر بدر د ستور فریدون د ستور بنداد ستور بشوتن میرسد و د ستور بشوتن در زمان خود موبدان موبد و در دار نجوم و ادبیات پهلوی سر آمد بوده است. دکتر مهربان هورمزدی در سال ۱۲۸۹ در کرمان متولد شد. پس از اتمام تحصیلات جون سال اول دورهٔ نهایی دبیرستان بوده، جزو نخستین گروه محصلین (اعزامی با اروپا) بلندن رهسپار گردید و در رشته برق و الکتریک با افتخار دریافت PHD نایل آمد.

۱۱۰

Figure 56: 1992 Payke Mehr Publication Report on Dedication of a Residential unit in Tehran in Memory of Dr. Mehraban Hormuzdi and his siblings for Zoroastrian Philanthropical use in Tehran

3.5 Rustom Kaikhosrow Soroushian Kermani and Winifred Audrey Sutherland[239]

3.5.1 Rustom Kaikhosrow Soroushian Kermani
1901- 1976 (Kerman, Iran - New York City, USA)

The man, later known as Rustam Kermani, was born Rustam Kaikhosrow Soroushian in the city of Kerman, Iran, in 1901. His father, Kaikhosrow, was the youngest of eight siblings. Kaikhosrow's older brother, Hormuzdyar, had married a Zoroastrian woman from the community by the name of Morvarid Darvish Dinyar. From that marriage, a daughter named Banu was born, but unfortunately, Banu was only a year old when her father died in an epidemic. Morvarid was still young, so the following year, she married Kaykhosrow, the younger brother of her late husband. In 1901, she gave birth to their son Rustam. Sadly, within a few years of his birth, Morvarid also died of an illness. Kaikhosrow remarried and went on to have six more children, Banu and Rustam's half-siblings.

Rustam and his siblings received their early schooling at the local Zoroastrian boys' school (amongst the first ones established in Kerman to provide secular education). As he grew older, Rustam also spent some time working at his Uncle Shahriar's trading company, thus gaining his first experience with business.

As a young man, Rustam joined the South Persia Rifles, a militia force aligned with Great Britain. This force had been organized during WWI, and a few Zoroastrian youths, including Rustam, enlisted, and he rose through the ranks. He had a few close calls during his military service. In one engagement with rebels in a mountainous area, his unit was ambushed. Only a few members of the unit got away; fortunately, he was one of the lucky ones. Later, he and some other members of his unit contracted malaria, so they were sent to Bombay, India, for treatment.

In the early 1920s, Reza Shah was elevated to the throne of Iran. Eager to modernize the country, Reza Shah encouraged young people to go to Europe and the US for higher education, especially in subjects like engineering and medicine. To this end, he initiated a program that provided financial assistance for talented students to study these subjects overseas, and after obtaining their degrees, they were expected to return home to help build the country's infrastructure. Rustam, who could speak English, was amongst those students. In an interview with the Zoroastrian publication, Hukht, Rustam credited the late Arbab Kaikhosrow Shahrokh (Zoroastrian representative in the parliament) with encouraging him to go to the US for studies. In 1926, he was sent to the US to study railroad engineering at Rensselaer Polytechnic Institute (RPI) in Troy, NY.

While at RPI, Rustam wrote to his father and asked for a few bales of Persian rugs to be sent to him so that he could sell them to his friends and professors. Soon, the rug business was booming, and Rustam decided to quit school and sell rugs full-time. He wrote again to his father

---

[239] The life story of Rustom and Winifred was narrated by Lisa Peterson-Grace of New York. She is the daughter of Karen Kermani, and the grand-daughter of Rustom and Winifred, and an educator by profession.

and told him to start manufacturing rugs in large quantities. However, he realized that he needed someone who knew how to mend and maintain the rugs, so he also asked that one of his younger brothers be taught the rug trade in order for him to come to the United States and help him with his business. His father selected Khodamorad, his younger half-brother, to begin training for this role.

In 1933, Rustam came home to escort Khodamorad to the United States. The two brothers arrived in New York City on September 29, 1933. They resided in the basement apartment of Alexander and Viola McKown on Lancaster Street. The McKown family were far more than just landlords; they helped the brothers in a multitude of ways. First and foremost, Mrs. McKown, who had recently lost her own son, acted as a surrogate mother to young Khodamorad.[240] In addition, she brought them to her church, the Trinity United Methodist Church of Albany, and introduced Rustam to her friends there, which helped him find a market for his rugs.

One of these Trinity Church families was the Sutherland family of Madison Avenue in Albany. Rustam visited the Sutherland house as part of a routine business call about cleaning the family's Oriental rugs, and it was there that he was first introduced to Winifred Audrey Sutherland, the family's youngest daughter. The two struck up a friendship, and they were married in 1939.

To a bystander, this marriage must have seemed like the unlikeliest of pairings, but according to friends and family, the match was successful on many levels. On a business level, Winifred's social connections provided Rustam with valuable contacts among the wealthy and socially respectable residents of Albany. She also provided financial help so that he could buy Van Heusen Charles Company, a well-regarded, century-old store dealing in fine China, jewelry and home furnishings. Before this purchase, Rustam had been selling rugs from a few small shops in downtown Albany, but now he could devote the fourth floor of the store entirely to the sale of Persian rugs.

On an emotional level, their personalities complemented each other: Rustam was a colorful extrovert, loud and willing to take risks, while Winfred was a thoughtful introvert who provided a calming influence. Despite their differences, they deeply respected each other: she respected his business acumen, and he respected her intellect and judgment. The couple soon welcomed two children: Peter Rustam, born in 1940, just a year after their marriage, and Karen, born two years later in 1942.

As the family grew, Rustam's business also prospered. In the latter part of the 1950s, Rustam traveled abroad for both business and pleasure. After one such trip in 1956, he was interviewed by The Albany Times-Union and stated that he had traveled "on business to observe

---

[240] Khodarahm, the youngest brother of Rustom and Khodamorad also came to the US few years later to help in the Carpet business in Albany. However, his stay in Albany was short, and after getting married, the couple left for the West Coast, where Khodarahm started his own carpet retail business in San Francisco.

his rugs being loomed… opened a school in his family name in the city of the same name in Iran, and visited with a foster child in Korea." The "foster child" was a child that Winifred had sponsored through a Christian charity, and she was thrilled to see pictures of the two of them meeting. After another trip, in 1958, he was again interviewed by the Times-Union, and he was pictured with his passport and some of the pearls he had purchased for his store while in Japan.

As much as he valued his business, Rustam also believed strongly in the importance of contributing to others. As previously stated, he funded the construction of a school in the county of Jiroft in the southern part of Kerman province. He also donated funds to build an assembly hall on the premises of the Zoroastrian temple of Kerman, which bears his name. In the U.S., he funded the construction of a chapel called the Kermani Chapel, which was built in the Trinity United Methodist Church in Albany. He also maintained ties with his homeland through the Near Eastern Foundation in New York City, and his name appeared in connection with a Royal visit to NYC in 1967.

In March of 1976, Rustam took a business trip to New York to collect a shipment of rugs. While on this trip, he suffered a sudden heart attack and passed away at the age of 75. Although he left behind a grieving family, he also left an enduring legacy. He had traveled halfway across the world from his homeland, leaving behind everything he knew. But in spite of the challenges he faced, Rustam built a prosperous business and a loving family. Moreover, he always remembered to give to others, donating generously to both his original community in Iran and his adopted community in Albany. From Rustam, his descendants inherited a determination to succeed, even in difficult circumstances, and a sense of responsibility to others.

3.5.2 Winifred Audrey Sutherland
1904 – 1997 (Albany, New York)

Winifred was born on November 7, 1904, to Willard and Anna Sutherland. The Sutherland family had arrived in Connecticut from Scotland in the early part of the 1700s, and they went on to settle in the upper Hudson Valley in New York State.[241] Winifred's ancestors fought in the American Revolution and later prospered as farmers and traders. Her father, Willard, had moved to Albany at the age of eighteen to work as a clerk. He became owner of a retail grocery business and then sold the business to become a partner with his brother, Charles, in the firm C.R. and J.W. Sutherland. The brothers were in the produce commission business, and while Willard retained a successful interest in the grocery business throughout his life, he also diversified into auto sales. Through his friendship with Charles Chrysler, Willard was able to establish the first Chrysler dealership in upstate New York, and he eventually acquired a Cadillac franchise as well.

As the youngest child by a full nine years, Winifred was the much-loved baby of the Sutherland family. Early in life, she showed great academic promise, and her family supported

---

[241] Information about Winifred's ancestry in America was sourced from the publication, "American Ancestry" for families settled in the Albany basin, volume 1, published by Joel Munsell's Sons of Albany, NY in 1887, page77.

her interests with a first-class education, unusual for a woman of her time. Winifred attended the Albany Academy for Girls and then Wellesley College, graduating in 1926. She continued her studies at the New York School of Library Service at Columbia University in New York City, graduating with a master's degree in library science.

After returning home to Albany, Winifred worked at the Harmanus Bleecker Library. During her time as a librarian, she became acquainted with Kenneth Roberts, author of historical fiction novels such as Arundel and Northwest Passage. Roberts was seeking information about local history, and she was proud that she was able to contribute information for several of his books.

During the 1930s, Winifred suffered the loss of her parents and her beloved older brother, Harry. When she met Rustam, she was undoubtedly ready to embark upon a new chapter in her life. While Rustam's background and heritage were certainly different from that of most men she had met, her intellect and curiosity made her fascinated to learn more about his culture and background.

Although their personalities and backgrounds were very different, this unlikely marriage proved successful for both Rustam and Winifred. On a practical level, Rustam possessed a great acumen for business, and Winifred's money and social connections helped him grow his small rug business into a thriving retail enterprise. On a personal level, they were devoted to each other, and perhaps because of their different backgrounds and abilities, they deeply respected each other as well.

Within a few years of their marriage, Winifred gave birth to two children, Peter Rustam, born in 1940, and Karen, born in 1942. She worked tirelessly to convey her love of books and learning to her children. She took them on frequent trips to New York City to experience museums and theater performances, and she read to them every day. Her son, Peter, went on to graduate from St. Lawrence University and served for several years as Board President for both the Albany Symphony and the American Symphony Orchestra League. In recognition of his service, he received an honorary degree from Russell Sage College. Her daughter, Karen, graduated from Vassar College and worked briefly as a teacher before giving birth to her own two children.

Winifred never stopped sharing her love of books with others. For years, she volunteered at Memorial Hospital, bringing a cart of books around to patients to ease their time in the hospital. She also sponsored the education of children in other countries through various charities. Like Rustam, Winifred taught her descendants the importance of sharing with others. By the time of her death in 1997, she had inspired many others to love books, music and learning as much as she did. Moreover, although she hadn't moved across the world like Rustam, she certainly had taken a risk in marrying someone from such a different culture and background. Both of them showed their descendants the importance of taking chances and having the courage to make their own choices in life.

Figure 57: 1940, Albany: Building housing Rustom's Retail Carpet and Luxury Goods Store

Figure 58: 1940, Albany: Rustom (seated on the right) and Winifred, seated across from him and his friends

Figure 59: 1952, Albany: Rustom and his son Peter, daughter Karen, along with his cousin, Khosrow Esfandiyar Soroushian, visiting from Iran

Figure 60: 1956, Albany Times Union Newspaper Interview with Rustom Kermani

Figure 61: 1970, Middle East-Iran report on Rustom Kermani School Dedication

Echoes of Survival

شماره ۳ - سال بیست و یکم
خرداد ماه ۱۳۴۹

هوخت
گفتار نیک

ای میهن عزیز من « ایران » فدای تو
معشوق من توئی و منم مبتلای تو
چشمم ز راه دور شب و روز سوی تست
دل می طپد همیشه به عشق و هوای تو

دهشمند نیکوکار ارباب رستم کرمانی
مقیم نیویورک

Figure 62: 1971, Cover Page of Hukht Publication in Iran carrying an interview with Mr. Rustom Kermani

167

3.6 Khodamorad Kaikhosrow Khodabux and Ruth Phinney[242]
3.6.1 Khodamorad (Rod) Kaikhosrow-Khodabux Soroushian Kermani
1920 – 2009 (Kerman, Iran - Albany, New York)

Khodamorad Kaikhosrow Soroushian was born in Kerman in 1920, the second youngest of six children of father Kaikhosrow and mother Khorshid Soroushian.

At the age of seven, Khodamorad was sent after school each day to the family's rug looms to learn the art of weaving, dyeing and repairing.

When he was 12, Khodamorad traveled with his 32-year-old half-brother, Rustam, to America on a purported "three-week vacation" that would last more than 35 years. At the time, Khodamorad had no idea he would never see his parents again. He would not return to his homeland for 35 years.

Young Khodamorad was marooned in Albany, New York State's capital, trying to learn English, attending public school half day and working in Rustam's oriental rug store repairing carpets for the rest of the day.

Hearing about Khodamorad's sparse existence in Albany, a wealthy local family, Alexander and Viola Albright McKown, who were also Rustam's rug customers, offered to take Khodamorad into their home and help raise him.

There, in the well-appointed and nurturing McKown household, Khodamorad quickly learned American manners, culture and social expectations for young men in America.

Khodamorad lived with the McKown family for several years. He continued to work in Rustam's rug store, attended Albany public schools and became a well-liked and competent student known to all as "Rod."

Following high school graduation, Khodamorad enlisted in the U.S. Army with plans to serve as an interpreter in the Middle East during World War II. A paperwork mixup sent Khodamorad to the South Pacific, where he served almost three years. He obtained his US citizenship on the jungle island of Guadalcanal.

After the Army, Khodamorad returned to Albany and worked for Rustam in the family's home furnishing and rug business for 14 years.

He married Ruth Phinney, and they raised three children: David, Karyl and Ronald.

Khodamorad eventually left his brother's employ and opened his oriental rug store, also in the Albany area.

While building his oriental rug business, Khodamorad generously gave his time, talent and resources to several local organizations, including the Albany YMCA and the Lions Club.

---

[242] This narrative was produced by Mr. Ronald Kermani. Ronald is the youngest offspring of Khodamorad and Ruth. He is a prize-winning journalist currently in retirement.

Khodamorad served in many capacities in those organizations for more than 50 years, receiving national recognition for his contributions.

He was the first person in the nation to receive the Lions Club International's highest honor, the Melvin Jones Award, in 1992. The prestigious award acknowledged Khodamorad's 50 years of behind-the-scenes work and his ability to shepherd capital campaigns from beginning to end.

His accomplishments at the Albany YMCA were equally remarkable.

Khodamorad served on the YMCA's board of directors for more than 20 years and was recognized as the top membership recruiter and fundraiser for the Y's annual Reach Out for Youth campaign.

To honor his 50 years of leadership and commitment, the YMCA awarded him its highest honor, Citizen of the Year, in 1996.

Khodamorad became a trustee of the YMCA, and his philanthropy continued. Kermani and his wife were instrumental in raising money to build the Bethlehem YMCA. The group acknowledged Kermani's efforts and contribution by naming the Bethlehem YMCA's state-of-the-art fitness facility after him and his wife.

Since he was 14, Khodamorad was active in local Masonic organizations.

He became master councilor of Demolay, the young men's fraternity affiliated with the Masons, and later earned that national group's highest designation, Chevalier, for his exemplary leadership.

Khodamorad continued his Masonic work by joining Masters Lodge No. 5 in Albany in 1946 and staying active in the lodge for more than 60 years.

The Grand Master of Masons in New York State awarded Khodamorad the Dedicated Service Award in 2002 for his decades of service to the Masonic order and its principles.

In 2007, the Masonic Lodge in downtown Albany named its library and meeting rooms in honor of the Kermani family and the four generations of Kermanis who have been active in Masters Lodge Number. 5.

Khodamorad was also a 60-year member of Trinity United Methodist Church in Albany. He also was a long-time member of the Men's Garden Club of Albany.

Khodamorad and his wife, Ruth, died in 2009.

3.6.2 Ruth Phinney
1921 – 2009 (Elizabethtown, NY – Albany, NY)

Ruth Phinney Kermani, an Albany resident and community volunteer for more than half a century, was born in Elizabethtown in upstate New York in 1921.

She graduated from Elizabethtown High School and from Albany Business College with a degree in secretarial studies. Ruth worked for the Army Corps of Engineers, the state Labor Department and the National Commercial Bank and Trust Co. in Albany during World War II.

Ruth Phinney and Khodamorad Kermani's first "introduction" -- years before they met in person at a dance -- was the work of fate and coincidence.

The Kermani family history in America began on page three of the Oct. 2, 1933 edition of the Albany Evening News.

The headline "Rug Merchant Leads Persian Brother Here" started the story about Albany, NY, oriental rug dealer Rustam Kermani bringing his 13-year-old half-brother, Khodamorad, to Albany. The article included photos of Rustam and his much younger brother.

One hundred fifty miles north of Albany, a 12-year-old girl recovering at home from a long battle with pneumonia read this article in the Albany newspaper.

She cut out the story and put it in her scrapbook because she had never heard of the nation called "Persia."

Eight years later and now a student at Albany Business College, this woman met a swarthy, handsome man at a dance in Albany.

He looked familiar.

He introduced himself.

She replied: "I know who you are."

He was the 13-year-old Persian boy featured in the yellowed newspaper article she had pasted into her scrapbook as a child.

The Persian boy and the girl from a small Adirondack town — Khodamorad Soroushian Kemani and Ruth Phinney — made a life together in Albany when he returned after serving in the Army in the South Pacific in World War II.

They were married in Albany in October 1945.

The couple raised three children: David, Karyl and Ronald.

Ruth was a homemaker who became very active in local charitable organizations.

She was a 63-year member of Trinity United Methodist Church in Albany, where she served as trustee and held several lay leadership roles for many years.

Ruth's considerable community involvement included years of volunteer work with the Albany Girls Club, Literacy Volunteers, Meals on Wheels and other charitable organizations.

She was also a strong supporter of the Capital District YMCA, which will recognize her philanthropy in April by posthumously bestowing that organization's highest award to her for her summer camp scholarship gift.

Ruth and her husband's decades of support for the YMCA were also instrumental in the building of the Bethlehem Area YMCA, which named that facility's family fitness center after her and her husband.

Ruth died in 2009. She was 87.

Echoes of Survival

Figure 63: 1939, Kerman: Khodamorad (second row, second from right) posing for a family photo before his departure for the US. Standing in the middle (dark suit) is Soroush Shahriar Soroushian

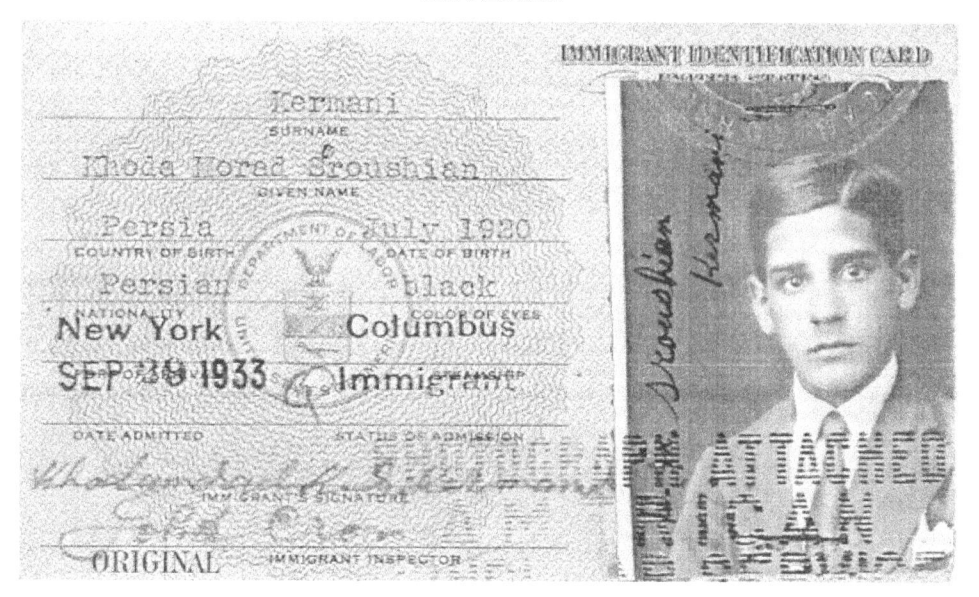

Figure 64: 1939, NY Harbor: Khodamorad's US Landing Permit

Figure 65 October 2, 1933: Albany Evening News Report Announcing Arrival of Khodamorad

Figure 66: 1945, Albany, NY: Khodamorad and Ruth's Wedding Photo (center of the photo))

Figure 67: 2023, Upstate New York: Ruth and Khodamorad's offspring, (L to R) Ronald, David and Karyl

Chapter 4
My Maternal Ancestry

In this chapter, I present a summary of the remarkable tale of the survival of my mother's paternal lineage, tracing back to the 18th century. Drawing upon scant information available on the physical settlements of earlier generations up to the mid-19th century, critical to their survival as Zoroastrians, as well as likely naming schemes used, I delve into the resilience and determination that characterized their journey.

From the tumultuous conditions of 18th-century Khorasan, where Zoroastrians faced escalating persecution and the looming threat of conversion to Islam, emerged ancestors such as Feridon Bahram and Firozeh Marzban. Their decision to flee their ancestral home in Neyshabur marked the beginning of a saga of survival against formidable odds. Setting out for the relative safety of Yazd, they embarked on a perilous journey, navigating the unsafe caravan paths and hostile forces to secure refuge for their family.

Their descendants, including Karshap Feridon and Morwarid Dinyar, inherited their legacy of resilience and determination. Witnessing the deteriorating conditions for Zoroastrians in Khorasan, they, too, made the courageous decision to seek sanctuary in Yazd, contributing to the establishment and revitalization of villages in the region.

As subsequent generations came of age, led by figures like Feridon and Firozeh, they were imbued with the values of self-sufficiency, vigilance, and unity, essential for survival in a hostile environment. Their leadership and courage ensured the safe passage of their families to Yazd, where they laid the foundation for a new chapter in their lineage's history.

The tale of my mother's paternal lineage is one of resilience, sacrifice, and unwavering faith in the face of adversity. It serves as a testament to the enduring spirit of the Zoroastrian community and the indomitable human will to persevere against all odds.

The naming schemes that were likely used were the basis of coming up with the forenames of the earlier generations. For the generation from the mid-19th century, onwards family information available was used.

4.1 Bahram Sohrab Viraf and Firozeh Marzban Rustom
4.1.1 Bahram Sohrab Viraf
1729– 1788 (Neyshabur, Khorasan – Ahmadabad, Yazd)

Bahram's ancestors had deep roots in Northern Khorasan, where they eked out a respectable living from their agricultural holdings near the city of Neyshabur. However, over time, the conditions for Zoroastrians, once the predominant population in Khorasan, deteriorated significantly. Moslem overlords resorted to violence and coercion in attempts to force conversion to Islam, leading to property seizures and threats of violence, compelling some to capitulate while others opted to abandon their livelihoods and flee southward to regions like Yazd, Kerman, and even India.

Echoes of Survival

The waves of invasions from Central Asia, beginning in the 11th century, exacerbated the plight of the general populace and Zoroastrians in particular. Sensing the looming peril, Zoroastrians resorted to safeguarding and concealing precious metals and coins underground to be unearthed swiftly in the event of pillaging by invaders or violent attacks from fanatical Muslim mobs.

By the 13th century, a systematic campaign aimed at marginalizing and purging Zoroastrians from Khorasan's urban centers pushed them into rural villages, where they were restricted to agricultural labor and trade. Despite these challenges, most managed to endure with dignity. However, as the project of Islamization gained momentum, particularly under the Safavids from the 16th to the early 18th century, conditions for the remaining Zoroastrians in Khorasan continued to worsen, exacerbated by the Sunni-Shiite rivalry that left them caught in the crossfire.

Gradually, Zoroastrian families began a steady exodus from their homelands in Khorasan, seeking sanctuary in Yazd, Kerman, or even India. This migration was fraught with risks, and not all refugees reached their intended destinations. By the time Bahram Sohrab and Firozeh Marzban's descendants reached adulthood and started families of their own, it became evident that fleeing was the only viable option for the survival and preservation of their lineage.

4.1.2 Firozeh Marzban Rustom
1734 – 1785 (Neyshabur, Khorasan - Ahmadabad, Yazd)

Growing up in close proximity to the bustling city of Neyshabur, Firozeh cultivated a strong foundation in reading, writing, and literature. Renowned as a center of learning, Neyshabur maintained its scholarly reputation despite enduring numerous devastations from waves of invaders that swept down upon it from the north and east. Firozeh's family, deeply rooted in the region, imparted to her a profound appreciation for religious traditions and history, instilling within her a keen sense of vigilance amidst the worsening conditions faced by her family and the remaining Zoroastrian community.

With her marriage to Bahram Sohrab-Viraf and the arrival of children, Firozeh's commitment to equipping her offspring with the skills necessary to navigate the perilous environment intensified. Recognizing the imperative to cultivate self-sufficiency and resilience in the face of adversity, she dedicated herself to instilling these values in her children, knowing that such instincts were crucial for their survival in an increasingly hostile environment.

4.2 Feridon Bahram Sohrab and Morwarid Dinyar Khosrow
4.2.1 Feridon Bahram Sohrab
1752-1799 (Neyshabur, Khorasan -Ahmadabad, Yazd)

In 1784, Feridon Bahram made the difficult decision to uproot his young family from Neyshabur, located in the upper reaches of Khorasan, and embark on a journey southward toward Yazd. His plan extended to encompass his parents and siblings, who remained in Neyshabur.

The relentless pressure on Zoroastrians to either convert to Islam or face persecution, coupled with the deteriorating security conditions exacerbated by increasing raids from Central Asian tribes, served as the impetus for the remaining Zoroastrian community in Khorasan to seek refuge elsewhere. Many found themselves clinging steadfastly to their religious identity, compelled to abandon their ancestral homes in a last-ditch effort to reach the safety of Yazd. While previous generations had also endured escalating difficulties, Feridon's generation found the situation increasingly untenable. The conversion of some neighbors to Islam under extreme coercion further isolated and demoralized the remaining Zoroastrians, amplifying the sense of vulnerability.

By migrating southward to the desert environs around Yazd, they effectively eluded the threat of Central Asian raiders. However, the climatic conditions in Yazd were notably harsher. Many migrant Zoroastrian families were compelled to undertake arduous tasks such as digging water wells, constructing qanats (underground aqueducts), and reclaiming land from the desert to cultivate fertile agricultural plots. Indeed, the genesis of numerous villages around Yazd owes its origins to the hard work and perseverance of these Zoroastrian refugees, including those from Khorasan.

Feridon meticulously planned his departure, liquidating his family's assets to serve as seed capital for their new life in Yazd. He also meticulously gathered intelligence on safe routes to navigate to their destination. Upon safely reaching the outskirts of Yazd, Feridon and his family settled in the village of Ahmadabad, where he purchased land and water rights and commenced agricultural endeavors. His young family, including Karshasp and his siblings, contributed as farmhands, playing a crucial role in ensuring the family's financial stability.

Feridon's parents, Bahram and Firozeh, lived long enough to witness their progeny's establishment in Ahmadabad. Their mortal remains were consigned to the Tower of Silence near SharifAbad, Yazd, perpetuating the enduring legacy of their family's resilience and determination.

4.2.2 Morwarid Dinyar Khosrow
1756 – 1797 (Tous, Ahmadabad)

Morwarid's family shared a familial bond with Feridon's, and shortly after marrying Feridon Bahram, the young couple became acutely aware of the escalating vulnerability faced by Zoroastrians around Neyshabur. Sensing the urgency, they diligently planned and prepared for their departure to the central regions of the country.

They were cognizant of the steady exodus of Zoroastrians abandoning their homes in Khorasan, seeking refuge in the villages surrounding Yazd. With a population of approximately 20,000, Yazd's desert-like climate and formidable terrain acted as a natural deterrent against invasions, making it an appealing destination for those intent on preserving their religious heritage.

Morwarid's own family was also in the midst of making arrangements for their departure. Once the plans were finalized, they departed in several groups to avoid drawing undue attention. Settling into their new environment around Yazd presented myriad challenges for the newcomers.

Arriving in the spring afforded them the opportunity to procure land and construct homes before the harsh winter set in. Meanwhile, the men of the family labored tirelessly to till the soil and sow new crops. They had managed to bring along sufficient funds, primarily in the form of silver coins from liquidating their assets in Khorasan, to sustain them until they could establish a source of income in their new home.

Morwarid, consumed with the responsibilities of raising her young children, educating them, and assisting with the farm work alongside the men, exemplified the collective effort of the new arrivals. Driven by a shared determination to ensure their survival and provide future generations with opportunities for a better life, they rallied together, embodying the ethos of resilience and unity.

4.3 Karshasp Feridon Bahram and Homayun Dinyar Parviz

4.3.1 Karshasp Feridon Bahram
1781-1838 (Neyshabur, Ahmadabad)

Karshap represented the final generation of his family to be born in Khorasan before the looming threat prompted their relocation to Ahmadabad in Yazd. Generations preceding him had their roots firmly entrenched in Khorasan.

Forced by deteriorating conditions for Zoroastrians in Khorasan, Karshap's parents and their siblings made the difficult decision to abandon their ancestral home and seek refuge in Yazd.

Karshap's upbringing was deeply influenced by his parents' tireless toil on the farm. They seized every opportunity to recount the hardships they endured in Khorasan and the necessity of fleeing to preserve their religious heritage.

Assisting their family as laborers on the farm, Karshap and his siblings imbibed the ethos of self-reliance cherished by their ancestors in Khorasan, who faced the looming threat of losing their means of livelihood. Fleeing to safer environs became imperative.

In addition to his agricultural pursuits, Karshap engaged in transporting both travelers and produce to Yazd city. Mastering the art of navigating travel restrictions, evading highwaymen, and circumventing the constraints imposed on Zoroastrians, he adeptly managed his ventures. Occasionally, his sons, including Viraf, would accompany him on these journeys, providing them with invaluable insights and experiences to draw upon in subsequent endeavors.

4.3.2 Homayun Dinyar Parviz
1789 – 1843 (Tabas, Ahmadabad)

Within a few years of Homayun's birth in Tabas, Khorasan, her family found themselves compelled to flee to Yazd, forsaking their ancestral home due to the deteriorating conditions faced by Zoroastrians. The resettlement in the village of Ahmadabad presented its own set of challenges. However, the family found solace in connecting with other families who had similarly sought refuge around Yazd. Despite their newfound sanctuary, they remained vigilant, mindful of the potential dangers posed by zealous adherents of Islam.

Growing up amidst these circumstances, Homayun and her siblings learned to stick close to fellow Zoroastrians and exercise caution around unfamiliar individuals, particularly those who hadn't earned their parents' trust through interaction.

It was during this time that Homayun crossed paths with Karshasp Feridon, forging an acquaintance that blossomed into marriage. Their union was marked by happiness, and through hard work and unwavering dedication, they nurtured their family. Their indomitable pioneering spirit served as a guiding light, instilling in their children a profound sense of determination and resilience.

Homayun ultimately outlived her beloved husband, Karshasp Feridon. Both of them breathed their last in Ahmadabad, where their mortal remains were laid to rest in the Tower of Silence near Sharif Abad, a site utilized by neighboring villages for such rites.

4.4 Viraf Karshasp Feridon and Khorshid Mehran Shahpur
4.4.1 Viraf Karshasp Feridon
1824 -1879 (Ahmadabad, Yazd City)

Viraf Karshap was born in the village of Ahmadabad, situated north of Yazd city. His initial visits to Yazd to transport produce from the village ignited within him a strong desire to relocate his family and establish roots in the bustling city. Despite being acutely aware of the prevalent discrimination and constraints faced by Zoroastrians in Yazd compared to the rural areas, Viraf remained resolute in his determination to thrive in the city.

Transitioning from the open expanse of village life to the more enclosed community of Yazd posed numerous challenges. However, Viraf navigated these hurdles adeptly, emerging as an independent merchant in the urban landscape. His involvement in advocating for the rights and representation of the Zoroastrian community led to his recognition in the annals of the newly established Nasseri Anjuman, marking him as a notable figure among the Zoroastrians of Yazd.

As the first generation of his family to actively engage in community advocacy, Viraf's pioneering example served as a beacon of inspiration for subsequent generations. His unwavering determination to surmount obstacles and achieve his objectives epitomized a pioneering spirit that left an indelible mark on his family's legacy.

4.4.2 Khorshid Mehran Shahpur
1828 – 1875 (Ahmadabad – Yazd City)

Khorshid Mehran, born in the village of Ahmadabad, formed a bond with Viraf from an early age. Upon reaching marriageable age, she wed her determined husband, Viraf, embarking on a journey to Yazd city for a new chapter of their lives. Transitioning to urban life proved daunting, requiring Khorshid to navigate the challenges of earning acceptance from her new neighbors.

With Viraf often occupied with his merchant endeavors, the responsibility of nurturing their children fell squarely on Khorshid's shoulders. She diligently imparted whatever knowledge she possessed to her offspring, including rudimentary literacy skills. Additionally, she grappled with the necessity of safeguarding her family against the hostility directed at Zoroastrians by Moslems zealous within Yazd City.

Tragically, Khorshid succumbed to a cholera outbreak, leaving behind her husband, children, and siblings. Her untimely demise marked a profound loss for her family and community, yet her legacy of resilience and maternal devotion endures.

4.5 Kaikhosrow Viraf Karshasp and Kian Feridon Rustom

4.5.1 Kaikhosrow Viraf Karshasp
1849 -1899 (Ahmadabad, Yazd City)

Kaikhosrow and his siblings reached adulthood while their parents grappled with the challenges of settling in the evolving Zoroastrian community of Yazd. Kaikhosrow, originally born in Ahmadabad, was brought to Yazd during infancy. His father's determination and commitment to the community left a lasting impression on him, which he endeavored to pass down to his own children.

Kaikhosrow and his siblings seized every opportunity available to receive a basic education, learning to read, write, and do arithmetic. Kaikhosrow assisted his father in transporting goods on donkey back and occasionally worked as a farmhand to contribute to the family's income, particularly to fulfill the burdensome annual Jazya tax.

Over time, Kaikhosrow managed to build upon his father's business, expanding its scope and reach. He then mentored his sole son, Rustom, instilling in him the same entrepreneurial spirit and determination to expand into trading, thus continuing the family legacy.

4.5.2 Kian Feridon Rustom
1848 – 1904 (Ahmadabad, Yazd City)

Kian was born in Ahmadabad to parents who had fled Central Khorasan due to the deteriorating conditions for Zoroastrians in the region. Her father, Faridon Rustom, had established close business connections with Viraf Karshasp, which ultimately led to Kian's marriage to Kaikhosrow, Viraf Karshasp's son. Following her marriage, Kian relocated to Yazd city, where she spent the remainder of her life. Within several years of her marriage, Kian bore children, including Rustom, her second child. She was greatly admired as both a mother and a wife, surviving her husband by five years.

Kian, along with her parents and husband, was included in the first accurate census of the remaining Zoroastrians in Iran during the 19th century, conducted by the celebrated Maneckji Limji Hataria.

4.6 Rustom Kaikhosrow Viraf and Mahasti Khodadad Firoze
4.6.1 Rustom Kaikhosrow Viraf
1863– 1917 (Yazd)

Observing his father's financial struggles, largely attributed to the limitations imposed on Zoroastrians in Iran, Rustom developed a profound sense of purpose and a resolute determination to surmount the challenges that lay ahead. He exuded dynamism, always in motion, propelled by his drive to succeed.

Under the guidance of his father and grandfather, Rustom honed a sharp business acumen. Starting as a small-scale merchant, he gradually ascended to prominence, establishing lucrative trade connections not only within Yazd but also extending to cities like Kerman. Moreover, he ventured into importing commercial goods from Bombay and Europe, further diversifying his enterprise.

Rustom fathered two sons, Kaikhosrow and Sohrab, and a daughter named Firozeh. Upon ensuring his sons received a foundational education, he actively involved them in the family business, ensuring they were well-versed in seizing trading opportunities and expanding operations whenever feasible. Entrusting his oldest son, Sohrab, with overseeing the Yazd business, Rustom personally assisted his youngest son, Kaikhosrow, and his young family in establishing and managing their trading endeavors in Kerman.

4.6.2 Mahasti Khodadad Firoze
1868 – 1913 (Yazd)

Mahasti, the second child of her parents, grew up in the Zoroastrian quarter of Yazd, near Rustom Kaikhosrow's residence. From a tender age, she displayed remarkable courage, determination, and daring. Despite the prevailing apprehensions surrounding the safety of young girls venturing outdoors unaccompanied, Mahasti daringly ran errands and procured farm produce and provisions from neighbors. Her boldness and resilience caught the attention of Rustom Kaikhosrow, leading to their eventual marriage. Their marriage ceremony was presided over by the head Zoroastrian priest of Yazd, after which Mahasti moved in with Rustom. Over the years, they welcomed two sons and a daughter into their family.

With Rustom frequently traveling for business, Mahasti assumed the responsibility of nurturing and caring for their children. As a devoted mother, she fostered strong emotional bonds with her offspring and imparted valuable life lessons. Additionally, Mahasti extended her support to relatives and neighbors to the best of her abilities. Tragically, Mahasti passed away several years before her husband. Her remains were laid in the tower of silence on the outskirts of Yazd, marking the end of a life marked by bravery, compassion, and unwavering dedication to her family.

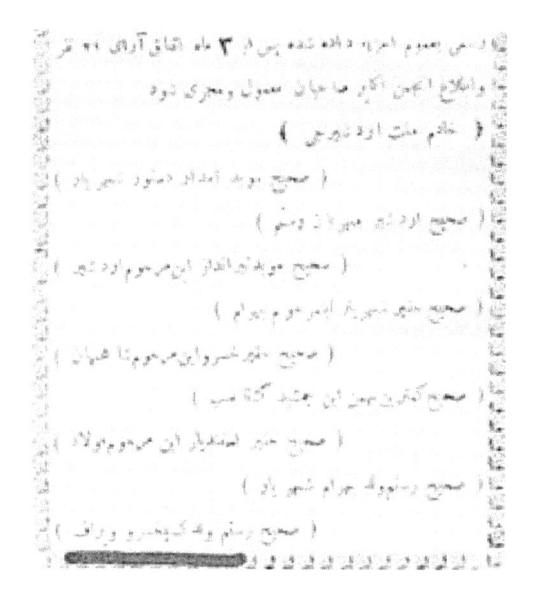

Figure 68: A page from Yazd's Naseri Anjuman Annual of 1893 indicating Rustom Kaikhosrow Viraf and Khosrow Shahjahan as signatories.

Figure 69: Descendents of Rustom and Mahasti family gathering in Kerman in 1934

4.7 Sohrab Rustom Kaikhosrow and Simin Khosrow ShahJahan
4.7.1 Sohrab Rustom Kaikhosrow
1891– 1960 (Yazd)

Raised by a stringent father who believed in early immersion into business, Sohrab and his younger brother, Kaikhosrow, gained valuable experience working alongside their father from a young age. While Kaikhosrow assumed leadership in the family's Kerman branch, Sohrab was entrusted with managing the operations in Yazd.

The Kianian brothers, in collaboration with the Soroushian brothers of Kerman (Soroush Shahriar Khodabux and Faridun Shahriar Khodabux), ventured into agricultural business, jointly acquiring farms and orchards across villages within the Kerman province. Over time, their partnership flourished, transforming them into major landowners not only in Kerman but also in two farming properties around Tehran.

Beyond business pursuits, Sohrab harbored a deep interest in community advocacy, following in the footsteps of his great-grandfather, Viraf. Possessing exceptional leadership skills and a persuasive demeanor, Sohrab ascended to a leadership position within the Yazd Zoroastrian Anjuman, spearheading the community's progress effectively. His adeptness in cultivating relationships extended to governmental agencies and Shiite leaders in Yazd, enabling him to thwart numerous attempts of forced conversions among Zoroastrian villages surrounding Yazd.

Despite his unassuming demeanor, Sohrab commanded immense respect within the community, engaging with individuals of all ages. His success in both community advocacy and business ventures was evident, with Zoroastrians traveling from other parts of Iran passing through Yazd would often find hospitality at Sohrab's expansive residence, located close to his father's house.

4.7.2 Simin Khosrow ShahJahan
1896 – 1973 (Yazd)

Simin was the only child of Khosrow ShahJahan and Mehrbanou Bahram to reach adulthood.[243]

Simin's paternal lineage, beginning with her father, unfolds as follows: Khosrow, the eldest son of Shahjahan, who was the son of Mehraban, the son of Goodarz, the son of Faridun, the son of Rustom, the son of Jamshid. Jamshid (1714-1769) was a prosperous trader from Northern Khorasan[244] who relocated his family to Ardakan in Yazd. His descendant, Mehraban, known as Mehraban-Khorasani, resettled the family in Yazd city, where they established themselves. Within a few generations, they had rebuilt their fortunes, with each successive generation expanding their involvement in commerce.

Mehraban-Khorasani's son, Shahjahan, and his wife, Firozeh, bore five sons and a daughter, Banu, all of whom reached adulthood. The five brothers - Khosrow, Parviz, Goodarz, Rustom, and Bahram - greatly expanded the family business beyond their father's operations in both size and scope. They established trade networks in major cities such as Tehran, Shiraz, Isfahan, and Bandar Abbas, engaging in commerce with Bombay, England, and France. By the early 20th century, they had become prominent traders in Iran.

Khosrow played a central role in the enterprise, handling business affairs with India and Europe. His capable brother Parviz, alongside Goodarz, managed operations from their Yazd headquarters. Rustom and Bahram oversaw business activities in other locations, such as Shiraz and Tehran. The Jahanian brothers' business also provided currency exchange and transfer services between Iranian cities,[245] as well as assisting Zoroastrians who had fled to India in sending funds to relatives in Iran. Although the Jahanian brothers' trading company eventually faced bankruptcy due to unforeseen challenges, their legacy endured. Descendants of Mehraban Khorasani were among the earliest Zoroastrians to migrate to Tehran and establish themselves in the capital.

---

[243] Her younger sister, Gohar died due to a cholera outbreak

[244] His trade activities tied in to the rather lucrative trade on the silk road. His ancestors had established trade connections.

[245] Under the Qajars, Banking services in Iran were fragmented and controlled by the British and the Russian interests, to the extent the legal tenders and currency issued in one city could not be used in another city. Some trading firms, like the Jahanian brothers, with operation in various cities, could provide the money transfer service. Under the Pahlavi, major banks were organized subject to uniform operation across the country using one national currency.

Echoes of Survival

During a business trip to Belgium in the early 20th century, Khosrow encountered a scholar of Iranian literature deeply versed in the poetry of Hafiz of Shiraz. Impressed by the scholar's knowledge, Khosrow developed a fondness for Hafiz. Upon returning to Iran, Khosrow sought out Hafiz's gravesite during a trip to Shiraz. Disappointed by the humble state of the poet's grave, Khosrow financed the construction of a grand mausoleum befitting Hafiz's stature. However, years later, a senior Muslim clergyman in Shiraz ordered the demolition of the structure upon learning that a Zoroastrian had funded it, resulting in damage to Hafiz's tombstone.[246]

Simin married the young Sohrab Rustom Kaikhosrow Viraf, but tragically, her mother, Mehrbanou, passed away within days of Simin's wedding. Simin's father also passed away a few years later. As the sole child, Simin assumed responsibility for the charitable organizations her father had established, including the Khosravi school for boys.

Figure 70: 1957 Yazd Airport: Sohrab Kianian (3rd from Right) leading the Zoroastrian delegation in welcoming the Shah of Iran on his inspection of flood relief operations in Yazd.

---

[246] The Pahlavis showed great interest in preserving all aspect of Iranian heritage. During their period the grave sites of past Iranian poets like Ferdowsi and Hafiz were adorned with majestic structures.

Figure 71: 1956 Yazd, Second row: Sohrab Kianian (1st Left), Simin Khosrow ShahJahan (1st Right) on the occasion of the wedding of their second son Feridon (2nd from Right) with Simin Mazdeh (second from the left), In the back row, left to right, Jamshid Soroushian, Homayun Sohrab Kianian, KhorshidBanu Sohrab Kianian, and Rustom Sohrab Kianian, Sitted in the front from left to right, Soroush Jamshid Soroushian, Mahvash Jamshid Soroushian, Mehrborzin Jamshid Soroushian

For the life stories of subsequent generations of this family, who endured despite the harrowing events that afflicted the Zoroastrians of Iran during the 18th and 19th centuries, please refer to sections 2.8 and 2.9 of this book.

Chapter 5
Conclusion

This narrative offers a glimpse into the life story spanning nine generations of a Zoroastrian family in Iran, spanning from the early 18th century to the early 21st century. The early generations of this family stood amongst a dwindling number of Iranians who preserved their Zoroastrian identity despite formidable challenges. By the early 18th century,[247] the Zoroastrian population of Iran plummeted drastically from approximately four million to a mere 90,000, mostly a consequence of Islamic intolerance towards non-Muslims. The number of Zoroastrian followers dramatically decreased from the beginning of the 18th century until 1856, when Maneckji Limji Hataria[248] conducted an accurate count, which revealed only 7,200 adherents remaining. This decline was primarily due to political unrest during the 18th century, which forced Zoroastrians from different regions of Iran to abandon their ancestral homes and seek refuge in desert areas, particularly around Yazd and Kerman.

Throughout the 18th century, political upheavals forced devout Zoroastrians from various regions of Iran to abandon their ancestral homes, seeking refuge in desert areas, particularly around Yazd and Kerman. Khorasan, traditionally a stronghold of Zoroastrianism, witnessed escalating tensions between the Safavid State, dominated by Shi'ite Muslims, and Sunni Muslims in the eastern flank, rendering the region increasingly unsafe for non-Muslims. Surviving Zoroastrians were predominantly driven out of major cities, retreating to safer rural localities where they engaged in commerce and agriculture, diligently amassing savings to navigate the uncertainties of life.

Upon arrival in the Yazd province, typically a temporary staging area, families endeavored to establish themselves and secure livelihoods. Over time their descendants would move on to safer localities with greater opportunities for prosperity in trade and business.

The families chronicled here exemplify those who prioritized survival in Islamic Iran, relocating as conditions demanded. They left behind ancestral livelihoods in order to safeguard their religious identity, facing hostility from Muslim extremists who sought their destruction. As the 19th century unfolded, conditions deteriorated further, prompting some families to risk all by fleeing to India.

---

[247] Genocidal acts, including mass or random killings of Zoroastrians, the abduction of their youth, the imposition of a head tax (Jazya), and the confiscation of their livelihoods and places of worship, were among the atrocities that pushed the Zoroastrian population to the brink of extinction. Facing relentless persecution, many were coerced into renouncing their faith and converting to Islam in order to escape the burdensome tax and secure some level of protection under local rulers.

[248] Maneckji Limji Hataria, dispatched to Iran from India as an emissary of the Persian Zoroastrian Amelioration Society, embarked on a comprehensive census shortly after his arrival in 1854. Traveling extensively from village to village in Yazd, to the cities of Yazd and Kerman, he meticulously counted the remaining Zoroastrian population. His exhaustive survey revealed a total of 7,190 Zoroastrians of all ages across Iran. Notably, this count encompassed 867 Zoroastrians who had managed to survive in the western province of Kermanshah.

The prevalent motif among the generations of the showcased families revolved around nurturing robust family values. Instilling in their succeeding generations a profound commitment to faith, family, and progressiveness was paramount. Equally vital was their preparation of children from an early age to confront the inevitable challenges and adversities awaiting them beyond familial boundaries—a crucial survival strategy. Additionally, imparting knowledge about commerce and trade, alongside encouraging active participation in these spheres, further contributed to their upbringing.

Those who remained in Iran persevered despite the challenges posed by fanatics. A branch of the family found footing in Kerman in the early 19th century, steadfastly preserving their Zoroastrian identity and upholding inherited ideals. Their arrival coincided with efforts to rebuild the shuttered city and the rebounding Zoroastrian community, culminating in the rise of this family to prominence by the century's end, contributing significantly to the city's revival.

The 20th century witnessed successive generations continuing the legacy of dedication to their Zoroastrian faith, country, city, and community. They played pivotal roles in the revitalization of the Zoroastrian community and the province, particularly during the Pahlavi Dynasty, which ushered in improved civil rights for minorities, absent for the preceding 13 centuries. However, the Islamic revolution of 1979 marked a turning point, prompting many younger family members to migrate to North America and Europe.

As the 21st century dawned, while some descendants maintain a presence in their ancestral land, the family's center of gravity has shifted to North America, with descendants predominantly engaged in professional pursuits.

Acknowledgments

I am deeply grateful to the following individuals whose unwavering support was instrumental in bringing this book to fruition:

To those who generously shared the narratives of their parents and grandparents, enriching this work with personal stories and invaluable insights:

I. Mina Hormuzdi-Amighi

II. Lisa Peterson-Grace

III. Ronald Kermani

IV. Vida Bahrami-Keyani

V. Mahdokht Shahriari

Special thanks to my son, Vishtasp Mehr Soroushian, whose meticulous editing greatly enhanced the clarity and coherence of this manuscript.

To the rest of my beloved family, Mehrbanou and Viraf, for their steadfast love and encouragement that sustained me through the challenging phases of completing this project.

Milton Keynes UK
Ingram Content Group UK Ltd.
UKHW030245011224
451916UK00011B/93